PRAISE FOR *YOU CAN SAVE THE ANIMALS*

"If animals could choose someone to speak for them, that person would be Ingrid Newkirk. Listen to her—and you will hear their voices."

— PAUL HARVEY AURANDT, **author, pianist, and composer**

"Ingrid Newkirk reminds us once again that we share with other animals the same desire to live, to have a family, to love, and to die without violence. I urge you to read this book and vow to do one thing every day that will bring life to a being who would otherwise die."

— JEFFREY MOUSSAIEFF MASSON, **author of**
Dogs Never Lie About Love **and** *When Elephants Weep*

"Ingrid Newkirk is one of the most important voices for compassion of the 20th century, and her new book, *You Can Save the Animals*, reflects the wisdom, urgency and pragmatism of her message. Read this book, share it with your friends. Learn to live by its injunctions."

— MICHAEL TOBIAS, **author, filmmaker, and ecologist**

"Ingrid Newkirk stands as a beacon of compassion and connection. Many of us want our lives to be statements that we care about all of life. She shows us how."

— JOHN ROBBINS, **author of** *Diet for a New America*
and founder of EarthSave International

"I thank God there are many options to reduce the suffering of our critter friends. Find them within these pages."

— BERKELEY BREATHED,
Pulitzer prize-winning cartoonist and author

"When I tell my students about the great peacemakers of our day— the real ones who demand nonviolence to all species—Ingrid Newkirk is among those whose deeds and words should be honored, studied, and put into practice. I'll be using *You Can Save the Animals* in my classrooms—heavily using it."

— COLMAN MCCARTHY, **syndicated columnist**
for *The Washington Post* **and director,**
Center for Teaching Peace in Washington, D .C.

"An invaluable work—should become the Bible for all those who care about animals."

—Jay D. Glass, Ph.D., neuroscientist and author of *The Animal Within Us*

"Unusually fair and clear-minded. If we all follow her reasonable, well-considered suggestions, we will soon see the end of cruelty to our fellow creatures."

—Rue McClanahan, Honorary Chairperson of PETA

"The thoughtless way animals are often treated in 'civilized' society scares even me! Read this book and learn some eye-opening lessons on how to turn cruelty into kindness."

—Cassandra Peterson (a.k.a. Elvira, Mistress of the Dark)

"The lives of animals are in your hands."

—Peter Falk and wife Shera Danese

You Can Save the Animals

251 Ways to Stop Thoughtless Cruelty

INGRID NEWKIRK

PRIMA PUBLISHING

PRIMA PUBLISHING and colophon are registered trademarks of Prima Communications, Inc.

All products mentioned in this book are trademarks of their respective companies.

Every effort has been made to make this book complete and accurate as of the date of publication. In a time of rapid change, however, it is difficult to ensure that all information is entirely up-to-date. Although the publisher and author cannot be held liable for inaccuracies or omissions in this book, they are always grateful for corrections and suggestions for improvement.

Interior design by Greg Smith

Library of Congress Cataloging-in-Publication Data

Newkirk, Ingrid.
  You can save the animals : 251 ways to stop thoughtless cruelty / Ingrid Newkirk.
     p. cm.
     Includes bibliographical references and index.
     ISBN 0-7615-1673-5
     1. Animal welfare.   2. Human-animal relationships.   I. Title.
HV4708.N493 1998
179′ .3--dc21   98-32055
                                                   CIP

99 00 01 02 03 HH 10 9 8 7 6 5 4 3 2 1
Printed in the United States of America

How to Order
Single copies may be ordered from Prima Publishing, P.O. Box 1260BK, Rocklin, CA 95677; telephone (916) 632-4400. Quantity discounts are also available. On your letterhead, include information concerning the intended use of the books and the number of books you wish to purchase.

Visit us online at www.primalife.com

MAY 12 1999

This book is dedicated to Linda McCartney, who had the resources to publish cookbooks and produce vegetarian fast-food meals, but unfailingly used a resource almost everyone has: her own voice. Whether at a political gathering, at a fashion show, or backstage, Linda asked everyone she met, "Are you veggie?" If anyone hemmed and hawed or said, "No," Linda would not let the person go without telling them exactly what animals endure in slaughterhouses and asking them to make the change to vegetarianism.

This book is also dedicated to Sir Paul McCartney, who has honored Linda by securing her legacy of activism. He, too, used his voice for the animals when he told the world that there were two things anyone lamenting Linda's passing could do in her memory: "Go veggie," he said, and give to animal rights charities or to groups that fight cancer without hurting animals.

Contents

APPENDIX A
Recommended Reading 219

APPENDIX B
Recommended Videos and Audiotapes 225

APPENDIX C
Recommended Groups 233

APPENDIX D
Recommended Web Sites 243

APPENDIX E
Recommended Products 245

APPENDIX F
People to Contact 249

APPENDIX G
Samples 251

Acknowledgments

Thanks for help with this book goes to everyone out there, including PETA's International Grassroots Campaign staff, past and present, who became "animal rights activists" by caring enough to do and say things to help stop animal oppression. Without such good souls, the What You Can Do sections would be only wish lists rather than great guides to where others have gone before and invitations to become part of a movement that's determined to achieve animal liberation.

Thanks, too, to PETA's Writers Group staff: Alisa Mullins, Carla Bennett, Paula Moore, Kathy Guillermo, and Alison Green; to PETA's librarian, Karen Porreca, and PETA's Caring Consumer Campaign manager, Robyn Wesley, who were invaluable sources of inspiration and information; to Anna West, who spent weeks digging into the PETA archives; and to Michelle Schreiber, who made the whole thing presentable.

As always, my gratitude to the extremely kind and clever Patti Breitman, who made sure this book happened.

Foreword

Bill Maher

My job is listening to people's opinions. I know that when four people discuss any topic, they're likely to agree on only one thing: Everyone else is wrong. This, I've found, is the human condition. Each of us tends to see the world from our own perspective, planting our flag on our individual hill and defending our point of view like it's a democratic territory under siege by the evil empire.

Rarely is the human perspective more self-serving than when dealing with animals. We can be altruistic; many people love their canine companions and let their cats sleep on their best bedspreads. But we don't like to be made uncomfortable. Just ask a friend who's about to cut into a slab of sirloin steak if he's ever been to a slaughterhouse.

If you fall into this category (most of us normal folks do to some extent), this book may make you squirm just a bit. But you won't be able to put it down. Who knew that macaws could play practical jokes on people? That an octopus could unscrew the lid from a jar? That animals are capable of acts so brave and so selfless that they should inspire humans to greater deeds? After reading these pages, you'll no longer think of animals as mere experimental subjects or livestock breeds or garden pests.

And thinking of animals as the remarkable individuals they are will change your life. Because once you do, you'll want to do something about it.

That's where Ingrid Newkirk gets down to business. This book is about *doing*. You can take a tiny step, a firm stride, or a great leap to change. You can start by clearing the animal-tested products from your bathroom cabinet or by coming down off the hill and handcuffing yourself to the entrance gate at a zoo. There are as many ways to make a difference in the lives of animals as there are personality types in a psychology text. Just find one you're comfortable with and start. You'll probably find, as I did, that the more you read, the more you'll want to stretch, try something new, speak up more.

There are great examples here: people who put their careers, even their own safety, on the line to stop an injustice against an animal. If they were embarrassed, if they were self-conscious, if they were nervous—who cares? They got past the things that often stand in the way of change. We can too. This book shows us how.

Now read and get busy!

Introduction

In 1980, I helped found People for the Ethical Treatment of Animals (PETA). PETA got started because of a young political science student named Alex Pacheco, who one day walked into the Washington, D.C., animal shelter where I worked and volunteered his services. As the beleaguered person in charge, I gladly put him to work.

Only a few months earlier, Alex had been aboard the Fund for Animals ship, *Sea Shepherd*. The vessel's captain, Paul Watson, had recruited the first group of marine mammal "warriors," Alex among them, to hunt down a pirate whaling ship called the *Sierra*. Over the years, the *Sierra* had been responsible for butchering hundreds of whales in international waters. After combing the Atlantic, Watson and the crew of the *Sea Shepherd* found the *Sierra* off the coast of Portugal. They trailed it from a distance until it berthed in Lisbon and, when its crew was safely ashore, rammed its bow. The *Sierra* went to the bottom, never to harpoon another Great Blue again.

In his backpack, Alex carried copies of Peter Singer's *Animal Liberation*, a book that had changed his way of thinking about animals. He loaned it to me, and as I turned the pages, I came to realize that deep in my heart, I believed, along with the author, that animals have a worth in and of themselves, that they are not inferior to human beings but are rather just different from us. They don't exist for us nor do they belong to us. I also realized that it should not be a question simply of *how* animals should be treated within the context of their usefulness, or perceived usefulness, to us, but rather whether we have a *right* to use them at all.

I came to see that although most of us grew up knowing and believing with all our hearts in kindness to animals, and wanting animals to be treated with decency and respect, something has gone wrong.

Luckily, we can fix the problem. After all, it is not as if we accept the psychopath who buries puppies alive in the backyard or condone the teenager who maliciously ties a firecracker to a cat's tail. We don't. We react with outrage and horror at such violence, because we recognize that animals are vulnerable and cannot adequately defend themselves against human wrath and callousness. So when we hear of such abominations, we picket the courthouse, demand heavy sentences for the perpetrators of such acts, and call for stricter laws.

However, the problems animals face are far larger than isolated incidents of abuse.

We have become, mostly unwittingly, participants in heinous cruelties to animals. These are *institutionalized* cruelties that affect billions of animals every year. We don't know how to begin to stop them because they don't take place on the public street. They happen out of sight, on the factory farm, in the slaughterhouse and laboratory, on the trapline, behind the Big Top, in jungles and forests, and even beneath the surface of oceans and lakes. Yet these cruelties are so ghastly that, unless we learn how to reject them outright, and take action to stop them, it will be difficult for us, when we look back on our lives, not to feel ashamed of what *our* species has done to all the others.

In 1977, a man was charged with liberating a dolphin named Puka from a laboratory isolation tank in Hawaii and releasing him into the ocean off Maui. The man said he had been driven to this desperate act, which cost him his career, by the attitudes of those around him in the science lab where he worked.

At his trial, the man said this: "I came to realize these dolphins were just like me. I watched the psychiatrists torment them and I watched the dolphins sink into deep depression, cut off from all that was natural and all that they had loved and wanted. I could not stand my own inaction any longer. I will go to jail with sadness that the world does not yet understand what I do, but my confinement will be nothing compared to what they have endured."

Luckily, no one has to go to jail to free the animals, although some courageous people will. There are legal ways to effect a change in attitudes, in hearts, and in minds. Ways to afford animals the dignity and respect they deserve.

My aim is to take you to places most people will never visit and to look at our interactions with animals in ways that are dramatically different for most of us. I hope to motivate and empower you in the vital changes that must come about. For you are the most important asset the animals have: You are their voice and their lifeline.

I will show you what you need to see so that you can know just how important you are to the animals. For the fact is that life, from the moment of birth to its invariably unsavory end, has become a nightmare for the gentle cows, frightened dogs, and displaced elephants who now find themselves facing such hardware as debeaking machines, decapitators, restraint chairs (such as those used by NASA to keep monkeys immobile for weeks on end), mechanized knives, shock prods, martingales (shackles that keep elephants' heads chained down to their front legs), and cranial electrode implants.

For these wonderful, sensitive beings, contact with humans comes not in the form of a hand reaching out to stroke them, but a bullhook or a whip meeting soft flesh. It comes when they are thrown against the side of the stainless steel cage that is their home, or when, old, sick and broken, they are kicked into the final transport truck.

When Alex and I formed PETA, we had no idea that it would grow to almost one million active members throughout the world, compassionate people who have switched from being sloppy shoppers to caring consumers. Our members don't sit quietly when animals need their voices; they speak out, politely but firmly. They don't accept cruelty; they object to it and get it stopped. And, thanks to them, great changes are occurring.

This book will link you up to that community of others who respect animals enough to make choices that affect them. Often simple choices, like which movie to see or which veterinarian or beauty salon to patronize. Sometimes, they're tougher ones, like what to do if your child's teacher insists that students dissect frogs. You will learn how to make your vote count, how to influence magazine publishers and television producers with a few strokes of the pen. Your neighborhood stores will begin to reflect your choices by adding items to their shelves and perhaps even subtracting unacceptable ones, thanks to you.

If you only do a few of the things suggested in this book, you should feel good about yourself. The more you do, the better you'll feel, the happier your companion animals will be, the healthier you'll become, and the more impact you'll have on the world around you. I'm positive of it.

I promise too that, after reading this book, you will be able to answer the question, "What did you do, in your lifetime, to help animals?" joyfully and without a second thought.

How to Use This Book

The novelist Henry James said, "Three things in human life are important. The first is to be kind. The second is to be kind. And the third is to be kind."

In order to be kind, one must *do*. There is no point in thinking good thoughts and not acting on them. There is no currency in wishing things were better but not rolling up one's sleeves and helping to change them.

Sometimes people tell me they feel so alone in their compassion. The fact is, they aren't. Let me give you just two of many examples:

A friend of mine who's a doctor was vacationing in Mexico when he spotted a man wearing an animal rights T-shirt. "Great shirt!" my friend said to the man. "Oh, I love it, but I only get to wear it here," the man said. "I'm a doctor back in the States and none of my colleagues believes in animal rights." My friend said, "I'm a doctor, too. Where are you from?" The man told him the name of the town. "But I know several physicians there who are animal rights advocates," my friend said, and named them. "I can't believe it," said the other doctor. "Not Charlie and Richard! I had no idea they cared about animals."

On a beach in France last year, I saw two boys catch a crab and put him in a pail and start to poke at him. Knowing only enough French to order a room and a drink, I was about to grab the crab and run for the water with him when I saw my companion, who speaks French well, walk up to the boys and start to talk to them. A moment later, a big man approached the group. "Uh oh," I thought, "that's their father. He won't like someone telling his children what to do." Suddenly, the boys ran to the water and let the crab go. When my companion returned, I asked, "What did that man say?" "Oh," said my friend, "he told them he wanted them to let the crab go too!"

No matter where you are or what you are doing, there are people who are as interested as you are in treating animals well, but who haven't said it or shown it. Often your action or words can make them see how easy it is to do the right thing.

A study on a college campus proves how vital it is to speak up for justice, no matter how awkward it may feel. In this study, a student researcher would approach someone and say, "One of the students received a letter containing racist remarks. Will you sign my petition to say we won't tolerate racism on this campus?"

Another student researcher, a shill who gave the appearance of just happening to walk by, would stop and listen, and then adopt one of two attitudes. He would say, "Well, how do we know the first student didn't provoke that remark?" Or he'd say, "Yes, we need to stop letting people be bullied because of their race."

Like it or not, in most cases when the student expressed concern and wished to sign the petition, the other student wanted to sign, too. But, in most cases where the student expressed doubt that there was anything wrong with the racist letter, the other student also thought it might be OK.

Our lesson is that we must be the first ones to speak up, *for* the animals, and *against* any cruelty. We will find others joining us, but we don't have to wait to be led.

In the late 1800s, the novelist John Galsworthy said,

> We are not living in a private world of our own. Everything
> we say and do and think has its effect on everything around
> us. If we feel and say loudly enough that it is an infernal
> shame to keep larks and other wild song birds in cages, we
> will infallibly infect a number of other people with that senti-
> ment, and in the course of time, those people who feel as you
> do will become so numerous that larks, thrushes, blackbirds
> and linnets will no longer be caught and kept that way. How
> do you imagine it ever came about that bulls and bears and
> badgers are no longer openly encouraged to tear each other
> to pieces, and carthorses are no longer beaten to a pulp.
> When a thing exists that you really abhor, I wish you would
> remember a little whether in letting it strictly alone, you are
> minding your own business on principle, or simply because
> it seems more comfortable for you to do so.

In his time, Galsworthy saw an end to many abhorrent
things done to animals in England. In my lifetime, I too have
seen enormous changes in attitudes and behaviors toward animals. There are veggie burgers on menus that once only fea-
tured steaks and there are close to six hundred companies that
have stopped testing their products in rabbits' eyes. It helps to
look back and recognize those advances when the task ahead
seems daunting.

Animal slavery will end, just as surely as women got the
vote and human slavery was abolished (those fighting for its
abolition almost unanimously believed they would never succeed). The only question is when. The more of us who get busy,
and the more each of us does, the quicker that day will dawn.

The beautiful thing is that activism is extremely easy and
takes countless forms. It can be polite, practical, and incorpo-
rated seamlessly into our lives. Or it can be exciting, avant
garde, and raucous. It takes all kinds of people and all kinds
of actions to get the job done. All that matters is that enough
of us do *something*, and all the bits and pieces will come together to make one glorious success story.

Please share the What You Can Do sections in this book with your friends, family, coworkers, neighbors, your doctor, and whomever is standing at the bus stop or wheeling a cart beside yours at the grocery store. No one needs a fancy degree to help animals: all you need is the desire to help, and you will make a huge difference.

Here are ten things you can do to help animals. More specific ideas are outlined in each What You Can Do section.

1. **Respect all species** and their wonderful attributes and beauty. Discover our mutual relationships and interdependencies, such as the ability to bond, feel pain, and enjoy food and physical comfort, so that as a society we can think of and treat animals as beings, as other nations, and as fellow Earthlings, not as property to be controlled, dominated, or disposed of at whim.

2. **Become a vegan, avoiding all animal products,** thereby sparing animals from the terrible abuses of the factory farm and the agony of the slaughterhouse, and at the same time helping to increase the Earth's productivity without destroying the environment.

3. **Work for the abolition of "entertainment" that exploits animals,** such as the circus and rodeo and cruel so-called "sports" such as hunting, fishing, and animal racing, so that this kind of treatment of animals can be put to an end.

4. **Educate yourself and others at work, in the home, and wherever you go.** Write letters to newspapers, work to change and enforce laws, picket, protest, and speak out for the animals in as many ways as you can.

5. **Be a fur-free and leather-free person,** thus avoiding the unnecessary killing of animals for vanity or greed.

6. **Buy only household products or cosmetics that are cruelty-free,** that is, not tested on animals, and that are environmentally safe.

7. **Support alternatives to vivisection** (animal experimentation), such as tissue culture and computer analysis.

8. **Volunteer at a humane animal shelter,** or donate money to an animal welfare organization.

9. **Adopt a dog or cat from a shelter** (not a pet shop or breeder) and give him or her a good and loving home. Have your dog or cat spayed or neutered, so that you contribute to the reduction of the overpopulation, homelessness, and consequent suffering of these animals.

10. **Simplify your lifestyle** by consuming less and recycling more, thus helping to curb development so you can help preserve wildlife habitat like rivers and shorelines, wooded areas, and ponds near your home, national forests, and even the rain forest.

From everyone at PETA, good luck in everything you do to help the animals. They need us all.

Thank you.

1

Who Are Animals?

This is probably the only time in this book that I'll mention a rhinoceros, but let me start with a true story about one. These animals are hard for people to understand. They aren't furry or big-eyed or easy to pet, and a person might be forgiven for imagining that a charging rhino could flatten you like a locomotive.

Anna Merz, the founder of the Ngare Sergoi Rhino Sanctuary in Kenya, has lived with rhinos for many years. She now realizes that these enormous animals live in a completely different sphere from ours. They are the Mr. Magoos of the animal kingdom, barely able to see a thing, and their world is dominated by smell and hearing.

Anna also realizes that "different" does not mean "stupid." In fact, the rhinos' communication system is quite complex. They use body language, a wide variety of calls, and even marking with urine or droppings to communicate. Perhaps most interesting, they use a highly complicated method of regulating their breathing, a sort of Morse code, to talk to each other.

Rhinos are not alone here. Behavioral biologists have only recently discovered "seismic communication" in Malaysian tree frogs: Male frogs use their toes methodically to click out messages, and female frogs vibrate to send electronic signals in the small saplings in which they live.

People may fear rhinos because they do not understand them, but Anna Merz says that fear is very much a two-way street, with most of the traffic coming from the opposite direction. "Most wild rhinos are obsessed with their *terror* of humans" because people have chased them, separated them from their calves, and slaughtered family members in front of them, cutting off their tusks for sale as aphrodisiacs.

The animals' fear makes close observation difficult. In the course of her work, however, Anna was lucky enough to raise and release a bull rhino called Makora, who had never witnessed an attack by hunters and so never learned to fear people. Over time, he actually came to regard Anna as a friend.

On one occasion, Anna was out with a tracker when the two of them saw a rhino moving very slowly toward them, looking very odd. When he got close, they saw it was Makora, and that he was completely entangled in barbed wire.

Barbed wire is terrifying to animals. When horses get tangled in even a little piece of the stuff, they invariably go wild with panic. Makora had recognized the sound of Anna's car engine and had come to her for help.

Anna got out of the car, and Makora, although trembling all over, gave her the greeting breathing. Somehow, Anna managed to get a handkerchief between Makora's eye and the jagged wire that was cutting into it, then took off her jacket and worked it under the wire that was cutting into his huge thigh. Anna and the tracker had no wire cutters with them, so the tracker used his cutlass and a flat stone to cut the wire, while Anna disentangled it as it came free.

Anna talked reassuringly to the big bull rhino for the forty minutes or more it took to get the job done. The whole time Makora stood stock-still, except for the tremors that shook his body.

When the last bit of wire fell away, he breathed a grateful good-bye and moved slowly back into the bush.

Anna knew she had witnessed an act of outstanding intelligence and courage. Wire is terrifying for animals to comprehend, yet Makora had known to come for help. Still more incredible was the control he had exercised over himself while he was being slowly extricated, although the process must have been painful to him. And, although Makora knew Anna's voice well, she had never before attempted to touch him.

Perhaps if we could sit rhino hunters down and get them to see that a rhino is not just an object to line up in their sights, not just a meal or trophy on the hoof, but a living, thinking, feeling *player* in what behaviorist Dr. Roger Fouts calls the "great symphony of life in which each of us is assigned a different instrument," it might be harder for them to raise their rifles to their shoulders and blow these magnificent beings to kingdom come. Perhaps not. But lightning-quick realizations do happen.

Take, for example, a case in upstate New York one winter when the lakes and rivers were frozen solid. Two hunters, a father and his son, were out looking for "game," when they came across a deer lying on the ice in the middle of a frozen river.

Seeing them, the deer struggled to get up, but the slippery surface prevented her from rising. Every time she struggled, she fell back hard on the ice, her legs splaying out from under her.

The hunters stood back and watched her trying to right herself, each time without success, until she seemed too exhausted to try again.

The father and son skated cautiously up to the doe. Like most hunters, they had never been really close to a live deer before, except to deal a final blow to their prey. The son, a man in his twenties, said later that when he bent down and put out his hand, he was afraid she would bite him. He reached out slowly, and the deer leaned forward and gently smelled the back of his hand, then looked up at him with her big eyes. The younger man began petting her.

The hunters found themselves in a predicament. Things were different. Somehow, they could not bring themselves to shoot this animal who, lying at their feet, as the son said, "looked like a big, old, sweet dog!"

The father and son found a nylon rope in one of their backpacks, and to their surprise the deer let them put it under her rump. Then, working in tandem, they started pulling the deer carefully across the ice toward the bank. It was hard work, and, about every ten minutes, they collapsed to rest, the three of them sitting close together on the ice until the father and son had their breath back. Then they pulled again, and the deer sat there quietly and helplessly, knowing they were all in this together.

When they finally got to the shoreline, the deer put her hoofs on the snow-covered earth, balanced herself, and stood. But now she saw the men as friends, rescuers, and was reluctant to leave. The three just stood there together, stock-still except for their labored breathing, until, eventually, the hunters decided they must shoo her away.

Later, the younger hunter appeared on television, showing his home video of the incident and saying nothing could ever be the same again. He can't hunt deer any longer because he sees them differently now.

If this wonderful sort of breakthrough happened every day to people actively engaged in harming and killing animals, we would have a peaceful revolution on our hands. Hunters and slaughterhouse workers and people who steal cats to sell them to schools for dissection would not see animals as inconsequential and unfeeling commodities or as enemies. Animals might come to be viewed in the way Henry Beston, the English philosopher, saw them. As members of "other nations, caught with ourselves in the net of life and time."

Most of us can't imagine picking up a firearm to slaughter a deer or a rhino. We never meet or come to know the animals *we* ourselves harm, directly or, far more likely, through strangers. Because we haven't really thought much about it, or don't imagine there is a choice in the matter, we buy products and services that provide the funds to pay others to put harsh chemicals down beagles' throats, to castrate lambs without anesthetic, to shoot mother orangutans out of trees, and to build tiny cages in which foxes and lynx live until their necks are snapped and their pelts turned into the fur trim on winter jackets and gloves. These experiences are all very real to the animals who aren't lulled into acceptance, as we are, by the myths about humane treatment and necessity, and who aren't distracted, as we are, by the pretty packages, alluring descriptions, and jolly music that surrounds almost everything we buy, from floor cleaner to circus tickets.

Although anyone who has taken Biology 101 would agree that animals are not inanimate objects, people often treat them as if animals have no more feeling than a desk or a chair.

Stop and look at the images of animals offered to us by fast-food companies. Animals are converted from flesh and blood into caricatures to make us feel comfortable about our complicity in their slaughter: Happy chickens in little aprons dance their way merrily across the sign above the fast-food restaurant; a cute baby pig wearing a chef's hat stirs the pot. Similarly, to nip our children's inquiries in the bud, the research industry sends colorful posters into the schools, dishonestly depicting the rats it poisons and kills by the millions as cute cartoon creatures, snuggled up in the cozy laboratory homes. And so it goes.

Walt Whitman saw things somewhat differently. He wrote,

I believe that a leaf of grass is no less than the journey
  work of the stars,
And the ant is equally perfect, and a grain of sand, and
  the egg of the wren,
And the tree-toad is a chef d'oeuvre for the highest,
And the running blackberry would adorn the parlors of
  heaven.
And the narrowest hinge in my hand puts to scorn all
  machinery,
And the cow, crunching with depress'd head surpasses
  any statue,
And a mouse is enough to stagger sextillions of infidels.

To the outside observer, the human race seems not to agree. It has separated the entire animal kingdom into two parts. Humans are given the status of gods. We can do anything we please. We can ride to hounds for fun or destroy scores of animals' habitats to build a new driveway or roller rink. Quite separate from us are all the other animals, be they our closest living relatives on the phylogenetic tree, the great apes with whom we share 98 percent of our DNA, or the tiniest beetle. We see them not as whole, complete, or important in their own right. In fact, they are viewed as inconsequential, allowed to live only if their existence serves some purpose to us, if they are pretty, amusing, tasty, or can pull great weights. We debase their nature, deny their needs, and reduce them to cheap burglar alarms, wind-up toys, hamburgers, or leather handbags.

Some rationalize their abuse, saying that humans are the cleverest animals on Earth, the only ones to put a person on the moon or write a symphony. True, but humans are also the only animals to devise an atomic bomb, invent concentration camps, and kill hitchhikers for sexual gratification. But what does it mean?

Grand and pompous statements about human superiority are reminiscent of the claims we read in history books, made by white slaveholders to defend auctioning children away from their mothers (for more than a century, some thought slaves were incapable of maternal love), and by powerful men determined to deny women any rights whatsoever ("You might as well give asses the vote," read one Boston editorial).

No doubt human beings, or at least some of them, are clever in ways other animals are not, although cleverness is hardly the criterion by which we decide whom to treat decently. If we did, many would be in deep trouble.

The fact is that animals often leave us in the dust, they are so amazing and awe-inspiring. Long before any human sailor made the discovery, albatrosses knew the world was round because they had circumnavigated it without benefit of even a compass. The tiny desert mouse is far superior at surviving in

Death Valley than the people who travel there, usually equipped with all manner of helpful gear, to test themselves against nature. These tiny rodents construct piles of stones around their burrows to collect the dew so they can take a drink when morning comes.

Name any animal and our silly prejudices fade in the face of their feats: Male Emperor penguins go without food for up to 145 days while guarding their eggs in the frozen tundra. Fruit-eating bats act as midwives for bats who run into difficulty giving birth and have been known to bring food to ailing group members. Some birds, like Indigo buntings, guide their flight by learning the constellations; other birds fix their position by the height of the sun and, if blown off course by the wind, reset their path by the phases of the moon and the rising and setting of the stars. Turtles "read" the Earth's magnetic field in order to navigate thousands of miles across vast, open oceans. Elephants mourn their relatives by cradling the bones of the dead animal in their trunks and rocking back and forth with them. Seals can absorb their own fetuses to prevent overpopulation during a time when food is scarce. Octopuses collect pretty objects and use them to decorate the walls of their subterranean caves. Chimpanzees seek out and use medicinal wild plants with antibiotic properties. Birds make clay by mixing water and mud to harden nests or as casts for broken limbs. A type of Antarctic fish can feed under the ice because they have the highest known level of serum antifreeze in their blood; salmon know the *taste* of their ancestral rivers; whales sing their histories down through the generations; dolphins can "see" through the human body. Ants form living bridges to get their fellows across streams. And there are dogs who can warn of impending seizures and detect cancerous tumors in their human companions.

Some of these traits and accomplishments can be attributed to nature or instinct, but they are no less impressive for it. After all, much of what *we* do is "natural" or "instinctive," too. Few people love their children or choose a mate based on careful calculation.

Ironically, animals are kind to us. Pigs have pulled children from ponds; canaries have flown into rooms where their guardians were sleeping, frantically warning them of fire; beavers have kept lost trekkers alive in the freezing forest by pressing their warm bodies against the hikers; dolphins have kept sailors afloat in shark-infested waters; and Binti Jua, a mother gorilla, and Jambo, a giant, silverback male, both won international admiration when they guarded and protected children who, in separate incidents, fell into concrete enclosures at a zoo. Fearing the worst, keepers ran to get tranquilizer guns with which to subdue the apes, but the apes recognized that these children needed their help and simply offered it.

Of course, dogs and cats, the animals we interact with perhaps more than any others, have saved our skins from everything from frozen lakes to armed attackers. They look after their own kind, too. Cat, dog, and mouse mothers will suffer burned faces and paws, crawling back into buildings to rescue their young. Take Sheba, the mother Rottweiler in Florida who watched helplessly from her chain as her owner dug a two-foot-deep hole in the backyard, dropped her live puppies into a paper bag, and buried them. Neighbors reported that they heard the heartbroken dog howl mournfully and strain at her chain all that day and night.

Almost twenty-four hours later, Sheba managed to snap her chain, break free, and dig the pups out of their grave. Some survived, and the owner was charged with animal abuse.

Why is it then that some people still refuse to attribute feelings to animals? How can love, loneliness, grief, joy, jealousy, or the desire to cling to life be thought of as singularly human traits?

Gus, a polar bear in a New York zoo, exhibited such misery from his confinement, including swimming endless laps in his pathetic cement pool, that he was prescribed antidepressants. Other animals in zoos are not so lucky. Wendy Wood, one of the first Jane Goodall Fellows at the University of Southern California, describes how chimpanzees develop autistic characteristics when denied opportunities to perform natural activities, like

8

playing, fighting, and looking for food, that they cannot do in a laboratory cage or inside a trailer in a traveling sideshow. The distressed primates pull their hair out and rock endlessly, day after day.

Even octopuses, casually dismissed as "stupid invertebrates," show their feelings. These mysterious sea creatures demonstrate their intelligence by learning how to unscrew a jar top to remove food, simply by watching the procedure. When given electric shocks, they show their desperation by biting into their own tentacles.

Altruism, too, is found in the other animals. In Carl Sagan and Ann Druyan's book, *Shadows of Forgotten Ancestors,* there is a hideous true story about monkeys who were fed only if they pulled a chain, electrically shocking an unrelated macaque whose agony was in plain view through a one-way mirror. Eighty-seven percent of the monkeys preferred to go hungry over pulling the chain, and one refused to eat for fourteen days. The authors write,

> The relative social status or gender of the macaques had little bearing on their reluctance to hurt others. If asked to choose between the human experimenters offering the macaques this Faustian bargain and the macaques themselves—suffering from real hunger rather than causing pain to others—our own moral sympathies do not lie with the scientists. But their experiments permit us to glimpse in non-humans a saintly willingness to make sacrifices in order to save others—even those who are not close kin. By conventional human standards, these macaques— who have never gone to Sunday School, never heard of the Ten Commandments, never squirmed through a junior high school civics lesson—seem exemplary in their moral grounding and their courageous resistance to evil. Among the macaques, at least in this case, heroism is the norm. If the circumstances were reversed, and captive humans were offered the same deal by macaque scientists, would we do as well?

Professor Frans de Waal, a primatologist who has spent decades watching chimpanzees taken away from their natural homes and kept in captivity, says, "An animal does not have to be human to be humane." De Waal's observations have taught him that chimpanzees have strong views about what is right and wrong and have a deep sense of justice. They believe in such concepts as sharing, and will not usually tolerate misbehavior in the group, literally turning their backs on those who step out of line.

We don't need these extraordinary examples to derail the myth that our own species is in all ways superior to all others. Many animals have much keener senses—clearer vision, better hearing, such acute senses of smell—you wonder how they tolerate sharing a home with human beings and their cigarettes, floor cleaner, and so on. They are also much faster than we slowly trudging primates.

One of the most infuriating arguments used to deride animals is that they can't speak—by which it is presumably meant that they can't speak a human language. Few of us, of course, can speak animal languages at all, but some animals have made serious headway with ours. Washoe is one such linguist. An aging chimpanzee who had mastered 132 American Sign Language signs by the age of five, she has a remarkable "vocabulary." Washoe was rescued from a research laboratory by behaviorist Dr. Roger Fouts and lives in a small group of others of her kind, including her adopted son, Loulis. Washoe spontaneously combines words to describe her experiences and desires, such as "You me hide" and "Listen dog," and invents names for her possessions, such as "Baby Mine" for her doll.

All this language among apes causes Douglas H. Chadwick to write in *The New York Times*, "Apes certainly seem capable of using language to communicate. Whether scientists are, remains doubtful."

Some people believe parrots just mimic what they hear, and they can certainly do that well, but the way they can put to use what they learn shows considerable intelligence and skill with language use, too.

A friend of mine has a rescued macaw who can copy almost any sound he has ever heard in the house, including her husband's voice. The bird will sometimes drive her mad. As my friend runs to answer the phone, there will be a knock at the back door, then, immediately, the front doorbell will ring. A second later, not knowing which way to turn, she will hear the words, "Can you get that, dear?" Of course, the bird is fully responsible for the entire commotion—the phone, the knock at the door, the bell, and the request.

I found out firsthand what a terrific sense of fun macaws have, when the Washington Humane Society asked PETA to temporarily house two that had been taken away in a raid on a badly run pet shop. Although these birds eyed us warily—they had good reason to, given what they had endured at human hands—they learned eight different laughs and greetings in a single afternoon, simply by eavesdropping. If you passed their room, you could hear them practicing to themselves.

At about 3:30 every weekday afternoon, workers from the factory below our office would start up the hill to the bus stop. Every day at that time, the birds would quietly move to the window and wait. When they spotted someone moving up the hill, two stories below them, they would start their game.

"Hello!" they would call out, just loud enough for who-ever was trudging up the hill to hear. The victim would look around, but see no one near him on the street. "Hello! Hello!" the birds would pick up the pace, using a slightly different tone, calling a little louder.

The man would cast about, baffled.

"Hello! Hello! Hello!" they would scream in unison.

Finally, the worker would look up, see the parrots and, in-evitably, relieved to have solved the mystery, say "Hello!" back.

The parrots became quiet as church mice. Whereas they had been completely intent on this game, now they concen-trated closely on grooming a nail or picking at a sunflower seed.

"Hello, there. Hello, birdies!" the man would call up.

The birds ignored him.

Giving up, he would move on. Then the birds would choose one of the laughs they had adopted as their own, drop all other sham activity, resume their positions, and wait intently for their next victim.

Alex, an African grey parrot with a large vocabulary of English words, which he can use in whole sentences, has used his language skills to try to save himself from unpleasantness. In one memorable moment, when he found himself about to be left behind at the vet's office, Alex urgently called out to his person, "Come here. I love you. I'm sorry. I want to go back."

Alex's avian relatives notwithstanding, most animals have throat and vocal chord structures that do not permit the same sort of speech humans make, and most use very different forms of communication than ours. Dolphins, for example, use echolocation, bats use sonar, octopuses and cuttlefish use fantastic color waves and patterns that ripple through their bodies, and bees flap their wings at varying speeds to give complicated directions to flower beds.

Some cetacean experts believe that dolphins may transmit whole pictures of events to each other in ways more sophisticated than we can fathom. But even those animals commonly despised out of sheer ignorance, the animals who bear the brunt of our prejudice, communicate in ways we are only just beginning to understand. Rats and mice, like elephants, "talk" at frequencies we cannot hear. Sadly, for them, cats are tuned into the same wavelengths. Prairie dogs' squeaks and chattering sounds are certainly components of a structured language, according to, among others, Professor Con Slobodchikoff at Northern Arizona University. Slobodchikoff converts the little rodents' sounds to sonograms, then uses a computer to correlate them to events. He has identified more than fifty words so far and realizes that prairie dogs can distinguish colors, shapes, and sizes, as well as tell a coyote from a German shepherd and a man from a woman. You can just imagine them warning each other to get back in the burrow quick, because "here's that insurance salesman from Prudential again."

One behavioral researcher at Yerkes, a huge primate laboratory in Georgia, Sue Savage-Rumbaugh, found that chimpanzees are so like us, they tell lies.

She reports that, when one baby chimpanzee in a sign language study broke a toy, the student who had been watching him quietly behind a two-way glass panel entered the room.

"Who broke the toy?" she signed to the responsible infant.

"He did!" the baby signed back, pointing to his innocent friend.

This story illustrates the perhaps painful fact that—while animals are not inferior to us in some grand way—they also have their own load of bad behavior.

We might well ask, as did the author of this verse:

Coat with fur,
Hat with feathers,
Lobster broiled alive,
Shoes and bags in sundry leathers
Of animals who've died.

Hunted, trapped, and torn apart
For me to satisfy
And, who am I? And what my rank?
That I may live
And they must die?

Let's explore where such thoughts will take us, and see how we can stop killing and hurting animals as an incidental part of our lifestyles.

CHAPTER

What Happens Along the Way to the Animals Who End Up as Dinner

A little girl got Lucie as a baby chick, the size of a Ping-Pong ball, from a man selling chicks under a bridge for a dollar apiece. By the time the girl got home, the chick was peeping loudly. She put him—Lucie was a rooster—in the basement in a shoebox with air holes and a tissue for a blanket, but the peeping didn't stop.

The next day the girl's mother, Barbara Munroe, realized the chick was freezing. She made a bed in her night table drawer and fitted it with a heating pad. Finally, Lucie went to sleep.

Barbara took to carrying Lucie around in her hand. He always wanted to be with people, so she kept him with her, letting him sleep with her. "The most amazing thing to me," says Barbara, "was the way Lucie adapted to suburban life, sitting in a car like a perfect gentleman or on the sofa while the family read or watched television." (Chickens are widely reported to enjoy watching television. In a study at the University of Edinburgh, their stress was reduced when they were exposed to just one half-hour of TV a day. The chickens looked forward to that one half-hour, and it made them "more well-rounded" as individuals and "less self-conscious.")

Leftovers were never acceptable to Lucie. When he was little, he would peck at Barbara's skirt impatiently while she made breakfast. Later, when he grew up, he would stand on a chair at the table and eat from a plate. He was always checking to see whether someone had something on their plate that he didn't have.

At about three months, Lucie went through an adolescent stage. He ran away when anyone tried to pick him up. However, he still liked to be in the same room with people and watch television with them.

Lucie used to be left outside during the day, but something must have frightened him, so he preferred to stay indoors. When Barbara would come home from work, she often saw him sitting on the back of a chair in an upstairs window, watching for her. By the time she got in, he was down in the kitchen, jumping up and down, greeting her.

If people in the house raised their voices, Lucie chimed in loudly. It was almost impossible to shout over him and usually everyone ended up laughing.

Lucie "talked" a lot. He had a lot of inflections, and his "mom" often thought she understood what he was saying. When she called him, he didn't always come, but he always answered.

Barbara's daughter kept her bedroom door closed. Lucie hated that, as he liked to be able to go everywhere in the house. If everyone in the family was downstairs and the daughter appeared, Lucie ran upstairs to see whether she had left her door open by accident and he could go into her room. Every once in a while the girl forgot to close the door. Lucie ran in and jumped on her bed but remained very quiet so as not to alert her.

All chickens have the potential of Lucie or more, if allowed to live a natural life in which they interact pleasantly with others. The same is true of all the animals we think of as "food." It is just that we never get to know them.

George Bernard Shaw once challenged a woman's appetite for chicken by suggesting that, instead of sitting passively and being served the dish, she slit the bird's throat herself. Perhaps that is a helpful challenge to present ourselves with when we consider ordering Chicken McNuggets. Most of us are too kind to wield the knife, but the tragedy is that, if we pay for the service, someone else will gladly wield it for us.

GIVE A LITTLE BIRD A BREAK

Chickens go from shell to hell as one of the most abused animals in the meat industry, which is truly saying something. Ducks, geese, and turkeys fare no better, but, because of sheer numbers (the average American will eat about five hundred chickens in a lifetime) chickens are truly in the soup. In fact, chicken soup is often the last resting place of their battered remains.

If you've ever known one, you know that a chicken is an individual with as much personality, or lack thereof, as anyone you could ever meet. Yet, can a personality develop if a bird is squeezed with tens of thousands of other birds into a stifling warehouse, unable to find room enough to stretch a wing, never to feel a breeze or the warmth of the sun? When the only regular human "contact" the bird makes is a glimpse of the person whose job it is to check the automatic feed and water troughs and to sling out the dead every day?

The life of a "layer" is even worse than that of a "broiler" because it lasts longer and because layers' beaks are seared off with a hot wire (the blades get red hot and both melt and cut through the beak, smoke rises from the beak—sometimes the cut is too high up to make eating normally possible again.) This is done to prevent the cannibalism that can occur in birds who are denied the room to establish a pecking order. The birds also experience chronic leg pain. They are kept in constant light to fool their bodies into churning out more eggs than is normal (a single egg on the breakfast plate means twenty-two hours of misery for the hen) and periodic "false moltings" mean farmers withhold *all* food from birds for up to *fourteen days.* Their hunger must be indescribable as they drop not only their feathers, but up to 30 percent of their body weight.

A PETA investigator who worked in the chicken sheds at a major poultry farm on the Delmarva Peninsula reported sick and injured chickens everywhere. Many had missing feathers, runny wounds, painful eye and ear infections, "frosted eyes" (blindness caused by ammonia from filth), swollen feet and knee joints, golfball-sized growths, wounds caused by sharp wires, and deformities caused by debeaking.

If workers paid any attention to "damaged" birds at all, it was to hold them by their heads and swing their bodies around to break their necks, slam them into a debeaking machine, twist their heads off, or simply step on them, breaking their backs or rupturing their internal organs.

Workers are not likely to be kind to the birds, but treat them carelessly and get irritated by them. There is a cruel game called "bagpiping," in which workers forcefully squeeze out a bird's feces and try to hit other workers with the mess. One of the supervisors observed by PETA investigators, swearing about a bird who had escaped during unloading, threw a board at the bird and missed, then kicked her four or five feet into the air. Another swore at a chicken he blamed for having made him twist his ankle, then lunged at her, throwing his whole weight on her, and punched her in the face.

Then there are the "downer birds." These are chickens who live with chronic leg pain, bent or bowed legs, brittle bones, rickets, "kinky back," or arthritis. Unable to walk to their feed and water, many die on the factory farm floor.

When the birds reach the age of sixty-five to seventy weeks, if they are layers, their egg production usually declines and they are auctioned off to companies like Campbell Soup Company. If they are broilers, life ends at six to eight weeks.

If they do not succumb to death when the cooling system shorts out in the summer heat, die from being pecked alive by psychotic housemates or from untreated illness or disease, "eating" or "laying" chickens' abbreviated lives come to an end after a nightmare ride. Smashed into a crate aboard a chicken truck, they will be jostled for hours in all weather to the slaughterhouse. There, the poor birds are hung upside down, screaming mightily and trying to right themselves as the conveyor belt carries them to their deaths.

A few years ago, four men accepted a $15,000 challenge from a British animal rights group to live like laying hens for a week. They didn't make it, emerging after just eighteen hours from a cage which had no provision for sanitation and which measured three feet square and six feet high. PETA has asked U.S. poultry executives to take a similar challenge and live for just one day like the chickens they profit from. So far there have been no takers.

As for the turkey, the bird Benjamin Franklin wanted to name as America's national bird, animal protection campaigners estimate that about 7 percent never get stunned, never get cut with the knife, and are dropped alive into vats of boiling water. Once fleet of foot and lithe, to meet the demand for breast meat, the industry has created turkeys with such unnaturally large chests that the birds' legs cannot support them for long.

Yet, removed from their living hell, they show delightful personalities and innately gentle natures. The *Miami Herald* reported about a local man named Sam Garcia who had bought a live turkey, intending to cut the bird's throat for Thanksgiving. What he got instead of a meal was "a relationship." According to Garcia, "Our family lost its stomach for a personable bird who likes children and gobbles back when you speak to him. We did call him 'dinner,' but now we call him our pal."

What a wonderful lesson for those children. Needless to say, it is to the animals' detriment that everyone isn't formally introduced to their intended meals before dinner. If we were, fewer axes would fall.

A STRANGE TASTE

Some have claimed that the kiss originated when our ancestors returned from the hunt, bringing mouthfuls of chewed meat to the young, the sick, and the elderly.

Today, meat represents the kiss of death to more than one million animals every *hour* in the United States alone.

These animals are suffering and being slaughtered not to feed the needy who have no other options, but to have tons of their flesh discarded on hotel room-service trays and into dumpsters by the most overfed members of a nation that can command endless varieties of foodstuffs by picking up a phone or driving to the supermarket.

What a bizarre state of affairs it is that people who love animals grow up eating meat. Although many young children are often repulsed by the stuff, they are usually persuaded by adults that the portion of flesh and bone on their plates is somehow different from Libby the Lamb of their storybook or they are told to remember starving children and make it go down the hatch.

After a while, we become addicted to the taste, for meat eating is habit-forming, just like smoking. If it were not, no one presented with the facts about health, the environment, or the animals would say, "I don't want to know, I could *never* give up my steak!" and people who bristle at the suggestion that they are anything other than humane "animal lovers" would not eat the objects of their compassion. That phenomenon was captured in this poem by Paulette Callen:

> Look! Cows! Stop the car!
> They are so beautiful! I will
> commune with cows! . . .
>
> and I think (not kindly, I confess):
> Commune with the cow
> that rots in your gut.
> Commune with her.
> For my car-mate
> had cow for lunch.

We are slow-thinking animals. It is not entirely our fault, but we can do better. Thanks to steady sales pitches and dishonest advertising, when someone asks, "What's for dinner?" the mental image automatically conjured up is that of the prepared pot roast or chicken drumstick, not of what went before it. No one thinks, "A pig!" and starts imagining what it must have been like for that animal at the moment when he watched his fellows being killed by the machine or the knife just ahead of him in that strange, frightening place. We are used to a world in which we accept the Oscar Mayer jingle in which children gathered around the "Wienermobile" sing gaily about how they would like to be a hot dog: a world in which parents scream bloody murder, not at the butcher and the company exploiting their children, but at the spoilsport idealist in the pig suit clambering atop the giant hot dog on wheels with a sign saying, "Pigs Are Friends, Not Food." It is all quite mad.

Animals aren't one thing and meat another. Each calf and turkey and duck and pig is real, as are their experiences. Here's a glimpse:

The truck carrying the cow was unloaded at a stockyard in Kentucky one September morning. After the other animals were removed from the truck, she was left behind, unable to move, probably because she had slipped and injured herself in the crush of animals being trampled. The stockyard workers proceeded to beat and kick her in the face, ribs, and back. They used the customary electric prods in her ear to try to get her out of the truck, but still she did not move. The workers tied a rope around her head, tied the other end to a post in the ground, and drove the truck away. She was dragged along the floor of the truck and fell to the ground, where she was left with both hind legs and her pelvis broken.

The cow lay in the hot sun crying out for the first three hours. Periodically, when she urinated or defecated, she used her front legs to drag herself along the gravel roadway to a clean spot. She also tried to crawl to a shaded area but could not move far enough, although she managed to crawl more than thirteen or fourteen yards. The stockyard employees would not allow her any drinking water; the only water she received was given to her by Jessie Pierce. Jessie, a local animal rights activist, had been contacted by a woman who had witnessed the incident. Jessie arrived at noon, giving the cow her first drink of the day. After receiving no cooperation from the stockyard workers, Jessie called the county police. A police officer arrived, but after calling his superiors, was instructed to do nothing and left at 1 P.M.

The stockyard operator informed Jessie at 1 P.M. that he had obtained permission from the insurance company to kill the cow, but he would not do so until Jessie left. Although doubtful that he would keep his word, Jessie did leave at 3 P.M. She returned at 4:30 P.M., by which time the stockyard was deserted and three dogs were attacking the cow, who was still alive. She had suffered a number of bite wounds and her drinking water had been removed. Jessie then contacted the state police.

Four troopers arrived at about 5:30 P.M. One trooper wanted to shoot the cow but was told that a veterinarian should kill her. The two U.S. Department of Agriculture (USDA) veterinarians at the facility would not euthanize the cow, claiming that in order to preserve the value of the meat, the cow could not be destroyed until a butcher was present. The butcher finally arrived at 7:30 P.M. and did shoot the cow—her body was purchased for $307.50. (Usually animals who are bruised, crippled, or found dead are considered unfit for human consumption and are used for pet food.)

When the stockyard operator was questioned earlier in the day by a local reporter, he stated, "We didn't do a damned thing to it," and referred to the attention given to the cow by humane workers and police as "bull crap." He laughed through the questioning, saying he found nothing wrong with the way the incident was handled.

The "incident" with the cow is not an isolated case; in fact, it is so common that animals in this condition are known as "downers."

There are lots of reasons to rethink what has become the standard American diet, among them the fact that producing meat uses up so much fossil fuel that it is actually more energy efficient to drive a car than it is to walk—if the energy for walking comes from a meat-based diet—and that more than half of all precious water used in the United States goes to raise and kill animals for the table. But, for me, that cow is the most powerful one.

Her life ended as I have described, but how did it begin? Her mother was probably artificially inseminated on what farmers themselves call a "rape rack," an unpleasant metal device in a cement-floored room. After her birth, she would have been taken away from the mother who loved her, and to whom her presence brought such comfort and joy, and sold at auction.

USDA inspectors can attest to how she was handled throughout her life. Even they, who see so many horrors, are appalled that animals are kicked in the face, electrically shocked on their genitals, and have sticks rammed into their rectums to move them along. (Pigs often have their snouts broken with a stout stick or baseball bat if they hesitate on the slippery ramps to the trucks.)

If you think back, you may have seen this cow, or others like her, staring out of the slats in the transport trucks that move animals to the slaughterhouse in all weather extremes, from snow to scorching heat. (Sometimes pigs freeze to the metal sides of transport trucks and their flesh is ripped off when they are unloaded.)

By the time she reached market and before she broke her pelvis, she would probably have been one of the 80 percent of cows who already have "carcass bruises" from abuse.

What would have befallen her in the chute or on the killing floor would have been terrifying, at best. In the first slaughterhouse I ever entered, I can remember being hit by the smell of warm death, the stench of hot, steaming blood and offal. To the animals, with their finely honed sense of smell, the sensation must be overwhelming.

If only our restaurants and kitchens had glass walls that allowed diners there to see meals being prepared from start to finish. In Gail Eisnitz's chilling book, *Slaughterhouse,* real-life USDA inspector Steve Cockerham describes seeing plant workers cut off the feet, ears, and udders of conscious cattle after stun guns failed to work properly.

"They were blinking and moving. It is a sickening thing to see," he said. In the same book, another USDA veterinarian, Lester Friedlander, tells us that meat inspectors are discouraged by USDA officials from reporting the mistreatment of animals, although the inspectors are the only hope the animals have. "Sometimes the wheels of justice turn slowly," Friedlander said, "but the wheels of justice at the USDA don't even turn."

A lot of people no longer eat meat but continue to use dairy products, not realizing that the "dairy cow" ends up in the same situation as the "beef cow." There are no retirement parties and retirement homes for the worn-out dairy cow. By the time she gets to the slaughterhouse, she is often on her last legs: Her teats may be sore and inflamed; just walking up the ramp may be more than she can manage. Vegans—people who don't use dairy products—are still a tiny minority of the population, while people who boycott veal are numerous. Yet, once understood, the connection between veal and dairy would seem to dictate that ethical transitioning consumers stop buying dairy products even before they give the meat counter the cold shoulder.

When I was seven, my mother came home from the supermarket and announced that she would no longer buy or cook veal. She had run into picketers bearing photographs. In Britain, the "veal crates," which are common in North America and other countries in Europe, are now banned, but then they were just starting to become popular. The calves were to be torn away from their mothers and raised in crates inside dark sheds so that their mothers' milk could be sold for human consumption. My father, who rather liked Veal Cordon Bleu—thin slices of white veal (white because the calf is purposely deprived of iron to induce anemia) wrapped in bacon and cheese—was the hardest hit. Of course, we all believed the suffering of veal calves was an isolated case. We never realized that our demand for *milk* products had created the nightmare and that there is a piece of veal calf in every glass of milk.

In our cheese-on-everything society, the mother cow is reduced to a milk machine. Her only potential source of joy, her calf, is kicked aside and prodded into a crate so we can steal the milk meant for him.

In the barns, veal calves are kept in elevated wooden stalls, their heads often chained. They reek of scours, a diarrheal disease common in intensive farming operations, and their knees are raw from falling and kneeling, falling and kneeling, on the hard metal gridwork or the wooden slats. People petrify them, and they scramble up when the feeder enters the barn, bucking at their chains, slipping in their own waste, and scraping their shins on the slats.

Here's what one former dairy farmer, "Paddy" McGrath, had to say: "Despite the most advanced equipment and technology which allowed less and less contact between man and beast, there were facts that could not be hidden: Cows have individual personalities and feelings. They love, mourn, and feel depressed or joyous just as we do. Replacing cows' names with numbers doesn't hide their individuality. Some soon became pets and often slipped their heads through the railings for a pat."

Cows singled out as sick or low producers go to their deaths earlier than the others.

Says Paddy, "So Mary-Anne (number 52) had to go. I looked at her big watery and gentle trusting eyes as she stood in the holding yard waiting for the truck to come and take her away. She called to her friends who were making their way down the lane to the grazing paddocks. She called until they disappeared behind the dust of hundreds of hooves, and a voice inside me cried out, '*Why* do we have to do this?' . . .'Because we have to live, don't we?'"

Paddy McGrath eventually realized he could live without killing animals. He left the industry and stopped eating meat and dairy products.

People who abandon milk products get a prize: They have a greater chance of avoiding bronchial, respiratory, and stomach complaints than do dairy consumers. Recently, a Finnish nutrition researcher, Teuvo Rantala, has linked the indigestibility of milk proteins to autism and depression. His own son, once withdrawn, violent, and unaffectionate, stopped having tantrums and began hugging his parents after milk products were removed from his diet. Rantala has shown that instead of breaking down into amino acids, milk proteins are partially broken down into peptides, which can leak across the gut wall into the blood and eventually penetrate the membrane that protects the brain, interfering with its development.

In Dr. Benjamin Spock's book, *Baby and Child Care*, the icon of childrearing warns parents to steer clear of dairy products and to make sure their offspring get the calcium and protein they need from beans, legumes, nuts, and plenty of green leafy vegetables, not from milk. Spock, once a "meat and milk man," credited pure vegetarianism with curing him of a debilitating ailment in later life. So, it turns out that advocating for the calf and his mother is a sound personal health move.

The animals aside, it is hard to understand why the filthy habit of meat consumption persists. Converting natural resources and plants into food by shoveling them down animals' throats is extremely inefficient. It uses six to twenty times as much plant food and the energy to grow it, not to mention causing the destruction of forest land and the depletion of topsoil, than were we to eat the plants themselves and forget the cow and chicken. It is also an environmentally destructive habit, sucking water out of the aquifers and causing more waterway pollution from animal waste runoff than any other industry.

Meat eating is irrefutably linked to heart disease, cancer, stroke, high blood pressure, and almost every other chronic disease except ingrown toenails. In some pig-producing states, like Iowa, radio stations warn residents not to drink the water on certain days because of contamination from intensive hog farm waste. Even Washington, D.C., city water has made people ill when bacteria from factory farms in other areas invaded reservoirs downstream. In a country whose citizens are rightly obsessed with their unhealthy and ever-expanding girths, vegetarian diets are more than 25 percent lower in fat than meat eaters'. However, whether or not we draw one of the many short straws in the health lottery, the animals always do, and only because we demand satisfaction for our insane craving to chew on their flesh.

A slaughterhouse manager once told me that it's foolish to care about animals because "they are stupid and dirty." After pointing out that animals are neither, I found myself wondering aloud that, surely, only a stupid person would stick a decomposing corpse in their mouth, and only a dirty person would lick their fingers afterwards.

IT'S A PIG'S LIFE

One November morning in 1996, a nurse, a veterinarian, an opera singer, a construction worker, and a member of the Australian parliament met at dawn outside a pig farm in New South Wales. Part of a rescue team of thirty-six activists who had become totally frustrated at the lack of action taken by the government over abysmal living conditions for pigs kept on factory farms, they marched through the fields and into one of Australia's largest piggeries, where they promptly chained themselves to the sows' stalls.

According to Patty Mark, the group's organizer, the noise from the pigs' screams was deafening. Two hundred and thirty thousand pigs were squeezed into individual concrete and iron chambers without room to turn around. As in the United States, where such intensive farming is considered standard practice, their total confinement had caused their joints to swell and produced painful leg and foot problems.

Some pigs were weak, some were dying. Some sows had bleeding wounds infested with maggots. Many were frothing at the mouth and biting their metal stall bars, signs of extreme distress. Pigs who were about to give birth tried to do what nature had taught them to do: make a nest. They were pathetic sights, virtually wearing their hooves out scraping pointlessly at cement.

Pigs don't cope well with the standard hog industry idea that breeding sows are nothing more than pieces of machinery whose function is to pump out baby pigs. Deidre Brollo, one of the people chained to the stalls, can attest to that:

Sitting there in the dark, it's impossible to forget where you are. Feeling the cold, smelling the stench, hearing the noise of teeth on bars, but seeing nothing. And while surrounded by pigs and people, I felt extremely alone. The sound became familiar over those hours of waiting, almost like rain on a tin roof, until dawn's lights brought home the reality of the situation. Frenzied bar-biting was accompanied by anguished faces and pitiful squeals. The pigs had woken to another day of suffering.

Soon we began to offer pieces of fruit and hay to the sows, something to ease the monotony and pain of their lives. Initially the sow opposite me didn't seem to understand it was food. She was happily destroying the hay, throwing it around and pushing it into the water trough. Finally she took a bite of the apple and that was it! She wanted more! I gave her all I had and she had a marvelous time. Then she gratefully accepted a good scratch under the chin.

Feeding time approached and the sows knew it. The noise became deafening as they awaited their one meal of the day. Some jumped up to put their front feet on the top bars and then struggled to get back down within the painfully small stalls. The bar-biting worsened. My sow screeched as she looked at me. Until this point I had felt numb and separated from the situation. All this came crashing down and I felt helpless, alone and so ashamed as the sow caught my gaze. I was human. Not something to be proud of at the moment, and somehow a victim of a world that doesn't seem to listen.

The shed seemed less like a prison at that moment and more like an asylum. Looking at these frantic animals, some mad, some pathetically broken, just sitting and staring, I understood the true tragedy of it all.

Because of the public demand for ham, bacon, ribs, and other animal parts, modern sows are driven beyond the breaking point. As with chickens, there is a big push to grow them as meaty as possible. All that extra weight causes painful leg problems, aggravated by brittle bones from lack of exercise. Painkillers are almost never given.

If their teats become infected and sore or raw from rubbing against the cement, that's just how it is. No one will rush over with a tube of salve or an aspirin. Although most state laws do not technically differentiate between cruelty to a dog and cruelty to any other animal, as Peter Singer, author of *Animal Liberation*, wrote, "Anyone who kept a dog in the way in which pigs are usually kept would be liable for prosecution, but because our interest in exploiting pigs is greater than our interest in exploiting dogs, we object to the cruelty to dogs while consuming the product of cruelty to pigs."

Having seen inside dog slaughterhouses in Asia and pig slaughterhouses in the United States, I can personally say that, while all animal slaughter for food is unjustifiable, it is difficult to join the chorus of Western voices raised against dog eating when we blithely tolerate equally hideous cruelties visited upon equally feeling animals in our own cheerfully named "packing plants."

Such thoughts led Dr. Donald Doll, a Los Angeles physician, to stop eating animals after hearing a radio station announcer blasting Vietnamese immigrants to California for eating dogs. Dr. Doll started wondering what made eating other animals right and couldn't come up with a logical answer.

This very odd dichotomy came home to me, too, when I was a humane officer in Maryland. My job was to bring prosecutions for cruelty to animals.

I had been called out to an abandoned farm and found the place in a mess. A dog had been left on his chain and had somehow survived, thanks to a bucket of dirty water. The horses and pigs had not. The barn was littered with broken bottles, left by the departing occupants of the farmhouse in the wake of a drunken party. In some stalls, the animals had cut their legs to ribbons on the shards.

Just as I was leaving the dark barn, I saw a movement back in a corner. Stepping carefully over to the straw, I found a little pig, too frail to stand. He couldn't have weighed more than a few bags of flour. I took him in my arms and carried him out into the fresh air and, laying him down under a tree, went to the pump to get some water.

He was too weak to raise his head, but he sipped the drops of water from my fingers, making little grunting noises of what could only be gratitude and relief. I sat with him, rocking him back and forth and talking to him until the van came to take him and the dog to the veterinary clinic. I had to stay to look for anything pointing to the whereabouts of the people who had done this to him and his fellows, so I could charge the family with cruelty.

That evening, driving home, I began to think of what I could cook for dinner. I had pork chops in the freezer. Then it hit me. How could I pay someone to hurt a pig, when here I was trying to prosecute other people for doing the same sort of thing? I didn't know then that pigs are routinely castrated without anesthetic and that they often have their tails severed to prevent injuries from their fellow inmates who have become enraged by confinement. I hadn't yet visited a slaughterhouse, but like anyone with a functional brain, I knew full well they must be appalling places if you happen to have been born an animal labeled "food."

For others, the revelations are more intellectual. Brigid Brophy, author of *Hackenfeller's Ape*, became a vegetarian "for the same reason I am not a cannibal. If you thought I would taste nice roasted or in a casserole, that would not give you the right to take away my life." She wrote:

You might argue that you were not endangering my species since there are plenty of (perhaps too many) human beings. You might argue that my life is of no value or interest to you and is a pretty dim sort of life anyway.

But the crucial question is not what value you set on my life and my enjoyment of it, but the value I set on them. Dim my life may be, but it is the only life I have.

And, like every pig and every sheep, chicken, herring, etc., I am an individual as well as a representative of my species. The fact that my species will continue to exist doesn't compensate me for the discontinuation of me.

Some animals (but, paradoxically, not as a rule those humans kill in order to eat their corpses) kill and eat other animals. So far as we can tell, they have no choice. Humans have choice and are very proud of it. Instead of killing animals on the grounds that they are intellectually superior to the animals, humans should stop killing animals and thereby demonstrate that they have more freedom of choice than the animals.

A human who supposes that he can't do without a diet of dead bodies of animals is deceiving himself. He is pretending to be a slave of habit and convention, whereas he is in fact a free agent.

HOOK, LINE, AND FACTORY SHIP

The word *animal* comes from *anima*, meaning "life." How odd, then, that many people do not consider a fish, a very animated being, to be an animal at all. Some people find protests over cruelty to fish laughable, although where an animal rates in our wildly arbitrary value system should have no effect on how we treat him or her.

I suppose this blind spot is what makes whalers in Norway and Japan (and the ones who used to harpoon these great beasts off the New England coast, for that matter) think of whales as nothing more important than uncooperative blobs of gray blubber, and so find nothing wrong with thrusting a harpoon into them. Certainly, fish and whales all thrash around with equal vigor and desperation when the metal sinks into their bodies, and both kinds of animals try with every fiber of their being to flee for their lives. But fishers and whalers don't "get it." Impervious to the animal's perspective, they can stand about, laughing and discussing the comparative worth of their new gum boots, while agonizing dramas are played out at their feet.

Why do people think differently about the salmon or sole they eat, on the one hand, and, on the other, the lion fish they gaze upon with awe and have their pictures taken with underwater while scuba diving in some tropical paradise? Or the guppies they view or keep and tend to in aquariums? For most people it would be unthinkable to eat that little fellow in the tank in the living room, but aren't they all fish?

I knew a banded ceverum long ago who lived in an aquarium in a country house. During the mornings, when the house was quiet, the fish spent his time at the end of the tank near the window, catching the morning sunlight on his fins and browsing among the reeds. But, at about 4:30 P.M., he swam to the other side of the tank and stared at the hallway door.

At that time of day, "his" man came home from work. Before the key turned in the lock, the fish began "pacing," swimming back and forth without letup, showing the sort of impatience you might see in a person drumming his or her fingers on a table top. Every few laps he paused and hung in the water, staring hopefully at the door.

Perhaps he sensed that the man loved him, as wholly inadequate as a man's love for a fish must be. In fact, the man had usually forgotten all about the fish until he reached the door, but then he remembered and rushed straight into the living room so as not to disappoint him. The fish jumped and wagged his tail like a dog, lifting about a fifth of his body clean out of the water. The man would gently scratch the fish's back, the fish offering first one side of his body to be petted, then the other, making little waves with the swishing of his fins.

The fish didn't know that, as a boy, the man had thrown cherry bombs into the creek when the carp were spawning and then killed them with blows from two-by-fours as they thrashed about on the bank. The fish didn't know that on summer days the man still caught and gutted fish from that creek and barbecued them just outside the window.

Not that the man would ever harm the fish in the tank, but, like most of us, he had a compartmentalized mind. Killing fish whom you don't know is just part of our culture.

The captive ceverum tried to make the best of what was otherwise a plain life. He cleaned rocks by rolling them about in his mouth, swam through the hair curlers fastened together to form a jungle gym, and tickled his back in the bubbles from the aerator. Once, he swam purposefully to the west end of the tank, seized a plastic plant in his tiny jaws, and dragged it back to his corner. The next day, when the man tidied the tank and put the plant back in its "place," the fish moved it again to the new spot he had chosen for it.

The fish had a sport. When the fish saw a cat tiptoe over the bookshelves to drink from the aquarium, he would lie in wait for her in the reeds. Experience had taught the cat to peer into the depths for any sign of an ambush, but the fish knew that and stayed quiet as a mouse. Only when the cat's tongue descended did the fish burst into action, propelling himself up through the reeds like a torpedo, hell-bent on taking a chunk out of that raspy organ. If she sensed the underwater eruption, the cat might get her first lap in before tongue and fish met. No blood was ever drawn on either side, but the contest was a welcome diversion.

The fish kept to himself, taking the presence of newcomers to his tank with all the dignity and despair of a librarian who finds a group of young bikers living among the shelves. He would puff himself up and shake his fins at them and give chase if they did anything truly appalling, but he never attacked.

In the end he outlived them all. Some died of "seasickness"—the trauma of sloshing around in the bag from ocean to distributor, in the truck to the pet shop, and then in the car on the way home; others succumbed to epidemics of "ick" which destroyed their fins, sending them spinning helplessly to the bottom of the tank, tiny vestiges of their graceful selves. Still more suffocated when power failures robbed oxygen from the water.

On the Saturday the tank cracked, there were only two other fish left. They were African "elephant noses," exotic fish with trunklike protuberances. The old ceverum accepted their presence; he and they kept as respectful a distance from each other as fish can in a modest aquarium.

The man had been at the movies and returned to find water all over the floor and still dripping from a crack in the glass. In the inch of liquid left in the bottom of the tank, three individuals lay on their sides, dying.

Rescue had to be effected without delay. The fish was whisked into a large pot. One elephant nose went into a saucepan, the other into a coffee pot; but this last little fish struggled, caught his long nose in the spout, and suffered a terrible injury. When the substitute tank was set up, the fish could not breathe properly or keep his balance. His companion helped keep him afloat, pushing him up against the side of the tank so he could reach food and air. But this didn't save his life. Within a week of the injured elephant nose's death, his companion died, too. After that, the old fish was alone again.

When I had first seen him, he had only been about half an inch long, and I was still eating cod roe on toast and salmon steak. But by the time the elephant noses died, he was six inches long and I had stopped eating others of his kind. As he had grown, so had my understanding that there might be something wrong with eating fish or pretending that they could be kept as living room decorations. Human amusement was not worth their barren lives and "accidental" deaths.

When the fish died, I found myself trying to imagine what his ancestral waters were like, where and how he had been captured or bred, and how sad it was that he had been robbed of his fish destiny.

Although some people fish to eat, which might be considered a necessity for bears, eagles, or certain aboriginal peoples, it is hard to imagine anything very noble about choosing to eat fish if you live in the land of a million more benign choices. Especially when one becomes aware, as announced by behaviorists at St. Andrews University, that fish value friendship, choose which fish to adopt as friends (they recognize their chums by both smell and appearance), and decide to swim with them instead of with other fish.

UP FROM THE DEEP

Most consumers get their fish without ever picking up a rod and reel, of course. Table fish, in the main, come from grocery stores and supermarkets, glassy-eyed or filleted, tidily frozen or "fresh," an odd term for a body that is busy breaking down. Most of this fish comes from fishing boats nicknamed "the bulldozers of the seas," trawlers as big as football fields that vacuum the oceans clean of most sea life, not only the target catch, but the "trash catch," including wonderful octopuses and cuttlefish, dog fish, turtles, and eels.

These boats—floating islands really—use satellite communications to track their prey and then drop huge nets, sometimes many miles long. The nets snag animals of countless species, including dolphins, seals, and sea otters. An estimated one million sea birds every year become entangled in fishing nets and drown. Some fishing outfits use underwater explosives to herd dolphins away from tuna nets, causing extreme pressure to fish and making internal organs shift, split, and even explode painfully.

When nets are dragged through the water, fish are squeezed together, suffocating, and the whole mess is bounced along, together with any netted debris, like rocks. The fish rub against each other and file away sharp scales, making their flanks raw. When they are hauled aboard from the depths of the ocean, they endure excruciating decompression, which can give their eyes that popped-out appearance and push their esophagi and stomachs out their throats. Due to the change of pressure, fish can also rupture their swim bladders when they are pulled rapidly from their watery habitat.

Up on the decks, the crew stab the fish with short, spiked rods and sort them, slitting their bellies and throats. The "trash catch" is dumped back overboard, often with a pitchfork, sometimes alive, sometimes badly injured, to die slowly or be picked up by a new predator. There is nothing humane about any part of the process.

One person who stopped eating fish for ethical reasons is Harriet Schliffer, a Canadian feminist who went fishing with her father for the first time when she was very small. As soon as she saw a fish reeled in, she couldn't miss the fact that this was an animal being hurt. Harriet was deeply upset that her father was doing something horrid to this fish and begged him to help the animal.

Other people abandon fish eating for health reasons.

Dr. Andrew Nicholson reminds us that "fish doesn't have a speck of fiber, complex carbs, or vitamin C." Another physician, Dr. Peggy Carlson, has written of fish, "It is loaded with chemical contaminants that nobody needs!" The National Wildlife Federation report on the risks of cancer from eating freshwater fish concluded that one weekly meal of a trout from Lake Michigan poses a cancer risk of one in ten. In another study, DDT was found in fatty fish tissue at nearly all sites tested, although it was banned more than twenty years ago. PCBs, also out of production since 1977, showed up in 91 percent of sampled fish and represented the highest cancer risk to fish consumers. Mercury turned up in 92 percent of fish studied.

Raw shellfish is one of the riskiest foods you can put in your mouth. An estimated 1 in 250 people who eat it gets sick. According to the Centers for Disease Control and Prevention in Atlanta, Georgia, shellfish is the single largest source of outbreaks of food-borne illness in the United States. The chance of contracting a digestive problem from fish is about twenty-five times greater than from beef and about sixteen times greater than from pork or poultry.

As for the idea that eating fish or fish oil is somehow good for your heart, the highest levels of omega-3 fatty acids, which are believed to reduce the risk of heart disease, do not come from fish. Four grams of flaxseeds pack a whopping 2,372 mg of omega-3s, walnuts also beat fish cold with 2,000 mg per few ounces, while tuna only contains 700 mg. The vegetarian sources have the added advantage of not containing metals, sewage, or toxins.

SNAILS, DUCK LIVER, AND OTHER INDELICACIES

"Gourmet" columnists are constantly waxing lyrical about some culinary "delight" that has invariably been painfully extracted from an animal. As if the horrors our race has dreamed up for the everyday kitchen are not enough, we are expected to drool over and to laud chefs who split open the backs of live lobsters, drip butter into their wounds, and then broil them to death. The days are gone when chefs took themselves as seriously as Monsieur Vatel, Louis XIV's kitchen man, who became so despondent at the prospect of preparing a dinner without the right ingredients to make lobster sauce that he ran himself through with his sword. But we are still expected to applaud the likes of Julia Child when they gaily cut holes in a fish's neck so as to stick the animal's tail through its body and out of its mouth, simply for effect. Lobsters are, by the way, widely believed to be fully aware of sensation when they are frozen alive or dropped into boiling water. Invertebrate zoologists tell us that these complex crustaceans have tens of thousands of bristles on their bodies that are touch-sensitive, and that they are not relieved of pain until their nerve ganglia are destroyed, fixing the tissue.

In my youth, I once saw a bin of live snails at an Italian market and decided to try to cook them. A helpful man in an apron put a couple of little shovelfuls of them into a brown paper bag and gave me his best advice. Off I drove, the bag on the passenger seat beside me.

About half an hour later, nearing home, I began to get the feeling I was being watched. I looked over at the seat beside me and there, peering out of the bag into the precipice below or up at giant me, were the snails. Having looked like nothing more than a cluster of shells when I bought them, the little horned beings had come to life, crawled up to the end of the bag, and managed to work their way out of it. Now they were sitting or standing there—it is hard to tell with a snail—escape weighing heavily on their minds.

I looked back and remembered the cooking directions. It said that the snails should be washed by swilling them about in a pan of warm water, then leaving them overnight in a deep pot of cold water. The next day, I was to get the olive oil sizzling, remove their tiny bodies from their portable homes, and toss them into the pan with some garlic, sauterne, and herbs. This was now impossible.

I drove as quickly as prudence allowed, raced the snails and their open bag to the back of my garden, deposited them gently on the grass, apologized, and went into the house. So much for escargot. When I went back to the garden the next morning, they had all disappeared. From then on, any delicious garlic-wine juice would have to be sopped up with breadsticks. After all, like tofu, snails don't have much taste in and of themselves. It's all in the sauce.

John Bunyan must have had a similar experience when he wrote of the snail,

> She goes but softly, but she goeth sure;
> She stumbles not as stronger creatures do:
> Her journey's shorter, so she may endure
> Better than they which do much further go.
>
> She makes no noise, but stilly seizeth on
> The flower or herb appointed for her food,
> The which she quietly doth feed upon,
> While others range, and gare, but find no good.
>
> And though she doth very softly go,
> However, 'tis not fast, nor slow, but sure;
> And certainly they that do travel so,
> The prize they do aim at, they do procure.

"My" snails had certainly gone, and they had procured the prize they sought: freedom.

Perhaps one of the most appalling cruelties in the name of the food business, and we certainly have enough to choose from, is in the production of foie gras, or fatty liver, prized by chefs and more commonly used in a sandwich paste or pâté.

Konrad Lorenz, the world-renowned wildlife ethologist, called foie gras production "a shame on all Europe," although today Israel and the United States are equally shamed. Lorenz was particularly incensed because he had adopted, or been adopted by, a flock of greylag geese during his studies in Switzerland, and had slept and swum with them as part of their family. Sir John Gielgud was so appalled about the treatment of ducks and geese used for foie gras that he narrated a video for PETA, denouncing foie gras and urging chefs and restaurateurs to withhold it from their menus.

In his video, Sir Gielgud described the intricate relationships among ducks and their amazing abilities by telling us:

> Anyone who has ever watched ducks bobbing underwater for food or skimming across a lake in a graceful landing would probably agree that these birds seem delighted to be alive. The diversity and charm of ducks are apparent in every facet of their behavior. Complex communicators, they begin early—even before hatching. Developing ducklings can be heard cheeping inside their eggs. After her ducklings hatch, mother duck devotes all her time to her young.
>
> Ducks have elaborate courtship rituals and have been known to develop caring, steady relationships with each other. (In his book, *Animail*, Cleveland Amory tells a wonderful story about a couple named John-Duck and Mary-Duck. Although it wasn't mating season, observers noted the two ducks were inseparable and that the male was extremely attentive to the female. Upon closer observation, it was discovered that Mary-Duck was completely blind. John-Duck had, in essence, become her "seeing-eye duck.")
>
> Ducks are natural athletes with remarkable physical capabilities. They are able to dive 100 feet deep and fly more than 60 miles an hour.

In the wild, they have been known to live as long as 18 years, but on today's foie gras farms, their throats are slit when they are just 3 months old.

What moved Sir John, who has always been fond of birds, was a videotape filmed by a PETA investigator at a New York foie gras farm. It shows the birds being violently force-fed by machine. Workers thrust long metal pipes down the birds' throats, then used a compressor to pump 3 kilograms (6.5 pounds) of cooked corn into their stomachs. Sometimes, the birds' internal organs simply burst; other times their necks ruptured from the sheer force and manhandling. Injury is so common on such farms that the people on the force-feeding line may be given a pay bonus if they manage to kill fewer than fifty birds during the process.

A few decades ago, foie gras production was limited to France and Belgium. Women living on farms would keep a duck or goose confined to their kitchen or barn, sometimes actually nailing the bird's feet to the floor or putting him in a small wooden box so he could not move.

After being blindfolded, a stick and long funnel were used to shove food down the bird's throat. Today, human ingenuity has resulted in a far more efficient, mechanized version of this abominable cruelty; we have moved thousands of geese and ducks onto factory farms, and the market is flooded with the canned livers of these dear birds.

Force-feeding isn't the only horror the birds endure. In addition to the three-times-a-day cramming (accelerated to every three hours, even throughout the night, during the last four days of the birds' lives), their wings often break when they are dragged roughly from their pens or cages and they suffer hideous injuries, the metal pipe sometimes penetrating the neck and making terrible wounds. They are also pathetic to see, because, so deformed and sick from overfeeding (their livers expand to six, seven, or more times their normal size), most cannot walk and must push themselves along on their wings.

Luckily, many airlines that once proudly listed foie gras on their first-class cabin menus have responded to Sir John's appeal and dropped it. Some stores have been sufficiently moved to stop stocking it, a few top restaurants no longer serve it, and treating ducks and geese that way to produce foie gras is illegal in Britain and Germany.

ACQUIRING GOOD TASTE

We are so lucky to have choices, endless choices, including the luxury of experiencing all the tastes we have come to enjoy, without causing harm and death to animals. Some men who are offered a vegetarian hot dog (or Not Dog) at a baseball game wrinkle their noses and look disgusted. How amazing that the same men would think it unremarkable to buy a hot dog into which have been packed blood, gristle, and the scraps of meat found around animals' noses and anuses and between their toes.

Although many new vegetarians don't want anything that reminds them of the old foods, and they eat a full, tasty, and healthy diet of dishes based on fresh vegetables, beans, legumes, fruits, and nuts, there exists now virtually every imitation meat and dairy product anyone could imagine. There are soy "ice creams," dozens of different brands of soy, rice, or nut "milks," and faux cheese and sour cream for those who love those flavors but don't wish to contribute to animals' suffering. The veggie burger market means a good investment as well as good eating, and there is soy "chicken," even "Tofurky" with stuffing and all the trimmings.

Some people are switching, not from meat to vegetables, but from "red meat" (cows, pigs, and lambs) to "white meat" (chickens, turkeys, and fish). I would give my eyeteeth to be able to find a way to quietly dye chickens red. Although the switch is usually "for health reasons," chicken is, in fact, far from a health food. It contains exactly as much cholesterol as beef, 25 milligrams per ounce (if you think that's bad, an egg is a cholesterol *bomb*, with a whopping 213 milligrams of cholesterol), and isn't much lower in fat, even without the skin. It contains no fiber and fills you out, not up.

It also makes bad mathematical sense, from a humane point of view, to switch from cows to chickens and turkeys, when you consider that it would take perhaps one hundred meals of beef to use up the meat from only one cow, whereas only three or four meals could be made out of the flesh of a single chicken.

Changes in the way we eat are indeed happening, as evidenced by the success of the veggie burger and the appearance of veggie hot dogs in ballparks. Nevertheless, millions of animals are being bred, hurt, and killed even as I write. Slaughterhouses may be carefully and deliberately built miles from our schools, homes, and businesses, but, unless we do our part to close them down, as Ralph Waldo Emerson remarked, "You have just dined, and however scrupulously the slaughterhouse is concealed in the graceful distance of miles, there is complicity." That is why our actions are vital. In the pages ahead, there is a wealth of information on things we can do to help, from where to buy "phony baloney" to how to protest when the Wienermobile drives into town.

Help Animals Used for Food

GO VEGETARIAN!

Good intentions are not good enough. It's easy to stop eating animals. Here's how:

- **Call a Hotline.** Call PETA's hotline at 888-VEG-FOOD for tasty, free vegan recipes, and buy or borrow a veggie cookbook. (See Appendix A: Recommended Reading.)
- **Order a Starter Kit.** Order the vegetarian starter kit from the Physicians Committee for Responsible Medicine (PCRM) by calling 202-626-2210, ext. 300. This helpful kit is available for $2.00.
- **Order Cookbooks.** Order PETA's cookbooks, *The Compassionate Cook*, or *Cooking with PETA*, through the PETA catalog or at your local bookstore. (See Appendix C: Recommended Groups for PETA's address.)
- **Subscribe to Magazines.** Subscribe to *Vegetarian Times*. A yearly subscription (twelve issues) is only $19.95. (See Appendix A: Recommended Reading for address.)
- **Join the North American Vegetarian Society (NAVS).** Individual memberships are $18, and family memberships are $24. (See Appendix C: Recommended Groups for address.)
- **Vegan Tips.** Check out our "Going Vegan" tips section at the end of this chapter.
- **Invest.** Invest in vegetarian businesses and food services.

■ **Enter Competitions.** Enter your vegan recipes into cooking competitions and bake sales, and make it clear that no animal ingredients were used. Dan Handley, a chef at the Virginia Beach Hilton Hotel, won a barbecue cookoff contest with his vegan recipe!

■ **Give Out Stickers.** On Halloween, give out vegetarian stickers with vegan candy.

■ **Act on Principle.** When bus driver Bruce Anderson stuck to his vegetarian principles and refused to give riders coupons for free hamburgers, he was fired by the Orange County (California) Transit Authority (OCTA). Anderson was reinstated when he won a lawsuit ruling that all vegetarians and vegans are entitled to protect their beliefs and rights.

■ **Be Encouraging.** Encourage others to become vegetarian by wearing a veggie button, baseball cap, or T-shirt and providing information to those who request it.

■ **Offer Suggestions.** Use suggestion boxes and fill in comment cards to promote veggie products.

■ **Show a Film.** Show *Diet for a New America* (available on loan from PETA for a $45 refundable deposit or from EarthSave) to school groups, friends, family, coworkers. (See Appendix C: Recommended Groups for EarthSave's address.)

■ **Donate a Book.** Donate a copy of *Diet for a New America* by John Robbins (or other vegetarian-related books) to your local library, put it on your own bookshelf to read, and lend to friends. Ask your book club to read it.

■ **Make a Display.** Do a library display on vegetarianism and factory farming.

■ **Use Your License Plate.** Advertise your veggie lifestyle on your car license plate. Sample phrases include "NO MEAT," "MTS MRDR," and "GO VEG."

■ **Exercise.** Promote vegetarianism when you exercise or compete. Don Lutz organized a pool team of vegetarians who have amassed more than two hundred titles in league and tournament competition and spread the word about animal rights everywhere they go.

■ **Have a Party.** Hold a tailgate party and serve Tofu Pups and veggie burgers. Also, ask your local ballpark to serve veggie dogs. The Oakland Alameda County Coliseum and Harbor Park stadium in Norfolk, Virginia, do. PETA can help.

■ **Feed Your Legislators.** Let your legislators try veggie food. Ask about hosting a vegetarian hot dog stand at lunch time at your capitol building.

■ **Raise Money.** Hold a yard sale, bake sale, car wash, or other event. These are easy and fun ways to raise money to run an ad or donate to your humane society or favorite animal rights group. Every summer, PETA hosts a combination yard sale/veggie hot dog and burger stand/clearance extravaganza called "Bonanza for the Beasties," and it is always an overwhelming success. One year, sales topped $3,000!

■ **Be a Helpful Guest.** When you're a guest, explain clearly what you do eat and what you don't. Many meat eaters are unaware that vegetarians eat no flesh whatsoever—no meat or chicken or fish. Let your host know this. If the dinner is very informal, you could help your host by suggesting some easily prepared, familiar meatless dish—a casserole or stir fry, for example. Even better, volunteer to bring a special vegan entrée for all to share.

IN THE WORKPLACE

■ **Share Food and Recipes.** Bring veggie food to share at your office, and give out recipe cards.

■ **Talk to Your Cafeteria.** Ask your office cafeteria to offer vegan food. If you attend meetings where food will be served (such as a professional workshop), request ahead of time that they provide vegan food for you. Be specific about what constitutes "vegan"—many people don't know. The Physicians Committee for Responsible Medicine (PCRM) and EarthSave offer vegetarian recipes for institutions. (See Appendix C: Recommended Groups for addresses.)

- **Request Vegan Gifts.** If your company gives employees free holiday hams or turkeys, as early as possible before the occasion politely ask that they switch to a vegan food gift.
- **Organize Others.** Get your coworkers involved in recognition of the annual Great American Meatout, coordinated nationally by the Farm Animal Reform Movement (FARM). Four thousand casino workers at the Trump Castle in Atlantic City enjoyed a veggie menu in their cafeteria. At a Michigan Chrysler plant, employees sampled meatless foods during a lunchtime vegetarian seminar.

DISCUSS, DEBATE, EDUCATE

- **Defend Animals; Show Pictures.** If you hear ridicule or criticism of animal rights, you can politely but firmly defend the validity of concern for animals. Point out that the circle of compassion does not start and end with people but should extend to all living beings who share the Earth. Try to reason with them. Explain calmly how battery hens and veal calves are treated, and show pictures if you can.

VOLUNTEER

- **Make Easter "Eggs."** At Easter, look around the craft shop for all the different "eggs" you can display, "hunt," and give as gifts. Craft stores offer a variety of "eggs" made from plastic, papier-mâché, wood, even glass. For young children and a fun party, use plastic eggs and colorful stickers that are appropriate for Easter. Card shops, fabric shops, even supermarkets carry fake eggs and other Easter decorations. Children can put stickers on these eggs, which can be hidden as is, or small trinkets or other treats can be placed inside. Parents can choose to save one or two eggs their children decorate each year. You can't do that with hens' eggs.
- **Talk to Your Animal Protection Organization.** If you belong to an animal protection organization that is still serv-

ing animal products at the table, urge the group to adopt an ethically consistent meal plan.

■ **Talk to Your Wildlife Protection Organization.** If you belong to an ecological or wildlife protection organization, make sure they are aware that becoming a vegetarian is one of the most important things an individual can do to conserve the Earth.

■ **Organize and Speak.** As a community volunteer, you can organize forums and speak at club meetings, church groups, public libraries, and service groups. Make these meetings interesting and informative by showing a video and handing out leaflets on factory farming and vegetarianism. Provide meatless recipes and samples of vegetarian food. Ask a local vegetarian or health food store to sponsor your effort and perhaps supply food samples and information pamphlets on the issue.

■ **Feed the Homeless.** Call your local homeless shelter and offer to get a team together to cook a vegan meal.

■ **Have a Picnic.** Advertise and arrange a vegan potluck picnic at your local park.

RESTAURANTS AND GROCERY STORES

■ **Display Stickers.** Help fellow vegetarians locate restaurants who offer veggie fare: Ask restaurants to display "We Serve Vegetarian Meals" stickers in their windows. (If they don't currently offer a vegetarian entrée or two, ask them to create vegan dishes for you, and bring them the recipes.) You may obtain stickers by sending an 8½" × 11" self-addressed, stamped envelope with $1 postage to EAT YOUR VEGGIES, c/o PETA. (See Appendix C: Recommended Groups for address.)

■ **Voice Objections to Lobster Tanks.** Tell managers of restaurants and stores that have live lobster tanks that lobsters have sophisticated nervous systems and can feel pain—whether it comes from boiling water or being ripped apart.

■ **Boycott Foie Gras.** Don't let 'em duck the issue! Ask specialty stores to take foie gras off the shelves, and don't patronize restaurants or gourmet shops that sell it. Show PETA's video (*Victims of Indulgence*) to anyone and everyone. Better yet, send a copy to a local restaurant or store that sells foie gras, telling them they won't be able to count on your business until they drop this cruel product. Also call your local gourmet markets to find out whether pâté tastings are planned. If so, take your case for kindness to the store manager. Discuss the cruelty and health issues of pâté and urge the store to cancel the event. If the store plans to go ahead with the tasting, demonstrate outside—armed with information and "faux gras," (non-animal foie gras) shoppers will perk up their ears and listen to your message.

■ **Use Frozen Foods.** Ask grocery stores to carry frozen veggie entrées, tofu, and soy milk.

■ **Promote Vegetarian Foods.** Ask local restaurants to highlight vegetarian entrées on their menus.

■ **Make a Vegetarian Line.** Ask your grocer to create a vegetarian line at the store so you won't have to put your groceries on a conveyor belt full of blood and salmonella leaked from packages of red meat and chicken.

■ **Try New Foods.** Broaden your eating horizons in ethnic restaurants that specialize in savory animal-free dishes and by trying new recipes in your own kitchen.

■ **Ask for Veggie Burgers.** Ask major fast-food chains to introduce veggie burgers and other alternatives to meat. Suggest that they accommodate the growing number of non–meat eaters. Tell them that salad bars are great but that there are also many other tasty fast-food meatless products available. (See Appendix F: People to Contact for addresses of the head offices of the world's largest fast-food chains.)

FLYING

■ **Ask for Vegan Meals.** When you make your flight reservations, inform the travel agent or airline representative that you want vegan meals. A few days before your departure, call the airline to make certain that your special meal request is still in the computer. There's still time (they need a day) for the airline to reorder the meals if your initial request disappeared.

■ **Support Animal-Friendly Airlines.** The following airlines have stopped serving and selling foie gras: American Airlines, United, Delta, Swiss Air, and Air Canada.

GET YOUR FAMILY INVOLVED

■ **Grill Vegan.** Grill up some tofu hot dogs and veggie burgers, and provide lots of good "fixin's" on the side (tahini sauce and grilled onions go great on the burgers) for your family, friends, and neighbors. Round out your menu with chips, a big salad, or a platter of raw vegetables with a tofu dip, and Tofutti ice cream cones.

■ **Cook Vegan.** Try cooking a different vegan meal every week for family and friends.

GET ACTIVE

■ **Provide Information.** Set up an information table at a fair, shopping mall, or other location that has a lot of pedestrian traffic. This is one of the most effective ways to reach large numbers of people. Include books, weighted-down leaflets (so the wind doesn't take them away), a collection tin with "Thank You" on it, a strutted card displaying buttons, plastic-covered posters, a display board about vegetarianism and/or your group with local information, a sign-up sheet with a pen on a string, and the name of your group prominently displayed on the front of your table. (You can order a Starter Table Pack including posters, bumper stickers, buttons, and a display copy of the book *Animal Liberation* for $15 from PETA.)

■ **Set Up Tables.** Find out where other groups in your community set up tables, and/or get a list of festivals and fairs from the Chamber of Commerce, Department of Parks and Recreation, or Tourist Department. (For certain locations you may need a permit from the mayor's office or police station.) Distribute literature about animal rights, the environment, health and diet, and the low cost of vegan meals.

■ **Join a Parade.** Find out when parades are planned and enter a vegetarian float. Remember, your message could be seen by millions if it's included in newspaper or television coverage.

■ **Hang a Banner.** Gather two or three friends to help you with a veg-friendly message from an overpass over a busy road or highway during the morning or evening rush hour. Be sure to hold it on the side facing oncoming traffic! Costumes add to the visual effect. "Chickens," "bunnies," and "cows" can be rented from local costume shops. Contact PETA for sample news releases or to borrow one of the following banners:

HOLIDAYS ARE MURDER ON TURKEYS

THANKSGIVING IS MURDER ON TURKEYS

CHICKENS: TORTURED, CRIPPLED, & KILLED. GO VEGETARIAN

CHICKEN MAKES YOU THICKEN, SICKEN, AND DEAD. GO VEG!

PORK BELLIES MAKE POT BELLIES

You can also make your own banner.

■ **Use Leaflets.** Literature can be left in hospital waiting rooms, health spas, beauty salons, on grocery store shelves, in "pet" shops, libraries, public bathrooms, on subway, bus, and train seats, and on car windshields.

■ **Protest the Wienermobile.** Call the Oscar Mayer hotline at 1-800-672-2754 to find out if the Wienermobile is coming to your area. Organize a demo to protest the Wienermobile's exploitation of pigs and children.

■ **Protest Ronald McDonald.** Greet Ronald McDonald with a poster (some activists have actually pied him!). Call McDonald's to find out if Ronald McDonald is coming to town. PETA can help you with props and tips.

■ **Write in Cement.** Instead of writing your name in wet cement, write, "Meat Is Murder."

■ **Use Stickers.** Label chicken packages in grocery stores with stickers (available from PETA) that say, "WARNING! This package contains the decomposing corpse of a small bird."

■ **Liberate a Lobster.** You may be able to persuade stores or restaurants to give you the lobster, especially if the lobster is large (old). Since lobsters require special handling, you may want to organize his or her liberation through PETA.

■ **Hold a Demonstration.** Even a one-person demonstration can do a lot of good. Someone wrote: "One hot summer day, as I drove up a busy highway in Florida, I noticed an elderly man at the stoplight. He was seated in a cheap aluminum lawn chair with a table, lemonade, and a sign that simply said, 'Don't buy a car here. They sold me a lemon.' One brave soul in the blazing sun, alone but bursting with conviction. I will never forget that man. More importantly, I will never buy a car from that dealer."

■ **Get Visual.** PETA activists drew attention to the ills of meat eating and killing animals for food at the National Maalox Pork Cookoff by clamping clothespins to their noses. Don McIntosh, 84, demonstrated at a meat-processors convention by holding a sign that expressed his disgust with their cruel methods. A vegetarian for thirty years, McIntosh says that he has been repulsed by meat processing since he was a boy. Easy and inexpensive to make, a protest sign pictured in a newspaper has the potential to send an animal rights message to millions of people.

■ **Hold a Vigil.** On Mother's Day, hold a vigil outside a restaurant that serves veal or outside a dairy plant. Coordinate a Spring Vigil for Chickens in your neighborhood this April or May. United Poultry Concerns (UPC) will provide you with handout literature, a sample news release, a public service announcement (PSA), and a Calendar of Events announcement. (See Appendix C: Recommended Groups for UPC's address.)

■ **Protest Conventions.** Protest meat industry conventions that come to your town. Let the public know about abuses like castration without anesthesia and narrow confinement stalls. Show them that "Meat Stinks!"

■ **Write to Your Elected Representatives.** Ask your congresspeople to stop subsidies to meat, dairy, and egg producers. Say that you are aware of the many risks to human health caused by a meat-centered diet and of the enormous cost to taxpayers of treating illnesses such as heart attacks, strokes, and cancer. Point out that livestock farming inflicts immense damage on the animals and the land. State your opposition to the mistreatment, restriction, and confinement of factory-farmed animals and the use of hormones, stimulants, tranquilizers, and antibiotics to control disease in the overcrowded pens. Point out that in consuming the flesh of these animals, people are also consuming an assortment of powerful drugs.

Letters should be short and simple. Ask that your letter be answered (it will be, as voters' comments are rarely ignored). Beware of misleading replies and respond to anything you disagree with. (Addresses are available from your local League of Women Voters; see Appendix F: People to Contact for addresses of United States and Canadian Departments of Agriculture.)

■ **Write to the American Veterinary Medical Association (AVMA).** Urge them to stand up for hens instead of the industry that profits from the birds' misery. Tell the AVMA to oppose forced molting. (See Appendix C: Recommended Groups for the AVMA's address.)

MEET THE PRESS

■ **Contact Your Newspaper.** Ask your local paper to write a story on the advantages of a vegetarian diet or the cruelties of the factory farm, or write a letter to the editor on the subject.

- **Contact Your Television Station.** Ask your local television stations to air a pro-vegetarian story.
- **Call Your Radio Station.** Jump into radio call-in discussions with animal issue tie-ins (for example, call in to a health show and offer information on vegetarianism).
- **Go to Animal Industry Sites.** Visit your local factory farm, stockyard, or slaughterhouse. Take photographs and document what you witness. Then publicize what you discover.
- **Write About Restaurants.** Write food editors and restaurant critics to suggest more vegetarian articles, reviews, and recipes.
- **Feed Disc Jockeys.** Deliver vegan "breakfasts in bed" to disc jockeys during their busy "drive time" morning shows to increase awareness of vegetarianism. When PETA did that, thousands of listeners heard the DJs say, "Yum!" after sampling the delicious meal and heard Robin Walker, who delivered the food, explain why vegetarianism is better for the animals, the Earth, and human health.

SPECIAL ACTIONS FOR YOUNG PEOPLE

- **Give a Speech or Write a Paper.** Research vegetarianism or animal rights. Danny Martinez of Huntington Beach, California, got an A+ when he chose to enlighten his classmates and teacher with an essay about meat consumption. After reading his essay to a school assembly, he was assailed by questions from students and teachers alike. Martinez, a vegetarian and long-time member of PETA, also spends free time placing cruelty labels on products that are tested on animals and vocalizing his strong opinions about animal rights. PETA has all sorts of information about various animal rights issues to help you with your research paper at school.
- **Make a Display.** Create a display about helping animals.
- **Use Fliers.** Copy fliers and post them on bulletin boards at your school and in your neighborhood.

■ **Talk to Your Teachers.** Ask your English teacher to have an essay assignment called "Animals Need Our Protection."

■ **Start a Group.** Start an animal rights group in your school.

■ **"Healthy Up" Your Lunch.** The Healthy School Lunch Action Guide has everything you need to approach your school district, food service personnel, teachers, parents, and students with information (including recipes, meal plans, food values). Contact EarthSave's Healthy School Lunch Program. (See Appendix C: Recommended Groups for address.)

■ **Boycott 4-H.** Don't participate in 4-H animal projects. The 4-H emblem is a four-leaf clover with an H on each leaf that stands for head, heart, hand, and health. Use your head, have a heart, give the animals a hand, and preserve their health (and yours).

■ **Clean Up.** Really shock your parents and offer to do the washing up for a week if they don't eat veal, eat more veggie food, or substitute soy milk for cow's milk.

■ **Make Art.** Enter art or poetry competitions and create a piece that speaks for animals or create a photo collage that shows meat for what it really is.

■ **Decorate to Liberate.** Mike Vallely uses his popularity to influence other young people positively. Every year thousands of skateboarding fans all over the world see the message, "Please don't eat my friends," painted on his colorful, unique deck. You can spread the word by decorating lunch boxes, lockers, motorbikes, and anything else you have.

VEGAN TIPS

■ **Dump Dairy!** For more information and recipe ideas, write to PETA for a "Cooking Without Dairy" recipe sheet.

■ **Try Taste-Alikes.** If you crave the taste of chicken or sausage, explore Loma Linda and Worthington taste-alikes made of soy, available at Seventh Day Adventist food stores, many major supermarkets, and health food stores. Some Chinese restaurants, like the Longlife Vegetarian

House in Berkeley and the Harmony in Philadelphia, specialize in wheat-gluten "chicken" dishes that would fool the most discerning diner!

■ **Go to a Health Food Store.** Check at your local health food store for Yves' "Fat Free Veggie Deli Slices," Tofutti's "Better Than Cream Cheese" or "Tofutti Cuties" (vegan "ice cream" sandwiches), Lightlife Foods' "Tofu Pups," Worthington's TVP "Vegetarian Burger," Imagine Foods' "Rice Dream" brand rice milk and "ice cream," and Soymage nondairy soy cheese.

■ **Veganize Your Recipes.**

Eggs When a recipe calls for eggs, simply leave the eggs out or use an egg substitute, such as the one made by Ener-g Foods (for the store nearest you carrying this product, call 1-800-331-5222). For breakfast, scramble mashed tofu with onions, mushrooms, and a dash of mustard, turmeric, and soy sauce. Soft or extra-soft tofu makes a great binder, as do bananas.

Milk Try commercially available vanilla, carob, almond, and plain soy milk (or rice milk or nut milk) for cooking, cereal, tea, coffee, and hot chocolate. Offered in vitamin-fortified and lowfat varieties.

Butter Sauté in water or vegetable broth, flavor veggies with lemon, "butter" toast with vegetable margarine. (For optimum health, use all fats sparingly.) Use gourmet mustards instead on sandwiches.

Cheese Try soy "cheese," available at health food stores. Great on pizza and sandwiches. Or cheese up your sauces and veggies with nutritional yeast flakes (also great on popcorn). Tofu can be used in vegan lasagna and cheesecake recipes.

Yogurt Try healthful fruit-and-tofu yogurts, available at health food stores.

Ice Cream Delicious tofu or rice "ice creams" are sweeter and healthier. Or try tangy fruit sorbets.

Hamburger Use texturized vegetable protein (TVP) in chili, "meat"-loaf, tacos, lasagna filling, spaghetti sauces, and

Help Animals Used for Food

What You Can Do

55

other recipes calling for flesh. Try one of the dozens of commercial tofu, tempeh, vegetable, and grain burgers available.

Seafood Eat sea *vegetables* instead of sea *animals*. There are about ten different varieties of seaweeds commonly available in the United States from most health food stores. Use *nori* as a wrap for avocado and cucumber sushi; try *wakame* or *kombu* in soups; or toast *nori* as a great salty snack.

3

Those Incredibly
Amusing Animals

On television I saw a hostage who had returned from Iraq. He was asked if he had been abused and he said, "Well, they took me from my home and family and freedom, and there is no greater abuse to anyone."

—A PETA MEMBER'S LETTER

Since the beginning of time, human beings the world over have used animals and their body parts as ready sources of amusement. Animals' bladders and heads were used as footballs long before their whole bodies were put to the test in the gory shows of the Roman Circus. Games requiring fewer and less exotic animals were popular in Europe until quite recently; bull-baiting and tying cats' tails together "in sport" were popular wagering activities throughout Europe well into the 1800s.

Today, although cockfighting is still legal in many countries and states, most animal fights have been rendered illegal, except in Afghanistan, Turkey, and Pakistan (where bears are still pitted against dogs, and international animal protection groups like the World Society for the Protection of Animals [WSPA] are raising a ruckus).

Animals are still dragged all over the field and paraded around for sport. For ceremonial purposes to mark the opening of games, doves are trucked in, held in cages until the magic moment, and then released to fend for themselves in strange surroundings or to try to make their way home (although the Olympic Committee has now switched to bird-shaped kites following complaints that disoriented birds released at the Korean games were burned alive in the Olympic flame). At county fairs, baby pigs race for food, and camels race because someone is digging them in the ribs with their heels. Overweight college students still hit and kick donkeys across gym floors in donkey basketball games. Ponies, denied water so they will not make unsightly messes, turn endless circles in children's carousels, and hermit crab races bring patrons into beach bars. What a state of affairs.

In Spain, the "proud tradition" of bullfighting has suffered a setback with the revelation that the bulls' eyes are smeared with petroleum jelly to blur their vision and the animals are given laxatives to debilitate them. All that must make it a tiny bit easier for the men and, occasionally, the women in the spangled outfits to stick their daggers into the bull's shoulders without too much risk. In the barbaric grand finale, as the crowd rises to its feet, the bull's ears are severed and presented to patrons as a trophy. The picadors' horses are often gored, occasionally to death.

Thankfully, there is light at the end of the bullfighting tunnel. Although television has made the bullfight accessible to more fans than could ever travel to see one, a large and ever-growing number of young people look down on such gruesome affairs as their "grandfathers' shame," and many tourist offices warn would-be fans that they won't enjoy them.

In North America, we have our own shames, such as, when the country was being settled, the mortifying way cowboys in the "Wild West" treated the miserable animals they herded on the way to slaughter. To that dim tradition of picking on those who can't defend themselves, we added new variations: We now have gay rodeo, black rodeo, and other games created by people who, themselves having experienced the sting of prejudice, should know better.

Aside from the more oddball events, the greatest cruelties we visit upon animals in the name of entertainment are institutionalized, just as they are in meat production and experimentation. The institutions under the microscope here are the zoo, the circus, the rodeo, and the animal racing industry. The image of these once harmless-seeming places and pastimes is fast being tarnished as the knowledge we have gained about animals has changed drastically in just a few human generations.

In 1849, Thomas Macauley was one of more than 150,000 people who camped out for days to see the first hippopotamus ever to be exhibited on British soil. He was amazed by the sight. Said Macauley, "I have seen the hippopotamus both asleep and awake, and I can assure you that, asleep or awake, he is the ugliest of the works of God."

Today, young people in North America or Europe, whose counterparts in 1849 would have thought a trip to the zoo or circus an experience akin to taking a trip to Mars, no longer get a thrill out of watching a hippo standing virtually motionless near a fake rock in an enclosure the size of their backyards or at a lion being controlled by a man in silly boots with a big whip. These children are afforded far more engaging hours of entertainment from a walk in truly natural surroundings or, for that matter, interactive video games and a myriad of other easily obtainable distractions.

In this chapter I offer a close look at what's wrong with the biggest animal entertainment institutions: circuses and zoos. In the What You Can Do section at the end of the chapter, you will find information about other cruelties, such as rodeos and racing.

ZOOS: FINE PLACES TO WALK AROUND AND GRAB A SNACK?

In 1991, Dale Marcellini, a curator of reptiles at the National Zoo in Washington, D.C., decided to do something truly interesting.

He turned his attention from zoo lizards to zoo visitors. He began studying what he calls "this huge population of animals we knew nothing about."

Marcellini and his colleagues watched and listened to more than seven hundred people over the course of a few summers. "Basically, we just tracked them," Marcellini says. "We'd pick them up at one of the entrances and tail them and record what they did."

The data Marcellini collected was quite surprising to zoo administrators because it exploded the myth that zoos are excellent ways to teach people respect and understanding for animals. The study showed that zoos are little more than backdrops for people's other preoccupations.

The visitors' conversations dealt, not with the animals at all, but mostly with their own lives. When people did comment on an animal, it was usually to remark on how someone they knew looked like that baboon or hippopotamus in the enclosure in front of them or to speculate as to how an octopus or some other animal could eat a person. The most common words used to describe animals were not words of wonderment and showed no respect or newly found knowledge of the species. Rather, animals were mostly described as "dirty," "cute," "ugly," "funny-looking," and "strange."

Marcellini found that almost 60 percent of visitors' time was spent walking from place to place, almost 10 percent was spent eating, and other chunks of time went to resting, bathroom breaks, and shopping. When visitors were actually milling around in exhibit areas, they spent less than eight seconds per snake and one minute with the lions. Pere David's deer, expected to be extinct when the last deer dies in the zoo, rated a mere twenty-seven seconds.

Marcellini concluded that people were "treating the exhibits like wallpaper."

It is not that zoos have gone downhill. Their origins never were anything to write home about. Originally set up as private menageries for the well-heeled, including Kublai Khan, Alexander the Great, Henry III, and Pope Leo X, zoos developed into moneymaking enterprises, places the public could visit, usually for a fee, to view the "weird and wonderful creatures" captured from then relatively novel expeditions to South America, Africa, and other "faraway" places.

When the Aztec ruler Montezuma's private zoo was unearthed, archaeologists found not only pumas, jaguars, and birds of prey, but the skeletons of albino and hunchback humans, people whose deformities had made them curiosities exotic enough to put on display. In about 1904, the Bronx Zoo put a Congolese Pygmy on display. He spoke no English and no one spoke his language, but everyone had a good gawk. At about the same time, some "Eskimo boys" from northern Greenland were exhibited in a traveling show, and, over the family's protestations, the skeleton of one Inuit's father ended up in the American Museum of Natural History. One can only imagine how future generations will shake their heads at today's practices and wonder how we could be so blind to the family relationships and rights of today's curiosities.

Early on, zoos figured out that adult gorillas, giraffes, and other animals are too strong and difficult to capture, so zoo collectors devised a simple plan: They shot all the adult animals in the family group and netted the babies. Most of the babies don't make it. Field zoologists and behaviorists, like Dr. Biruté Galdikas, estimate that for every primate who arrived alive in the West, eight or more perished, succumbing to untreated injuries or illness, dehydration, and malnutrition at the holding stations, cruel transportation through the jungle, and the trauma of overseas shipment. It is a shameful toll.

Removed from their real mothers, baby gorillas and other great ape infants grow up, bottle-fed, diapered, and baby-talked to until they reach puberty. At that point, a chimpanzee is at least ten times as strong as the strongest man and can lift him off the ground, something a chimpanzee juvenile, trained to walk on a harness and leash, illustrated perfectly by running up a tall tree and pulling his handler up the trunk behind him.

At puberty, the combination of these animals' powerful hormonal drives and their phenomenal strength dooms them to sudden banishment from human company. After years of being mollycoddled and treated as precious little people, the chimpanzees suddenly find themselves booted out of the house, dumped in a barren cage, and treated like dangerous beasts.

Added to this traumatic upheaval is the often horrifying experience, for an ape raised as a human being, of coming face to face for the very first time with others of his own kind. Washoe is a chimpanzee who was raised to eat at the table with her human "parents." She lived as part of a human household and went to the drive-in for ice cream. She wore diapers, played in the yard, and was taught American Sign Language. When she matured, Washoe was introduced to other chimpanzees and nearly went into cardiac arrest. Frantic, she signed to her humans something along the lines of, "Washoe want out! Let Washoe out! Big dirty black hairy dogs here!"

As for marine animals, whales, dolphins, and orcas usually come to the aquarium in this way: They are kidnapped from their pods and families at sea by "aqua cowboys," men who use speedboats to corner a whole group of sea mammals and then net the babies. Like ape infants raised in captivity, these babies have missed the mothering skills nature intended them to learn in the bosom of their real families. When they themselves give birth in captivity, they can be frightened and confused by the presence of the new life form that has suddenly appeared before them, not knowing what to do with it and not realizing they are meant to suckle and nurture the infant. The result is the sort of article you see in the newspaper that reads, "Zoo/aquarium keepers step in to save baby (whale, panda, gorilla) when mother abandons her."

Of course, the cycle is perpetuated if the baby whale, panda, or gorilla survives. Most do not.

A ZOO BY ANY OTHER NAME . . .

As for education, although the majority of big zoos have finally done away with such debasing and silly shenanigans as dressing chimpanzees up in human clothing and making them have tea parties or juggle, zoos have a long way to go to redeem themselves. Nor do they live up to all their public relations talk about breeding endangered species to preserve the gene pool. It is estimated that only 5 percent of the world's ten thousand or more zoos can honestly claim to do anything whatsoever for the "conservation" of animals, not that there is so much as a mousehole of habitat left into which to reestablish these endangered animals.

Some zoos recognize that they do not have the best of reputations, but instead of doing an about-face and putting their money into habitat protection *in the animals' disappearing homelands,* or setting up programs in Africa and other countries that would provide an incentive for native peoples to stop poaching and encroaching, they simply change their names.

When one zoo in New York decided to call itself a "conservation park," it prompted a local radio commentator to remark that, given the zoo's wretched record of animal care, "That's like a bunch of rapists deciding to call themselves a dating service."

Existing zoos would perform a valuable service by evolving into desperately needed sanctuaries for displaced wildlife—the elderly bears dumped by a bankrupt circus, the baboons left on the New York docks by a traveling show that sailed back to Russia, the gorilla who spent twenty years in a cage in a shopping mall before activists persuaded the owner to let him go. Instead, the majority of zoos still treat animals as commodities, moving "specimens" about as if they were lifeless portraits in a traveling art exhibit, and separating lovers of many years standing, simply to provide a new mate for some other zoo's "collection."

In August 1996, I wrote an editorial that appeared in newspapers in several states. I wondered what would happen to a gorilla baby then at the Brookfield Zoo in suburban Chicago. His mother is Binti Jua.

Binti herself had captured international headlines, and a great deal of fuss was being made over her. What had happened was this: A three-year-old boy had fallen into the zoo's gorilla pit as his own mother watched helplessly. The boy tumbled over the wall and landed in the dry concrete moat that divides the gorillas from the public. He lay there motionless while onlookers screamed because several large gorillas were in the enclosure, including a male silverback weighing in at many hundreds of pounds of sheer muscle.

Binti was not small either, and a gasp went up from the crowd as the fall got her attention and she began to head for the moat.

Before anyone could stop her, Binti had clambered down into the pit and picked the human child up. Very gently, she cradled him in her arms, despite the weight of her own child on her back. She headed directly for the gate through which her keepers came and went and deliberately set the boy down there, then waited for help. The child recovered.

Binti was not the only gorilla to show such concern for the young of her captors' species. A few years earlier, a huge male silverback named Jambo had performed a similar act, using his body to shield from younger males a child who had fallen into an exhibit on an island off the coast of France. Both gorillas had revealed that a soft heart beats inside that King Kong chest.

I asked in my editorial whether the zoo was likely to return the favor and save *Binti's* child. The answer is probably a resounding "No!" for if past practice is any guide, the baby will not remain with her mother and family as would happen in nature. It is too early to tell yet, but the baby will probably be lent, swapped, or sold to another zoo, perhaps even shipped overseas to spend his life in confinement elsewhere. For in the zoo's eyes, a baby gorilla is not an individual or part of a gorilla family unit. He is marketable goods to be displayed, bred, shuffled about, and used.

Compassionate people might question the wholesomeness of zoos if they knew that many zoos enjoy cozy and very hush-hush relationships with research departments at universities, allowing experiments on animals to be conducted on zoo premises in buildings that are off-limits to the public, and sometimes shipping animals off to labs. I remember, years ago, learning that the Detroit zoo had sent a group of crab-eating macaques to terminal research when they became "unstylish." They replaced them with an exhibit of trendier snow monkeys. Zoos often compete for public attention by entertaining and providing ever more titillating species rather than by educating about those animals unlucky enough to be common or out of vogue.

Some zoos have gone so far as to buy certain exotic reptiles and primates on the black market when trade in them is illegal, and some dispose of their "surplus" lions and other animals by sending them to cheap, rundown traveling shows in South America or even to game ranches to be shot for a fee. So much for respect for the animal kingdom.

NOT EVEN A NICE PLACE TO VISIT

Then, there is life in the zoo. The Born Free Foundation in the United Kingdom has done its homework on what the animals feel about captivity. The foundation's opinion, based on studies by investigators who spent three years traveling to over one hundred zoos across Britain, Europe, and North America, is that the animals go mad. Deprived of their natural homelands, natural social structures, and outlets for many of the skills that have naturally evolved in their species, animals develop abnormal "stereotypic behavior," "psychosis," or "zoochosis."

This means that animals try to compensate for their great loneliness, their frustration, boredom, and the loss of control over their lives by making repetitive and obsessive movements. They bob their heads up and down constantly, rock back and forth, walk in circles wearing dirt trails through their enclosures or indentations in the cement of their cage floors, suck their bars like popsicles (factory-farmed pigs do this, too), throw up and repeatedly eat their own vomit, and mutilate themselves, say by picking on their arms even after they have created bloody wounds.

Dr. Phil Murphy, head of Clinical Psychology for Mental Handicap in Norfolk, England, told reporters that such behaviors "can still be found in institutions caring for our severely mentally disturbed patients." Of course, a zoo fits just that description.

Sometimes zookeepers resort to medication to treat the misery zoos cause. A case in point is Gus, a famous polar bear housed in New York's Central Park Zoo. Gus came to the public's attention in 1994 when he became the first "zoo animal" to be given Prozac. For over four years, this very depressed bear had spent almost every waking moment swimming, back and forth, back and forth, in the small cement pool in his enclosure. Perhaps the viewing public enjoyed the look of the "icebergs" constructed in Gus's enclosure, but to a lonely, bored bear a long way from home they were just big meaningless pieces of fiberglass that had not slowed his descent into madness. We are told that the Prozac helped. But Gus is still swimming—alone—back and forth and back and forth.

In aquariums, like the much-touted one in Baltimore Harbor, dolphins and other sea animals routinely die of stress, sometimes physically manifested in ulcers. Dolphins and orcas can develop a drooping dorsal fin before noticeably losing weight or dropping dead; some marine mammals develop vision problems from the chlorine and other chemicals put in their tanks, some develop nutritional problems from the diet they are fed (zoos depart so far from the animals' natural diet that they have been criticized by their own keepers for feeding low quality "straw" to grazing hoofed "stock," and horsemeat to naturally vegetarian gorillas).

The stress animals in aquariums experience is, one presumes, caused in large part by never having freedom or privacy. Enormous sea animals are kept in tanks that, compared to the hundreds of miles they may travel in their true homes, must be like living in a bathtub. They have to breathe and drink their own diluted urine and the waste of the others in the tank with them; they are unable to use their sonar, which, in captivity, simply bounces off the tank walls; they can never jump in the waves or choose a mate; and they can never escape the noise of tens of thousands of visitors, whose steps vibrate through the cement walls of their tanks all day long, every day.

Zoos and aquariums are antithetical to our more recent understanding of our place in nature—not as its master, but as one part of a whole. They show children shadows of animals, defeated beasts who are not behaving as they should, and they teach all the wrong lessons: that it is acceptable to imprison animals, to deprive them of free flight and travel, to forbid them the chance to establish their natural territory, to breed and separate them as we, not they, please; and to let them go nuts from a great loneliness of spirit.

A truly educational experience might be one in which human beings returned to the zoo to appear as exhibits. Actors have performed in this role at the Baltimore, Maryland, zoo, at a zoo in Canada, and in France. The purpose was always the same: to inspire introspection about our own roles in the great web of life.

In the future, we may see robots replace the conventional zoo, like the 439-pound virtual reality gorilla developed by the Georgia Institute of Technology. To interact with him, you put on a headset, step into a computer-generated gorilla habitat, and meet up with a gorilla troop. If the "visitor" behaves properly, she or he may be rewarded with a grooming session from a motherly female.

Until those happy times arrive, every summer, during peak zoo visiting time, volunteers from PETA and other animal protection groups can often be found standing on the sidewalks outside zoos like the National Zoo in Washington, D.C. They are there to hand out pamphlets, urging visitors to "Be a Zoochecker." The pamphlets contain a series of boxes visitors can check off whenever they see an animal whirling in circles or showing some other zoochotic behavior. Realizing such problems exist allows parents and their children to reevaluate their opinions about zoos and to focus on the plight of the animals.

Many will never see the zoo in quite the same light again.

DEAR RANI,
AND HOW TYKE ESCAPED

Rani was the first captive elephant I ever met. Every single day for many years she stood outside the Asoka Hotel in New Delhi, India, from sunrise to late at night, waiting to be prodded into action whenever a tourist fancied a ride. She wore a jewel-encrusted cloth mantle over her head and her brown and pink skin was painted with an intricate pattern of paisley and dots.

When I first saw Rani I couldn't have been much taller than her knee, but she was extremely gentle with me even when she could see that her handler, Ram, had succumbed to the midday heat and conked out under a bush. She allowed me to hang on to her legs and would gently blow air into my hair and down my neck to cool me in the blistering heat or hold my wrist in her trunk and sway slowly back and forth.

If business was slow, Ram would dig the bullhook into Rani's neck, just behind her ear, to make her kneel. Then he would hoist me into the pretty wooden *howdah* on her back. I would kick my legs over the edge of the little box as Rani lurched up and forward, then lumbered slowly down the hotel driveway and into the street. I remember the air was choked with the fumes of unfiltered fuel from the hundreds of little putt-putt motorcycle cabs and decorated trucks fighting it out on the street. Even high up on Rani's back, I could feel the carbon particles in my throat. I didn't think how much worse it must have been for her.

In fact, I didn't think about the quality of her life at all until one day when I asked Ram where Rani had come from and he explained that young elephants are taken from their families and "broken." He described how they must be chained and beaten until they learn to listen and behave. (It wasn't until the mid-1990s that I saw a *National Geographic* special on American television showing men carrying out exactly that barbaric and inhumane system. Since then, I've learned that deep in the jungles of Thailand, elephants are also chained down, flat, to the ground and beaten in preparation for circus life in the United States.)

Rani died, long before I had learned that elephant calves left unmolested in the wild, like orca infants, stay at their mothers' sides for a decade or longer; that elephants cradle their lost relatives' skulls in their trunks; that they use tools as flyswatters, to sweep paths, even to draw pictures in the dirt and scratch themselves in inaccessible places; that they communicate in rumbles at frequencies so low humans cannot detect the sounds without sophisticated equipment.

There are between two and three thousand "Ranis" held captive in the beastwagons of Western circuses and in private collections. Sometimes the elephants stop behaving like windup toys and crush the bones and breath out of a keeper, make a break for it, go berserk, and head for the unreachable hills. Most simply endure. Their spirits were broken during capture and, later, God help them, when they were trained for the ring. Many are drugged to calm them down. Otherwise, they would all use their immense strength to fight back against the human hand of tyranny. They would refuse to be kept chained between performances like coats on a rack, refuse to be backed up ramps into railroad cars and into trailers like so many cars being parked out of the way.

In just one week, in Queens, New York, nine elephants from the Clyde Beatty Cole Bros. circus suddenly broke away from their handlers. As they broke free, the spectators' adrenaline levels shot to the tent top in pure terror. But this time, the elephants were subdued and shackled before anyone got hurt. It was the second incident that summer. "Debbie," one of the elephants involved in the Queens incident, was one of two elephants who had run amok some weeks earlier, smashing through a plate glass window in downtown Hanover, Pennsylvania.

Three times in the summer of 1995 a "circus elephant" went berserk and crushed her captors. "Flora" crushed the skull of a Moscow Circus interpreter minutes before a planned appearance on the Regis and Kathy Lee show. In Honolulu, a twenty-one-year-old elephant named Tyke deliberately stomped her trainer to death, waving his body aloft in her trunk afterward, then injuring spectators as she tore out of the Circus International tent and into her death by gunfire. It was the second elephant attack at that circus in a week. The summer before, Janet, an old elephant who had been kept on repeated doses of tranquilizers, tore out of the Great American Circus ring in Florida, carrying a box full of children on her back. She was shot forty-seven times by an off-duty police officer before she died. Police officer Blaine Doyle, the man who pulled the trigger, said, "I think these elephants are trying to tell us that circuses are not what God created them for."

Janet, the elephant shot in Florida, had appeared under several names. It is in fact common, when an elephant starts to "act up" or "go bad," to pass him or her on to another circus under a different name or to keep them and start calling them something else to deflect attention and, presumably, to escape liability. This ruse goes back many years. Hannibal, who was brought to the United States in 1824, killed at least seven people, and when he went on a rampage was stabbed repeatedly with pitchforks, a technique that couldn't have helped improve his disposition.

While the pachyderms' polite protestations have sometimes turned desperate, circus proprietors remain complacent, sitting in their counting houses counting out their money while their habits of slugging and drugging uppity elephants worsen the problem.

Elephants have the largest brains of any mammals on the face of the Earth. They are creative, altruistic, and kind. Imagine what it must be like for them to be ordered around, courtesy of a bullhook, every moment of their lives. They live over seventy years in their homelands, but their average life in captivity is reduced to fourteen years. Because of stress, traveling in boxcars, and being stabled in damp basements, many captive elephants have arthritis, gammy legs, and tuberculosis, a strain that is contagious to their keepers and to children who ride on their backs.

Left to their own devices on their own turf, as it should be, elephants enjoy extended family relationships: aunties baby-sit, mothers teach junior life skills such as how to use different kinds of leaves and mud to ward off sunburn and insect bites, babies play together under watchful eyes, lovemaking is gentle and complex, and elephant relatives mourn their dead. In captivity, of course, elephants are deprived of all such experiences. Life under the Big Top means performing heavy manual labor, paying attention to your trainer, feeling his "mahout stick" (a wooden rod with a cruel pointed metal end) bite into your flesh. Don't stumble or falter even if you feel tired or ill. Obey, obey, obey. It means leg chains between acts, including "martingales," shackles that are used on males during "must"—a time of sexual desire—and in cases of severe disobedience, to fasten the elephant's head to his front feet. It means the loss of all comfort and warmth from your father and mother, your siblings and children. It means having no long-term friends.

Behaviorists tell us that elephants can and do cry from loss of social interaction and physical abuse. Yes, cry. Small wonder these magnificent beings can't always keep from going mad—waiting in line night after night, eyes riveted on the man with the metal hook, then circling to the music in their beaded headdresses.

Civil rights activist Dick Gregory took up championing the plight of elephants in circuses and traveling shows in 1998. Standing outside Madison Square Garden on the opening night of Ringling Bros. circus, he told passersby, "Elephants in circuses represent the domination and oppression we have fought against for so long," and urged them not to buy tickets.

Of course, other animals suffer in circuses. It is only common sense to realize that leopards don't jump through flaming hoops because they find it enjoyable, orangutans don't skate around in a dress and roller skates because it is comfortable to do so, and bears don't choose to spend their Decembers riding a bicycle over a barrel. The muzzle, the neck chain, the whip, the chair, the bullhook, and the electric shock prod clenched in the handler's palm make that deduction easy. So does a little basic understanding of animals' very natures. Orangutans are arboreal, their feet turn inward, and they have difficulty standing upright for very long; tigers and lions are afraid of fire and avoid it at all costs; and bears' biological clocks tell them to hibernate when cold weather comes.

Since you can't explain to wild animals like brown bears what the point is of holding sticks in their paws and walking along a trapeze line suspended thirty feet above the ring, how do you make them do this? To say, "With love, patience, and understanding," stretches the limits of P. T. Barnum's line, "There's a sucker born every minute." Chances are, you do it by introducing the fear of something even worse and more frightening involving any implement from a gun with blank cartridges to an electric shock or a red-hot poker. The circus business is not a gentle trade.

In his book, *The Circus Kings,* Henry North Ringling writes, "It is not usually a pretty sight to see the big cats trained . . . When he (the trainer) starts off they are all chained to their pedestals, and ropes are put around their necks to choke them down and make them obey. All sorts of other brutalities are used to force them to respect the trainer and learn their tricks. They work from fear."

That is exactly what PETA's investigator found at Tiger's Eye Productions, a circus training school in Florida, when he responded to a whistleblower complaint. Videotapes of training practices there show big cats being dragged around on chains, hit with broom handles and fists, slapped and punched across the face, and having ax handles shoved down their throats. The cats were trucked in thunderstorms and left in open cages in the fierce Florida heat at gas stations and other cheap venues where the trainer was paid to perform as part of sales stunts.

In Taiwan in the spring of 1998, I visited the compound and later met with performers from the American International Circus, a hodgepodge of circus stars from all over the world. When I sat down with the Russian woman who ran the bear act, unbeknownst to her I had already seen her miserable, dull-coated bears in their small, barren, and rusty traveling cages, including one female bear who had become "unmanageable" and who sucked her teeth constantly, a sign of severe stress.

"Natasha" answered my questions with great charm. "Where did she get her bears," I asked. "They are all orphans," she smiled. "I rescue them when they are found without mothers in the woods." She was so used to saying this that the words came out without hesitation. "What happens to them when they get old?" "I send them to a wonderful retirement park, just outside Moscow, so they can live out their old age," came the pat reply. "Is it difficult to train them?" "No, I raise them as my babies. They love me. To them, I am their mother. With little treats, they learn their tricks from me when they are very, very small." "Do they ever give you trouble?" "Trouble? To their mother? Never!"

Later, when Natasha had left, the ringmaster, a burly Irishman, sat down to coffee with me. He had no idea I was with an animal protection group. I told him I was impressed that Natasha could manage such big bears.

"Oh, that woman's tough as nails," he said. "She has a little iron bar that never leaves her hand. When one of those bears gives her any lip, she smashes him on the nose with it. One of her assistants mouthed off at her a few weeks ago and she knocked him out cold. No one messes with her."

LIKE FAMILY

Bobby Berosini, once a performer on the Las Vegas strip, loved his orangutans, too. At least that's what he told everyone, referring to the apes he used onstage as his "children." "I am their dad" was one of his catch phrases.

Yet, what kind of "dad" was he? Octavio Gesmundo, a dancer in the casino act before Berosini's, had heard what he described as "awful sounds" coming from behind the curtain just before Berosini entered the spotlight. After hearing this commotion night after night, Octavio decided to set up a hidden camera backstage.

Berosini starred in two shows every night, bringing on the orangs in their little sparkly boxer shorts, making them sit on upturned tubs, wiggle their backsides, and give the finger to the audience in the smoke-filled room. What Octavio recorded, every night, twice a night, for eight nights in a row, was Berosini and his assistants secretly beating the animals with a metal bar, pinching their shoulders, pulling their hair, and punching them in the face just before the orangs were walked onstage.

Later, in court (Berosini sued Gesmundo and PETA for allowing the tapes to be shown on television!), Berosini, referring throughout the trial to the orangs as his "kids," told the judge that such behavior is acceptable because "you have to get the animals' attention." He likened the "discipline" he doled out as "nothing more" than what a parent would do to get the attention of a misbehaving child in a supermarket.

Gentle animals, orangutans are known in their homelands of Borneo and Sumatra as "people of the forest." The Berosini orangutans spent their lives in isolation confinement, totally dominated by their handlers. Using one of the oldest tricks of circus lore, between acts Berosini kept them stored, individually, on a bus in solid metal containers. He had air holes drilled into the boxes near the top. The orangutans' only "freedom" came when Berosini opened the doors to clean the boxes or to give the orangs food. The only other excursion was generally the hour or so when the animals were "performing" on stage. Berosini cultivated their absolute dependency, making sure they knew he held the key to everything in their perverted lives: He was the man who could let them stand up after being hunched over for hours on end in their boxes, the man who decided whether they would starve or receive nourishment, the man who could ease their thirst.

Burning for revenge, Berosini filed a $20 million lawsuit against Gesmundo, PETA, and others, for invasion of privacy and libel. While at first gaining the upper hand with his "my children, the orangutans" line, the tide of public opinion and subsequent court rulings went against the entertainer. His credibility eroded before his eyes as more and more people saw the tapes and heard a litany of testimony of abuse spanning ten years. While Berosini told jurors he had only "tapped" the apes with "a little wooden bird perch," one eyewitness described picking up the instrument used by Berosini to strike the animals and recalled, "It was similar to a heavy-duty welding rod, approximately sixteen inches long." Yet another eyewitness reported watching in horror as Berosini "repeatedly punched an orangutan with both fists." Another reported hearing Berosini yelling at the orangutans and watching the bus in which they were kept rock back and forth as he heard them being beaten.

Berosini's career hit the skids, the USDA compelled him to build enclosures for the apes, the U.S. Fish and Wildlife Service took away his license to buy and sell endangered species, and he found himself out of work and facing more than $1 million in legal fees and a huge judgment.

Things started to get a bit rocky for other members of this old circus family, too. Berosini's niece, Brigitte, was bitten on the neck and face by a five-hundred-pound tiger during her Las Vegas act, and at almost the same time, Berosini's brother, Otto, ran into trouble. Government authorities found nine of the big cats Otto used in his own circus act living in small traveling crates on an Indian reservation about fifty miles outside Las Vegas. A leopard found in a pool of vomit and lions suffering from urine burns were taken into custody by the government. Pasha, one of the tigers, who had been lying in her own excrement, too weak to stand up, dehydrated, and suffering from abscesses and infection, died shortly afterward.

BIG NAMES BLAST THE BIG TOP

The big circuses love movie stars to be seen at their openings, but many stars are too wise to touch such an event with a barge pole and reject lucrative offers to appear in such shows

75

as the "Circus of the Stars." Steve Allen, Mike Farrell, James Coburn, Doc Severinsen, and Zsa Zsa Gabor showed how much they objected to the domination and abuse of animals by unhesitatingly condemning Berosini; *Golden Girls* star Rue McClanahan, PETA's honorary chairperson, flew to Las Vegas with *American Top Forty*'s icon Casey Kasem, comedian Kevin Nealon, and baseball great Tony La Russa, all at their own expense, to stand up for the apes.

Gérard Dépardieu, Juliette Binochet, and other celebrities have signed a letter to Prince Rainier of Monaco, asking him please to bar animals from appearing in the dreadful "International Circus Festival of Monte Carlo." Every year, the beastwagons of notorious circus families roll over the mountains, bringing a sad collection of landlocked sea lions and monkeys in frilly dresses to perform for the Grimaldi family, its guests, and paying customers. Among the participants are the Chipperfields. (Mary Chipperfield was charged with multiple counts of cruelty to animals in 1998, the same year one of her sons shot a caged tiger to death in a fit of rage while working with Ringling Bros. in the United States.)

Box office superstars like Alec Baldwin and Kim Basinger speak out vociferously against the exploitation of animals. They have both attended hearings against the carriage-horse trade, protesting how overworked these poor worn-down animals are, toiling in the heat, their noses at tailpipe height in the traffic. Kim has appeared before the United States Congress to appeal for stricter laws to protect the victims of entertainment and, in 1998, wrote personally to the USDA on PETA's behalf in the case of Kenny, an elephant used by Ringling Bros.

Kenny came to Kim's attention when a whistleblower called to relate that, although just three years old, the little Indian elephant had already been separated from his mother and was traveling and performing for Ringling.

Ringling was fully aware that Kenny had become ill, yet they still forced him to perform. Even when Kenny was "wobbly" on his feet and "wailing," he was taken into the ring and made to do two shows. By the third show, Kenny made it into the ring, but couldn't perform. He died later that day and Ringling had his body hauled away.

Kim Basinger immediately asked the United States secretary of agriculture to investigate the case. He did just that and charged Ringling with negligence under the Animal Welfare Act. Ringling settled the case, paying $20,000 under a court agreement.

Alec Baldwin says it took him years to realize what circus life must be like for the animals. In an *Animal Times* article he wrote for PETA, he appealed to compassionate people not to go to animal circuses, but instead to ask themselves four simple questions: (1) Where did these animals come from? (2) How are these animals kept between shows? (3) What would they rather be doing? and (4) What will become of them in the end?

It is unlikely that any of the answers would make us feel comfortable about supporting the continuation of any animal show. For example, in the case of an elephant, the answers are probably: (1) The lush Indian jungle. (2) Shackled constantly by their front and back legs (or inside a dark train boxcar traveling between towns). (3) Walking among the trees, bathing in the river, feeling the sun on their backs, being with their families. (4) They'll probably be sold to a cheap zoo and die lonely and sad.

Of course, the answer to "How are they kept?" is "Beyond abysmally" in the case of many of the less attractive and endearing animals unlucky enough to end up in a circus. In *The Rose-Tinted Menagerie*, an exquisitely researched and very moving book about life for animals in the circus, the author, William Johnson, describes how crocodiles are kept for most of their lives in total darkness in minuscule tanks and boxes, the lids kept on, the animals' mouths taped shut.

How much better, then, if we are to have circuses at all, to have ones composed entirely of human performers: jugglers, tightrope walkers, fire-eaters, clowns, acrobats, and daredevils who are there of their own free will.

There are umpteen animal-free circuses, but perhaps the most amazing is the Cirque du Soleil. This enormous circus, which performs all over the world, is known as "the circus of the next century," and it so beautifully costumes its performers and choreographs its acts in ways that highlight human talents and feats that its audiences leave the Big Top spellbound.

There is another unexpectedly refreshing aspect to the animal-free circus. It hits you immediately: the absence of the sawdust the old-fashioned circuses use to sop up animal waste! In fact, the only smell in an animal-free circus is that of fresh popcorn.

THERE'S NO UNION FOR ANIMAL ACTORS

Caring moviegoers need to be on their toes—sometimes all the way up on them and striding out of the theater—if they see anything on the screen they suspect could be animal abuse. They may be right. Consumers should be aware, too, for when animals are part of a commercial or a print advertisement, if the animals are real, so too may be the problems that commonly accompany their use.

The most common abuses occur behind the scenes, when animals are trained and housed, not when they are on the set where lots of people have a chance to see what is going on. Nonetheless, abuses happen there too.

Whistle-blowers from films and filmed advertisements have complained of animal "actors" collapsing from the heat of the bright arc lights, being deprived of food, being prodded and goaded, and being scared by the clapboards or gunfire. Abuse can be as subtle as forcing cats to stay awake for hours so as to be able to get them to fall asleep "on cue," or the use of a "tie-down," an invisible filament wrapped around an animal's waist and attached to an unseen anchor.

Even though the use of "trip wires," rigged to make animals fall, is prohibited in the United States, many westerns are made overseas, in Spain, Portugal, and other countries where no restrictions apply.

Other abuses include chickens being gratuitously run over in movie chase scenes, and even being killed on the set when the movie becomes a real-life "snuff film," with goldfish vacuumed out of the water and tropical fish tanks purposely smashed in fight scenes. Cats have been drowned after being tied to a raft in a "river adventure," small animals are sometimes given no choice but to fight their natural enemies in contrived encounters, and rats have been killed after being put in liquid oxygen for underwater scenes.

Sawed-off pool cues and blackjacks have been used on film sets to keep chimpanzees and other animals in line. The orangutan who starred as the lovable "Clyde" in Clint Eastwood's *Every Which Way You Can* is believed to have been beaten to death during filming. An autopsy showed that the gentle ape died of cerebral hemorrhage.

Unless you are watching a nature show, most apes you see on television or in the movies are babies. In the rain forests, they would not leave their mothers' sides for eight or more years. In Hollywood, they are props, involuntary "actors" who will be washed up and discarded as too strong and willful to handle when they reach puberty.

Primate behaviorist Dr. Roger Fouts recalls a conversation with movie producers who were considering adding live animals to a film they were making. "I told them that the traditional circus method of training chimpanzees has been referred to as the 'two-by-four technique,' meaning that the animal is beaten into capitulation. I also explained a common method is to keep the young chimpanzee in a small box and only take him out to act or for training."

Even the presence of a big star doesn't always guarantee compassion. Kevin Costner made headlines for reasons that must not have made him or his agent very happy after filming his box office bomb, *The Postman*. According to a newspaper report, film crew members complained that when horses used in the film were dyed dark brown or black, there were so many horses and therefore so much dye to apply that the process took too long: The horses' skin had become irritated and the horses began kicking and biting from the irritation and whinnying from the pain.

Another complaint reported in the press was that the horses in *The Postman* were forced to gallop again and again over treacherous rocky ground covered with rocks so sharp that they sliced vehicle tires open. A news magazine reported that one horse had a cut three inches long on his leg and that his leg bone was exposed.

There is also the matter of where the animals come from. For one of the *Batman* movies, for instance, easily stressed penguins, native to Antarctica and the sub-Antarctic islands, were shipped to California and kept on the set for months, then harnessed into "missile" gear. To make *Babe II*, primates were shipped all the way to Australia.

There are some safeguards. Filmmakers are required to ask the American Humane Association (AHA) to review scripts and make recommendations or even to be present on the set or on location during filming. To get the AHA "seal of approval," or "end credit disclaimer," the filmmakers must meet certain reasonable standards, including not killing or injuring an animal for the sake of the production and not treating an animal inhumanely to force a performance. The AHA also requires that all hunting and fishing scenes be simulated; that animals in performing stunts be "properly trained"; and that all animals receive exercise, rest, and veterinary care if sick or injured.

AHA's influence has been a great help to many animals used in movies, but in this age of animatronics, robotics, computer simulation, and special effects, there is never an excuse for bringing "wild" or "exotic" species into the act at all. If Robert Redford can use mechanical salmon in the fishing scenes from *A River Runs Through It*, other filmmakers can do the same.

As for commercials, few are as offensive as the Marlboro ad that shows a calf being flipped onto his back by a cowboy with a rope, but there are many close seconds, including other

Marlboro ads that use horses. On the other hand, there are the gorgeous ads by companies like Giro, maker of sports helmets, that show the love between dogs and their people; and those by the Schott Glass Company, highlighting how animals—from ants to birds and deer—show true friendship. These are all a joy to see, for they show real-life relationships without interference.

After all, what is more beautiful at every level than respecting animals by filming them, unobtrusively, in their natural environs? It is a sign that we respect the objects of our interest and that we realize that they, too, have other things to do, other places to go, families to raise, and lives to live.

Animals in Entertainment

....

ZOOS

- **Find Alternatives.** Choose an alternative to zoo visits. Put on your hiking boots and observe animals' natural behaviors on their turf instead of behind glass and steel. Rainy-day activists and less adventurous types can learn from *National Geographic* specials, travel videos, and zoology or nature books, as well as from visits to the local nature center or by subscribing to wildlife protection organizations.
- **Boycott Roadside Zoos.** Never pay to visit a roadside zoo. Instead, write a letter to the local newspaper, the Chamber of Commerce, and the state's tourism department voicing your objections to such cruel exhibits. Ask for their intervention and support in getting roadside zoos improved or dismantled.
- **Draw Public Attention.** Sandra Van de Werd of Amsterdam spent more than thirteen days in a cage in front of Artis Zoo, one of the most famous and cruel zoos in Holland, to protest conditions there. Heightened European awareness of the plight of animals in captivity led to the proposal for a revolutionary "zoo" without animals.
- **Be a Zoochecker.** When you visit the zoo, take a questionnaire with you and return it, completed, to PETA. (See Appendix G: Samples for a questionnaire.)
- **Write Letters.** Write to the zoo director and ask any questions you may have, like what happens to the baby animals

when they get big, or why are some animals in cages that don't look natural, or where have all the animals come from.

■ **Create Alternatives.** Students: If your class ever goes to the zoo, ask for an alternative assignment, or ask your teacher to give each student a sheet of zoocheck questions so that the whole class can be zoo sleuths. (See Appendix G: Samples for the questionnaire.)

MARINE THEME PARKS

■ **Return Captive Dolphins and Whales.** Join the growing list of people and groups demanding the return of captive dolphins and whales to their families. Researchers know where in the oceans most orcas' families are. Help send the captives home to them.

■ **Watch Local Aquariums.** Monitor your local aquarium's activities. If aquarium officials are considering an expansion or want to add (or replace) a dolphin to their "stock," protest vigorously—to city officials, local legislators, and in letters to publications. Suggest a display of animal models, aquatic plants, and coral reefs instead. When friends and relatives visit, steer them away from the local aquarium, which serves as a prison for fish and marine mammals. Instead, show them your city's museums and historical sites, or catch a movie.

■ **Educate Travel Agents.** When you make hotel reservations, tell your travel agent that you will not stay in any place that features a dolphin swim program.

■ **Write to the Government.** Write to the U.S. Fish and Wildlife Service and your congressperson to ask for a ban on any capture and confinement of marine mammals. (See Appendix F: People to Contact for addresses.)

■ **Join Organizations.** Join organizations like Earth Island Institute, the Animal Welfare Institute, and the Sea Shepherd Society, who fight to protect marine mammals.

RODEOS

- **Educate Sponsors.** Tell rodeo sponsors that you will not patronize them or their "entertainment," and get others to join you.
- **Read Reports.** Eric Mills worked hard on a fifteen-month campaign with a coalition of California activists who were victorious in getting the Hayward Police Officers Association to abandon rodeos as fund-raisers. The campaign culminated with a gut-wrenching six-page report on rodeos sent to the Hayward Area Recreation District Board of Supervisors. Others fighting the rodeo blight can contact PETA for a copy of this influential report to use in their own fight.
- **Pass Local Ordinances.** Ask your local government officials about the procedure for introducing a city or county ordinance. Then find sympathetic citizens and officials to back you. Many individuals have made changes on the local level. After two members of the Pittsburgh, Pennsylvania, group Animal Advocates attended a rodeo and videotaped numerous blatant abuses, such as repeated shocking and beating of animals in the chute and a bull's hind leg being shattered during a bucking event, the city of Pittsburgh effectively banned rodeos by forbidding the use of spurs, bucking straps, and other cruel devices. The footage was later shown on national television, educating millions of viewers. Rhode Island is also among those states that have passed laws to protect rodeo animals.
- **Demonstrate.** Demonstrate and leaflet outside rodeo events. PETA has great fliers you can use to educate countless people.
- **Join Parades.** Crash the parade. In Davie, Florida, a red convertible Cadillac joined a procession including a float sponsored by the Professional Rodeo Cowboys Association. Entered in the parade by members of ARFF (Animal Rights Foundation of Florida), the convertible's original noncontroversial decorations were replaced along the route with

banners reading, "Rodeos: Cruelty for a Buck." The car's "cowboys" and "cowgirls" handed out anti-rodeo fliers and a "horse" waved to onlookers, including the mayor.

RACING

■ **Adopt a "Retired" Greyhound.** Contact the National Greyhound Adoption Network (650-327-0631) for help in finding local groups in your area that find good homes for greyhounds. (See Appendix C: Recommended Groups for addresses.) David Cantor of Pennsylvania took Bruno, his adopted ex–racing greyhound, to a news conference to protest a bill to legalize greyhound racing in the state. While Cantor circulated literature, Bruno provided gentle, silent testimony to the cruelty of the greyhound industry. The bill did not receive even one vote—after seeing Bruno on television and in newspapers, compassionate citizens could not imagine condemning tens of thousands of dogs like him to death every year.

HORSE-DRAWN CARRIAGES

■ **Boycott Carriage Rides.** Don't be taken for a ride. If you see horse-drawn carriages in any city, please write your objections to the local paper, the chamber of commerce, the board of trade, and the mayor. If the carriage-horse operation is affiliated with a hotel, tell the manager too.
■ **Report Abuses.** Report any abuses, for example, overwork, overheating, lameness, beating, or overloading, to the police and humane society.
■ **Educate Customers.** Talk politely to potential customers about how hard these animals work and ask them to reconsider.

THE BULLFIGHT

■ **Boycott Bullfights.** If you're traveling to Mexico, Spain, or Italy, help spare the pain of the thirty thousand bulls who are killed in the arena each year. Don't attend bullfights; encourage others not to patronize them; and avoid purchasing souvenirs that depict any aspect of bullfighting.

■ **Distribute Leaflets.** Write to PETA to receive free leaflets in Spanish and English to distribute at your hotel and in the airport.

■ **Protest Bullfights.** Protest "bloodless bullfights" if they appear in your city (within the past few years, this spectacle has occurred in Chicago; Phoenix, Arizona; Houston; Artesia, California; and Dodge City, Kansas). Write your objections to local papers and legislators.

COCKFIGHTING AND PIT BULL FIGHTING

■ **Call the Police.** If you see evidence of illegal cockfighting or pit bull fighting, call the police. If you live in a state in which cockfighting is legal, write letters to legislators and local papers.

"ACTORS"

■ **Boycott Theaters.** Walk out of a movie or play if you are offended at how animals are portrayed, or see a scene containing cruelty to animals. By doing so, you alert others that what happened is ethically indefensible. Let the manager know that you would not have attended if you had known there would be animal cruelty. Ask for a refund or return pass. If the explanation is firm but polite (remember, it's not the theater's fault), most managers will be obliging and may also learn something.

■ **Contact Companies.** When you see a movie, or even an advertisement for one, that shows questionable activities involving animals, write or call the film or television companies involved.

■ **Write to Critics.** Ask your local movie critics to include real or perceived animal abuse in their reviews. PETA has written to more than one thousand critics nationwide. Your efforts will initiate interest.

ANIMALS IN ADVERTISING

■ **Help Give "Awards."** Every year, international ad agencies vie for the coveted Kelly awards for excellence in advertising. But they dread PETA's Litter Box awards, given to companies that reek of a lack of compassion and respect for animals. Fortunately, for every company that chooses to exploit, degrade, and otherwise abuse animals, there are good guys who sell their products and warm consumers' hearts at the same time. When you see an advertisement that depicts animals in a manner that is anything other than respectful or compassionate, write to the advertiser and explain that such tactics discourage consumers from buying. Please send a copy of the advertisement to PETA as a Litter Box or Glitter Box nomination.

■ **Support Compassionate Businesses.** Let businesses know you support compassionate advertising with your consumer dollars.

CIRCUSES AND OTHER ANIMAL ACTS

■ **Educate Children.** Children are the group to which animal circuses try hardest to appeal. Most children have a natural affinity for all living beings and are upset when they learn about cruelty. Take them to see shows whose entertainment value comes from amusing and unusual *human* performances.

■ **Protest Traveling Animal Acts.** Get traveling animal acts to take a detour past your town. Take your message to the sponsors (business owners and managers and radio and television stations). Inform promoters about the problems with animal acts and urge them to withdraw their support. Many sponsors care about animal suffering but just aren't aware. Urge them not to repeat sponsorship the next time the show comes to town.

■ **Pass Legislation.** Take your concerns to your city council. Encourage your local humane society to get involved. Hollywood, Florida, passed legislation banning all animal acts and exhibits.

■ **Watch Videos.** Show a video to friends, coworkers, and members of your activity groups. Ask for *Cheap Tricks* from PETA (See Appendix B: Recommended Video and Audiotapes.)

■ **Demonstrate.** Demonstrate or leaflet dressed as a clown, riding a unicycle, or using a friendly smile. You're sure to reach many people. When the circus came to town, Jirleen Sandhu, Melba Lowe, Lisa Ferrell, and several other activists in Richmond, Virginia, were prepared with a protest on wheels! They drove around and around the arena with a "tiger" caged in the back of a pickup truck and a sign reading, "No One Read This Prisoner His Rights."

■ **Write Letters to the Editor.** Write letters to the editors of your local papers telling them why you won't attend a circus that forces animals to perform tricks. (See Appendix G: Samples for a sample letter.)

■ **Use Video Cameras.** Use a video camera to record any mistreatment of animals when a circus unloads or parades through your town. Take your evidence to the media, the police, and your local humane society.

■ **Report Cruelty.** The Burlington, Vermont, mayor's youth office chose not to invite back the Great American Circus after receiving several reports that a trainer had beaten a baby elephant with a shovel prior to a performance. According to eyewitness Jennifer Blow, "He was hitting the elephant, fifteen or twenty times." Jennifer is a fine example of how much it helps to document and report cruelty whenever and wherever you see it.

■ **Write to the Shriners.** Appeal to the Shriners, a major circus sponsor, to hire only animal-free circuses like Cirque du Soleil, Cirque d'Ingénuité, Circus Smirkus, The New Pickle

Family Circus, and Earth Circus. (See Appendix F: People to Contact for address.)

■ **Speak Up.** Jim Sicard of Florida sent a letter to the publishers of *American Heritage Dictionary* protesting the use of a photograph showing tigers performing in a circus to illustrate the entry "circus." They agreed to remove the photograph from future printings of the dictionary. Linda Geant of Chicago solicited help from her local activist phone tree, animal control chief, and a sympathetic columnist to stop a bear wrestling event at Chicago's Club Land, dashing plans for a private party where twelve men would be invited to wrestle a bear. Warned animal control chief Pete Poholik: "If the event takes place, I'll either make an arrest or confiscate the bear. It's illegal and cruel to torment and tease an animal. The bear was not only declawed—he had no teeth!"

■ **Protest to Management.** Take the plunge. Protest to management of any fair where mules are diving (a traveling act in which mules are forced to climb up a ramp and jump into a pool of water from a height of 30 feet), as well as to your local humane society and department of animal control. Heather Gray and Debbi Liebergot made a splash at Tim Rivers's diving mule show when they jumped into the diving pool and refused to get out. Other determined activists across the nation leafleted fairgoers and reported the show to local authorities.

■ **Be Creative.** Karen Medicus of the Animal Rescue League of Martin County, Florida, didn't sit quietly when she heard Tim Rivers's High Diving Mule act had been booked at a local Toyota dealer. She voiced her concerns to General Manager Mark Jacobson, who not only canceled the act (to the tune of the contractual $3,600) but also generously offered to donate $50 to the Animal Rescue League for every car sold.

4

There's Nothing Sporting About Hunting and Fishing

You ask people why they have deer heads on the wall. They always say, "Because it's such a beautiful animal." There you go. I think my mother's attractive, but I have photographs of her.
— COMEDIAN ELLEN DEGENERES

In the fall of 1988, a Michigan deer hunter came upon a buck and a doe standing side by side in the forest. When they did not run from him, he raised his rifle and killed the buck. In spite of the shot, the doe remained motionless. As the law did not permit shooting does then, the hunter approached her. To his amazement, she allowed him to walk right up to her; it was then that he saw she was blind.

Further inspection revealed a large area of fur worn away from the buck's left side and a similar area on the doe's right side. By pressing his side against hers, the buck had led her through the forest and cared for her. When he saw the hunter, the buck had chosen to stay beside her, although he could have run. How marvelous if the hunter had felt even a portion of the buck's devotion.

One has to wonder what makes grown men (and a few women) want to shoot and kill animals. That thought was heavy on my mind as I sat in the stands at a park in Hegins, Pennsylvania, waiting with a group of activists for the right moment to disrupt a live pigeon shoot.

The Hegins pigeon shoot has to be seen to be believed. Tame pigeons are brought to the site in crates, kept in a shed overnight, then shoved into little boxes on a playing field. The "trapper boys" stuff the birds into the boxes, then pull the strings that release the birds at intervals so that paying guests can shoot at the birds, scoring points for every kill. The trapper boys' other job is to gather up fallen birds who are still alive and stuff them, wounded and dying, into a sack (they will be ground up and used for fur-farm food) or, if the boys can be bothered, wring their necks.

A fair number of the hunters, although they wear shirts proclaiming their marksmanship, couldn't hit the side of a barn. At one point, I saw a pigeon fly out of the box, land on the ground, look around in confusion, and then get shot. Although the man with the gun could not have been more than thirty feet from her, his aim was so poor that he succeeded only in shooting off her legs.

A little boy in front of the stands who had watched this poor pigeon get shot and turn end over end like a badminton shuttlecock turned away from the slaughter and hid his eyes. His father saw him shy away from the scene and, not willing to stand for such sissiness, turned the boy around to face the shoot. The boy started to cry.

"Watch!" the man said.

The boy turned again, buried his head in his father's pants and sobbed, but it did no good. His father took his little shoulders forcefully and spun him back to face the field.

"You *will* watch!" he said.

I couldn't watch any longer, so off we went, over the fence, out onto the field to stop the shoot, at least for a while, to set as many pigeons free as we could, and to get carted away to Pottsville Prison for a couple of weeks.

BIRTH CONTROL BY FIREARM

The main argument hunters offer in defense of their grisly hobby is that hunting helps control wildlife populations. We are asked to believe that animals are so out of control and nature so inept that hunters have to sacrifice their weekend golf games to do the ultimate favor for deer and grouse and ducks: blow them away.

Hunters are such good wildlife exterminators that, in a single year, about 25,000 black bears bite the dust, as do ten million ducks, thirty million rabbits, and as many squirrels. Canada geese, who break formation if one of their flock is hit, with two geese going to ground to guard and protect their fallen friend, lose more than one million of their kind each year to hunters' guns. And, the humble mourning dove, who is not starving, overpopulated, known to attack small children, or engage in any other transgressions, apparently needs more "help" than most animals: This gentle bird has the dubious distinction of being the most hunted animal in the United States, with an annual death toll of more than fifty million.

Perhaps the cruelest part of hunting is that it makes widows and widowers. Geese mate for life, as do ducks.

Chief Luther Standing Bear of the Oglala Sioux once said, "Only to the white man was nature a 'wilderness' and only to him was the land 'infested' with 'wild' animals and 'savage' people. To us it was tame. Earth was bountiful and we were surrounded with the blessings of the Great Mystery." In hunting magazines, hunters describe the most benign animals as wild, terrifying, threatening, and oversized, rather than as timid beings who flee for their lives at the first hint that a human being carrying heavy artillery is coming after them. "Sport" is a misnomer, of course, given that the animals are out there with no defense other than their hooves (which they use to run away) or claws (for trying to climb out of reach), and that today's hunters are equipped with all-terrain vehicles, tree stands, walkie-talkies, high-powered weapons, high-powered scopes, binoculars, sock warmers, hip flasks, moose urine to deflect their smell, camouflage clothing, and even camouflage toilet paper. And only one-half of the players in this "sport" are in it voluntarily.

As far as the "We must kill them because there are too many and they'll starve" argument goes, often the populations of deer and other "edible" species are purposely "exploded" in order to cater to hunters, sell more hunting licenses, and provide more recreation for residents and special interest visitors.

Game "management" programs are actually game propagation programs, designed not to reduce or restrict the animals' numbers but to fool desirable species into overpopulating. The most obvious is to shoot only males and to protect females so they can keep on bearing fawns. Another favorite trick is to plant far more tasty vegetation or browse than a region would normally support. Left to their own devices, deer "read" the available food supply and reproduce based on how much there is to sustain their herds. If it is a good year, a doe may have one fawn or twins. If faced with nutritional stress, a doe may simply not ovulate, and bucks will reduce their sperm count. If disaster strikes, a doe can reabsorb her fetus. When state wildlife departments (composed almost solely of hunters) fool the deer, the birth rate goes up.

"Game management" operates so much to the detriment of animals that, in Michigan alone, just one state game program *added* about 1.5 million whitetail deer. Rather disingenuously, when the figures were announced, hunters took to the airways to lobby for extended hunting seasons and bigger bag limits to reduce the very problems they had created: traffic accidents caused by deer browsing near highways and loss of ornamental shrubs.

OUT OF CONTROL

Edward Abbey dealt swiftly with the psychological aspects of hunting when he wrote, "I was once a sportsman. But I grew up." The inability to curb aggression and the belief that it is acceptable to kill for pleasure are a frightening phenomenon. Luckily, less than 6 percent of the U.S. population hunts, and, of them, I'd guess that about .00001 percent do so because they have no other way to feed their families.

Columnist Carla Bennett believes she has found the answer to why some of this 6 percent hunt. She has unearthed many supporters of the theory that some hunters are trying to compensate for other problems in their lives. Ms. Bennett quotes Dr. Karl Menninger of the Menninger Clinic, who describes hunting as the product of "erotic sadistic motivation"; Dr. Joel R. Saper, a University of Michigan professor who feels hunting "may reflect a profound, yet subtle, psychosexual inadequacy"; and Washington, D.C., clinical psychologist Margaret Brooke-Williams, who theorizes that "hunters are seeking reassurance of their masculinity." Interestingly, clinicians report that the incidence of wife-beating is always at its peak the day before hunting season opens.

Reading hunting magazines, as *Esquire* contributor Joy Williams has, seems to substantiate the view that all is not well in the minds of at least some hunters. Much is made of the chase, the anticipation, and the conquest. Take this example from a popular outdoors periodical: The hunter has used a sex lure to draw a buck to within convenient shooting range. "The big buck raised its nose to the air, curled back its lips, and tested the scent of the doe's urine. I held my breath, fought back the shivers, and jerked off a shot."

Whatever lurks in the hunter's psyche, the effect of his all but irresistible habit on his victims is deadly. Hunters have rendered extinct, among others, the dodo, the great auk, the Florida black bear, Sherman's fox squirrel, the heath hen, the eastern elk, and the passenger pigeon. Hunters also wound countless animals. In fact, hunters call crippling "a by-product of our sport." According to the Texas Wildlife Commission, bowhunters, whose weapons pack 1,500 pounds of pressure, expend an average of twenty-one arrows before shooting and keeping a deer. The bowhunters themselves report a 50 percent or higher rate of animals wounded and lost (not that all hunters look for or trail the animals they injure). This means animals stagger off to die of blood loss, starvation, thirst, and infection.

Trigger-happy hunters also "harvest" nonhunters (one woman in Maine was killed in her own backyard by a hunter who said he thought her white gardening gloves was the fur on a whitetail deer's rump): pesky game wardens who object to the use of infrared night sights and off-season shooting; cows and horses grazing peacefully in fields; each other; and even themselves. In one notable case, a hunter committed inadvertent suicide when his weapon went off while he was bludgeoning a wounded deer to death with his rifle butt.

HUNTING IN THE WATER

Human beings generally have a very unfair way of thinking about animals. Favored animals go into one category and less fortunate ones, like fish, go into another. There are many people who abhor hunting on grounds of cruelty, but who haven't realized that their "peaceful pastime" is nothing more than hunting in the water.

That's why lots of people who "love animals" also fish. I certainly did, standing in my bare feet in the crashing surf of Florida's Gulf Coast years ago and casting my line for sea trout. I hated catching the fish, not, I'm sorry to say, because I recognized what they were going through, but because they stunk when they died, because I hated having to wrestle them to remove the hooks, and because catching them disturbed my otherwise happy experience: enjoying the feel of the water, the sound of the waves, and the warmth of sweet sunshine on my skin. At some level I must have realized that my entertainment was less than pleasant for the fish, because, when I did catch them, I either threw them back in or killed them quickly. But I kept on fishing.

The English poet John Wolcot wrote,

Enjoy thy stream,
O harmless fish;

And when an angler for his dish,
Through gluttony's vile sin,
Attempts, a wretch, to pull thee out,
God give thee the strength,
O gentle trout,
To pull the rascal in!

THE EYES HAVE IT

The Chinese philosopher Lin Yutang chided, "To comprehend
the organs of the horse is not to comprehend the horse itself,"
but he could have been writing about any animal. For hundreds of years, elephants were nothing but tusks and tasks.
They hauled logs and provided scrimshaw and piano keys.
Even whales were thought of as big gray blubber masses,
good only for parts—oil for lamps and bones for corsets—
rather than as something more than the sum of those meager
parts. Today, if you look at a whale's eye in a photograph or in
one of the posters sold by the Cetacean Society or Greenpeace,
you know there is *someone* inside that almost featureless body.

Once someone opened a book and showed me a picture of
a pair of very wise, familiar eyes, surrounded by wrinkled,
wizened, sun-weathered skin. It made me think instantly of
an old peasant woman I knew who gathered wood on the
slopes of a mountain in the Kulu Valley. They were clearly the
eyes of a tribesperson who had spent her entire life outdoors,
the sun having carved deep furrows into that knowing face.

It turned out that I was wrong. The eyes so full of life experiences and hard times belonged to Siri, an aging elephant
confined to a small enclosure in the Burnet Park Zoo in Syra-
cuse, New York. The book was her story, as told by her keeper.
He had found Siri drawing in the dirt with a stick and had
given her some blank art paper and crayons, which the elephant liked immediately. Siri's work had been praised by the
great Willem de Kooning and his wife, who found them "full
of flair, decisiveness and originality" and called Siri "a
damned talented" artist. The keeper had been fired from the

zoo and missed seeing her and being with her. Perhaps Siri missed him too and that was reflected in her eyes.

One evening, driving into Philadelphia, I stopped my car beside the Schuylkill River to enjoy the water and relax. Two men were fishing on the riverbank, but I was glad to note they were not catching anything. Or, any*one*, I should say, for a fish is not a thing. Then, as dusk fell, I saw one of the men wrestling with what looked to be an enormously long fish. He seemed to be having a hard time, so I walked over to him to see what was happening. When I got there, I realized he had caught an eel.

There was a five-pronged metal gaff, with separate sets of barbed hooks attached to the prongs, embedded in the eel's throat. As the animal wriggled, the man pulled and twisted at the gaffs, but succeeded only in making a bloody mess. I asked if I could hold the eel still because the procedure was not going quickly. The man agreed.

I took the towel the man had been using to clean his fish knife and wrapped it around the eel so I could hold his long body up to the light from the nearby lamppost. The eel's face was now level with mine. That allowed the man to use both hands to open the eel's mouth wide and to use his pliers more effectively, but the going was still tough because there were so many hooks.

Suddenly, the man lost his patience and yanked hard on the gaff set. In a split second he had pulled the eel's throat clean out of his mouth. The eel and I made eye contact at that very moment.

There was no mistaking the look on the eel's face: shock, horror, sheer fright, and terrible pain. He could have been a dog, a child, the man fishing, or me.

My friend, who had come up behind me, seized the eel and crushed the animal's head quickly with a rock to end his suffering.

Afterward, the man and I had a chat, but he was unable to relate to the experience in the same way. To him, the encounter with the unwanted, inedible eel had simply been a waste of time and bait. He offered me a beer and eventually we said our good-byes. As I drove out of the parking lot he was tying a piece of raw bacon to the gaff, ready to have another go.

It has been years, but I still can't shake the look in that poor animal's eyes. He was used as an object to satisfy the recreational whims of members of a species capable of playing chess with computers, devising elaborate games, doing crossword puzzles, and reading great books.

He had been hurt terribly and then killed, not by perverted juveniles on drugs or evil sadists on a crime spree, but by a man who seemed respectable, decent, and polite. The miserable deed had been carried out, not in secret, down a dark alley, but in the open in a public place. It had happened a million times before, in much the same way, or worse, and it would happen as many times again. All for nothing.

I was not upset because I am a vegetarian. I was upset because I had witnessed a hideous cruelty. I was also upset because I knew, from talking to him, that the man, while inured to the eel's suffering and that of the fish in his bucket, would have been as upset as I was if what happened that evening had happened to a horse or a dog or another being he related to and who is not associated with his "sport."

DOWN AMONG THE FISH

Fish are so low on the totem pole that they get even shorter shrift than chickens, and that is saying something. Yet fish are communicative and sensitive animals.

Fish certainly have a neurological system like ours and the brain capacity to experience fear and pain. And, while pain is a mental event that cannot be accurately measured, it only makes sense that pain, a biological necessity, is not a singularly human trait. Without the ability to feel pain, fish, like us, would perish.

Fish also have on their backs sensory hairs that register vibrations and electrical fields: they have taste buds in their throats, as well as in their lips and noses; and they use their mouths much as we use our fingers, to pick things up and feel them. In fact, their mouths are so exquisitely sensitive to stimuli that any pain they experience is especially acute. They like to play in air bubbles, as dolphins do and, like bears, they enjoy the sensation of rubbing their backs and bodies along the edges of rocks and tree trunks.

When people who fish think about being more humane, they usually "move up" from killing fish to practicing "catch-and-release." As Ellen DeGeneres says, that's like running down pedestrians in your car and then, when they get up and limp away, saying "Off you go! That's fine. I just wanted to see if I could hit you."

Sadly, catch-and-release may not help much. Fish not only suffer injuries from hooks, but two other physiological phenomena occur: The tremendous stress of being caught causes lactic acid to build up in their bodies and can weaken and kill them and handling them to remove a hook destroys the protective coating on their bodies that shields them in the water. An Australian study found that when fish are chased, confined, or otherwise threatened, they react as humans do under stress: with increased heart and breathing rates and a burst of adrenaline. In other words, just as we do when we're under stress.

AN ODD CATCH

Fishing certainly hurts fish, but it does more damage than that, as many hikers and park users have found out firsthand.

One spring, a couple walking their dogs in a Virginia park noticed a movement in the bushes around the lake. When they investigated, they found a seagull tangled up in fishing line and struggling to stay alive. He was upside down, very close to the water, and had to try to keep his head up to save himself from drowning. The line went around both his wings, over his shoulders, crisscrossed over his back and around his legs.

The seagull also had a barbed fishing hook embedded under his wing. It took the couple nearly an hour to untangle the bird, cut off the barb, and remove the hook.

Every year, people who fish leave behind a trail of tackle victims that includes millions of birds, turtles, otters, seals, sea lions, bats, and other animals who suffer debilitating injuries or slowly starve to death after swallowing fishhooks or becoming entangled in filament line. In fact, officials with the Virginia Marine Science Museum Stranding Team say monofilament fishing line is one of the top three threats to sea animals, along with plastic trash—including discarded bait containers and lures—and propeller and boat strikes. On riverways, the toll can be even higher.

In Britain, one study found that, in just two weeks, anglers discarded or lost 36,000 pieces of line totaling six kilometers *in an area just two kilometers long.* Fishing line is designed to be strong enough to defeat a struggling fish, long enough to reach far from a boat or pier, and virtually impervious to the elements. And you'll find it everywhere fishers have been, on beaches, at the edges of rivers, and drifting around in the water, waiting to ensnare a passerby. In Florida, where fishers on piers often joke about how many pelicans they've caught, 85 percent of the birds taken to the Suncoast Seabird Sanctuary are there to be treated for injuries from fishing line and hooks. Another study found that the cause of a mysterious illness in otters was the presence of indigestible plastic bait worms clogging up their intestines.

I doubt an aboriginal fisher is reading this book, so I think it is safe to say that we can easily find something else to eat and some other way to pass our time.

It may be hard, at first, to care about what fish feel, but we know they do feel. If we can't justify impaling dogs on barbed hooks and dragging them into the water, how can we justify doing the same sort of thing to a fish?

What You Can Do

Hunting and Fishing

- **Check Out Wildlife Groups.** Before you support a "wildlife" or "conservation" group, ask if it supports hunting. Such groups as the National Wildlife Federation, the National Audubon Society, the Sierra Club, the Izaak Walton League, the Wilderness Society, the World Wildlife Fund, and many others are pro-hunting.
- **Make It Difficult.** Deny hunters land to hunt on. Encourage your neighbors, especially those who own large tracts of land such as farms and ranches, to post "No Hunting" signs every hundred yards. Explain to them that aggressive human hunters with their powerful weapons are far more dangerous than wild animals who invariably flee, even if surprised.
- **Apply for Licenses.** For hunts that issue a limited number of permits, apply for permits yourself. The permits are usually awarded through a simple lottery system. People in nursing homes love animals too. Follow activist Janet Palomis's lead by signing them up for *free* senior-citizen hunting licenses. Each license obtained by a nonhunter saves lives that a real hunter might have taken.
- **Create a Hostile Environment.** Create an environment that's hostile to hunting. Spread deer repellent (available at feed and hardware stores), or hang little mesh bags of human hair (from a salon or barber shop) two or three feet above the ground along deer tracks, warning deer that humans have invaded their terrain. If hunters use dogs in

your area, sprinkle a female dog's urine in heavily hunted areas, or spray a solution of chopped garlic cloves soaked in water or diluted lemon juice on leaves and trails to throw dogs off the scent. Remove the food piles hunters sometimes leave as bait in hunting areas, and scatter human hair or urine over the area.

■ **Feed the Animals.** Some areas outlaw the hunting of animals who are "baited." Before one hunting season, activist Dorothy O'Brien turned herself in to state game authorities for feeding local ducks and geese, thereby making their slaughter illegal.

■ **Get Hunts Canceled.** Look for announcements of scheduled hunts in newspapers and magazines. Contact the sponsors or local authorities and ask that the hunt be canceled, both for human and other-than-human safety. Circulate petitions in neighboring areas and picket the entrance to the hunting grounds, or arrange a peaceful civil disobedience action against hunting violence.

■ **Work Your Community.** Develop strong anti-hunting sentiment in your community by writing letters to the editors of local newspapers, meeting with neighbors, and getting on talk shows. Post anti-hunting fliers in parks and other community areas. Let your neighbors know that federal law recognizes that wildlife "belongs" to *all* people, most of whom don't hunt.

■ **Pass an Ordinance.** Encourage your municipality to pass an ordinance that bans the use of weapons within its limits in the interest of public safety. Lobby for laws that require hunters to carry written permission from landowners to hunt on private land. Ask your congressional representatives to introduce bills prohibiting hunting and trapping on national wildlife refuges and all public land.

■ **Be a Hunt Saboteur.** Chrissie Hynde of The Pretenders joined a group of "hunt sabs" in the woods of Maryland. Hunt saboteurs distract hunters with conversation and use other carefully chosen, nonviolent methods to stop hunters in their tracks.

- **Stop Pigeon Shoots.** Kay Lair and Nancy Patterson delayed a pigeon shoot by more than three hours by chaining themselves to the entrance gate of the National Skeet Shooting Association (NSSA) near San Antonio, Texas. A towing service finally cut through the heavy chain with a hacksaw and blowtorch and police arrested the activists, who arrived at the jailhouse to discover many people expressing their support. Lair's and Patterson's action was seen by television viewers as far away as Seattle, Washington. All charges were later dropped, and the NSSA has not held a pigeon shoot since.

- **Put Your Foot Down.** At a party, Anita Monical showed anti-hunting literature to wives of men who were planning to go bear-hunting with her husband the next day. When the women announced that they would not put bear meat in their freezers or hang bearskins on their walls, it took just five minutes for the men to call off the hunt.

- **Look for Traps.** "I'd do it again," vowed Joy Roelofsz. The Army Corps of Engineers construction inspector was threatened with a $500 fine and three months in jail for releasing a coyote from a leghold trap. She'd heard a chain rattle in the bushes and found the yearling coyote. "I started talking to her. She was so smart, she laid there and let us release her foot. It had to hurt because we had to wiggle it so much." All charges against Roelofsz were dropped.

- **Do Something Else.** Don't get hooked on fishing. Go hiking, canoeing, snorkeling, or bird watching, or read a book in that waterside folding chair.

- **Eat Vegetarian.** Never buy or eat fish. Send for PETA's free vegetarian recipes for delicious, nutritious (and cheap!) meals or ask your health food store to stock "Tuno," a soy tuna fish taste-alike.

- **Use Your Feet.** Collect unwanted fishing tackle from friends and family after *you* convince them to stop fishing. You can use the gear for a "Stomp out cruelty" demonstration. (Wear sturdy shoes!)

- **Display Stickers.** Use PETA's "Fishing Hurts" stickers in highly visible places.

- ■ **Organize a Demonstration.** To find an appropriate venue, check your local paper for any fishing tournaments and hunting events or find a highly fished location or a bait, gun, or tackle shop on a major road.
- ■ **Write a Letter to the Editor.** Many people have really just never considered that there might be anything wrong with fishing. A letter in the paper can open many eyes to the suffering of these animals. It can just be a few simple, sensible, heartfelt lines. (See Appendix G: Samples for a sample letter.)

Pet of the Month
or Friend for Life?

THY SERVANT, A DOG?

Man's best friend *isn't*, in many parts of the world. In Korea, the Philippines, Vietnam, and mainland China, dogs are kept in the burning sun in small cages behind restaurants, tin cans shoved over their muzzles, their forelegs often broken and tied behind their backs. They are "tenderized" by being beaten while alive, strangled to death, and skinned for their meat. In some of these countries, dog soup, like rhino horn and tiger penis, is considered an aphrodisiac. In Thailand, dog-hide factory trucks trawl the streets, offering to trade plastic buckets for live dogs to be slaughtered and made into bags, drum skins, and golf club covers.

I grew up in India, where, although dogs are not eaten, the mange-covered and starving stray animals are so common and so pathetic, they can't help but capture your attention. Even when I was supposed to be admiring the jeweled walls of the Taj Mahal or concentrating on where to place my feet on the icy paths of the "Everlasting Snows," the helpless wandering dogs could not be ignored. The animals I couldn't see fared worse. In the pounds, death was courtesy of a crude electrocution machine that seared the skin and set the dog's hair on fire or via blows from men with billy clubs. In light of our treatment of them, it is particularly humbling to read a Press Trust of India report about how stray dogs on the streets of Calcutta kept a night-long vigil protecting an abandoned baby from harm and then waited outside the police station she was taken to, apparently concerned over her fate.

In Taiwan, a rich country with a large Buddhist population, one would think animals would fare much better. The truth is quite the opposite. Death for dogs in the pounds can come from live burial (digging a pit and throwing the dogs into it), electrocution of their metal cage with the dogs inside it, poison-laced food, starvation, or drowning. In Keelung, in April 1998, I rescued eleven dogs from the drowning tank and extracted a promise from the Minister of the Environment to immediately stop all drowning in that area. The city administrators have been good to their word, but in other pounds, like Sanchung and Tu Chung, the cages are still filthy and overcrowded, food is scarce if available at all, and the attitude of the workers toward the old, dying, and diseased dogs they "care for" is revulsion that translates into meanness and cruelty. Pressure is still desperately needed to bring about reforms.

I used to harbor the illusion that in Europe and North America, at least, animals were all well treated. But we have plenty of room for improvement here, too, to say the least.

In Baltimore, Maryland, there is an organization called Alley Animals. They have seen it all, right here in America: animals with festering wounds from slingshots and bottles, animals made lame and terrified of human beings, cats with elastic bands embedded into their necks, kittens blinded and used as bait in pit bull fights, dogs with nails so long they have grown back into the pads of their feet, abandoned Easter rabbits, a rooster wearing a broken ankle leash, even a green iguana, now the "most common new exotic throwaway pet," according to news reports.

The group operates simply and on a shoestring. When dusk comes, its volunteers drive an old beat-up station wagon into the most rundown parts of that sprawling old city. Their job is to find the animal waifs and strays who creep from their hiding places when the city gets quieter and they know they are less visible to juveniles armed with free time and a rock or a firecracker. The animals are searching for that little morsel of food or the puddle of rainwater that can keep them going for another day.

In many alleys, the volunteers are known, and out from the boarded-up buildings and storm drains come animals, mostly cats, who are grateful to receive something clean and nourishing to eat.

One evening, volunteer Alice Arnold and her partner for that night's trip, Eric, were just pulling out of an alley where they had put out food when Eric said, "Did you see that puppy?"

Eric pointed, amid the trash, to an overturned reclining chair. Alice squinted and saw what he was talking about. A tiny head was sticking out ever so slightly, her reddish-brown fur almost blending in with the color of the old chair in the alley's black shadows. The stuffing had come out of the chair and the puppy had gone in, claiming the interior as her shelter from a world that had rejected her.

The puppy had very quietly watched as Alice and Eric arrived at the alley and then backed up to leave. No doubt she was fearful of the noise the car made and worried that people were so near to her safe place. She didn't realize that the car offered hope. Alice cringed at the thought that she had almost driven away, oblivious to the little life hidden in the discarded furniture, needing help.

Within a week of little Stuffing's rescue, it was obvious that she was very intelligent and lovable. After a few weeks, she had gained weight, become paper-trained, and was doing wonderfully, snuggling up in bed every night with her new human being. Alice says that, to look at her now, no one would ever guess that this happy little girl spent the first months of her life eating from trash cans, sleeping inside an overturned chair in the middle of an alley.

Alley Animals and similar groups can't round them all up, but they can make a dent in the suffering, a dent that matters to each individual they save. In the What You Can Do section, you will find details of how to start your own Community Animal Project. It doesn't have to be on the scale of that of Alley Animals or of PETA (which builds dog houses, and provides straw, spay surgeries, vaccinations, and even food to needy animals in low-income areas), but in every community there are homeless and neglected animals who would give their eyeteeth to have a friend.

A GOOD RELATIONSHIP IS HARD TO FIND

Most people don't think the problems of strays and chained backyard dogs have anything to do with them. But they do. The biggest nightmares plaguing domesticated animals in our society do not involve wanton acts of violence toward them. Rather, they are acts of thoughtlessness by otherwise intelligent and caring people who simply do not understand what or who, exactly, a dog or cat is and what they need.

It is easy to pick five major contributors to the Mastiff-sized headaches facing dogs and cats the world over. They are casual acquisition; overpopulation; ignorance of animals' needs, and underestimation of the depth of their feelings; carelessness; and improper placement when an animal is given away.

HOW MUCH DOES THAT DOGGIE IN THE WINDOW SUFFER?

Pet shops that sell animals, rather than just supplies, are part of the problem, not the solution. They contribute to the high mortality rate of birds, reptiles (the decline in the population of the North American box turtle is directly linked to the pet trade), and small rodents. They also compete directly with pounds and shelters and are busy creating more animals at a time when overpopulation of dogs and cats is at a crisis level, with too few good homes available.

Pet shop sales contribute to abandonment, whether on the street or at the shelters. Since anyone can plunk down a credit card in any pet store in virtually any shopping mall and walk off with a "pet," that cute little puppy in the window often goes home with someone who has given the proposition only fifteen minutes' thought. An animal should be a lifetime commitment, not an impulse purchase.

The idea that overpopulation is someone else's problem is naive and false. Sadly, the majority of people who keep a young animal into adulthood do not get the dog or cat "fixed" at sexual maturity because they don't act quickly enough or because they think it acceptable to have at least one litter. After all, they surmise, they can place the offspring. However, for every home they find for the new puppies and kittens, they create one fewer adopter who might go to the local pound or shelter and rescue an equally precious animal waiting on death row. Of course, that's not counting the following generation of puppies and kittens who will be born to the females of that litter very shortly, for sexual maturity arrives in a matter of only a few months for dogs and cats.

People who buy stuffed toys have no demands placed on them, but people who buy a live animal find out they have just adopted a baby. Animals make noises, make messes, require feeding and watering, and have a score of vital needs that can interfere with a person's own interests. If that is boring, tiring, or doesn't fit into the purchaser's schedule, out the animal goes, now confused at suddenly losing his or her home and newly accepted family and probably psychologically traumatized for having been yelled at for doing what comes natural to a baby animal.

When I worked at the Washington Humane Society, a little dog was turned in to a metropolitan Washington shelter because she ripped things up when the family went to work. Tracing her back through three failed homes, we discovered that she had been locked in an apartment during a fire in the building and had suffered from smoke inhalation before being rescued. While her last family had been furious at her behavior and unwilling to try to correct it, the little dog had been desperately trying to communicate the fact that she was terrified of being left alone in the house for good reason based on her past experience.

GETTING RESPECT

It is not just "pocket pets" or "exotics," like lizards, snakes, and prairie dogs (whose need for everything from a daily misting, to ultraviolet light, to room to unwind and move about), or birds (pity the poor macaws and lovebirds who are kept in cages and denied their basic desires to fly and be part of a flock) who are misunderstood. Cats and dogs are often treated as if they are not individuals in their own right, but accoutrements to a human lifestyle, who must fit in or be modified. For example, cats are commonly declawed to preserve the furniture, although declawing—a misnomer if ever there was one—means removing not the claw, but the first section of each toe—bone, ligament, and all—and is a painful surgery with the potential for subtle lifetime problems.

Dogs and cats are expected to fit *our* plans always. Dogs are yelled at not to tug on their leashes. They are pulled by the neck or told sharply to "come along" when they might rather look around or stop and smell something. How many people take the dog out for a walk only when it is absolutely necessary, rather than think when *the dog* would like to go, just for his or her pleasure? How many times do you see people hurrying their dogs on their walks, resenting the few minutes it takes for them to move their bowels or urinate, even if it is the only excursion they will get all day?

When two dogs meet in the park, some owners never consider allowing them to sniff and socialize, even for a moment.

They pull them away from that cherished little contact with others of their own kind.

People talk and laugh and call out to each other from room to room, but if dogs bark in fun or to warn their people that a stranger is approaching, they are told to be quiet.

If people are eating from a dish of snacks at dog nose-level, why is the only person not allowed to try this tantalizing appetizer the dog whose nose is smacked away when he or she tries to join in?

Could the man who tells you his dog is perfectly fine not relieving herself for the ten hours he is at work and traveling there and back be able to comfortably withhold those functions himself every day? And whatever gave anyone the idea that the way to toilet train any living being is to rub her nose in her own mess?

OFF YOU GO! GOOD LUCK!

Cats and dogs are often sent out unattended. Sometimes they don't ever come home. Not that they have decided to go live somewhere else. Some are abducted, others are found dead or injured. In a world of tractor trailers, psychopaths, intolerant neighbors, juveniles out for a lark, strange animals, rabies (in some states a six-month quarantine is required if a dog or cat returns home with a scratch or bite from an unknown animal), leghold traps set for other animals, and storm drains that flood suddenly, the animal's disappearance still seems to come as a surprise to many people who "love" their animals.

"But he wants to go outside," "But we live on a very quiet street," "But it's cruel to keep her in" are the silly justifications that could never be used by someone dispatching their toddler into the street.

The way we learn not to let the dog or cat out unaccompanied is usually by way of disaster. In Pompano, Florida, lost dogs and cats were found in a storage warehouse used by a pit bull training school. In Washington, D.C., a cat let out for her daily stroll returned covered in hot cooking grease. In

California, a woman searching for her two cats found both with arrows shot through them. Before I knew better, my cat went missing for three days and finally crawled home to die on my backdoor step, her lung collapsed and her ribs broken. Prince Charles's favorite terrier disappeared into a rabbit warren and was never found, despite a massive search and the inevitable fanfare that would have greeted the dog's rescuer.

MOVING OR MOVING ON

Over twenty million dogs and cats every year are unceremoniously dropped off at U.S. shelters, which, if well run, are certainly much better options than casually passing a dog or cat on to the first person who answers an ad or says they'll take the animal. No one can explain to these once-secure dogs that their people are moving, divorcing, or being transferred abroad. And how could anyone explain that, unlike a child or human loved one, this "member of the family" isn't important enough to accommodate?

Elsie and Bob Anderson of California found out the hard way that not all prospective adopters of unwanted animals are what they are cracked up to be. The Andersons had rescued countless animals from the nearby desert, pulled the cactus needles and porcupine quills out of their skin, built them back up to health, and placed ads for permanent homes.

An impressive, lonely old lady took two of their dogs, but turned out to be the mother of a licensed dog dealer who sold them, and at least fourteen other dogs from the "Free to a good home" ads, to a laboratory. A few of the dogs were still alive when they were traced, but many of their teeth had been mysteriously knocked out, and they were debilitated and scared to death. The others had been experimented on and killed. What must the ordeal have done to the survivors? How could they rest, or trust that they would be safe ever again?

Barry Herbeck is a Wisconsin man who was arrested after answering "Free to good home" ads in his local newspaper. But he was not caught soon enough. People say Herbeck always seemed a model placement because he brought his two young children with him to their homes, and the children fell in love with the animals. That helped Herbeck obtain numerous dogs and cats. Animal bodies were later found in the dumpster behind Herbeck's workplace and a dead sodomized cat was found inside Herbeck's home. Herbeck's arrest arose from the torture killing of a dog he punished for making a mess by taping her mouth shut and sealing her inside a plastic trash can. She reportedly whimpered for over a week before she died.

JUST OUT OF REACH

There are other forms of torture that are simply accepted in our society. I'm sure readers of this book would never chain up a dog as if he or she were no more than a bicycle. But in every town there are dogs who spend their whole lives on chains, watching forlornly from a distance as the family comes and goes and life passes them by. They are scared to death out there in thunderstorms or blizzards. They are hot in summer, cold in winter, and thirsty when their water bowl, if they have one, overturns or freezes. Their sicknesses go undetected because no one pays them any real attention, and their unfulfilled longing to be part of a "pack," a family of dogs or humans, makes them lonely indeed.

Dogs like this need a friend like Linda Tyrrell at PETA, who, in addition to her own full-time responsibilities, works with her staff to build waterproof dog houses, buy straw, and make neglected dogs comfortable. These dogs need their own neighborhood watch: They need someone who asks permission to walk them, makes sure they are all right, even looks out for them in case of a flood or fire, for, hideous thought that it is, people evacuate during emergencies, leaving their animals behind without even bothering to expend the one minute it would take to unclip the chain or open the pen door and give their animal a fighting chance. Dogs drown, swimming to their deaths in the rising waters, in every single flood, just as surely as caged birds are left to succumb to pneumonia and hamsters are abandoned in their cages.

THEY TOOK THE SCISSORS
TO HIS WINGS

> When his wing is bruised and his bosom sore—
> When he beats his bars and he would be free;
> It is not a carol of joy or glee,
> But a prayer that he sends from his heart's deep core,
> But a plea, that upward to heaven he flings—
> I know why the caged bird sings!

That poem, by Paul Lawrence Dunbar, the son of two run-away slaves, is a reminder of how impervious we can be to the desires of others. Without much of a thought, we take a blade and cut the wings of beings who were born to fly, to soar, to float on currents and feel the sun and wind on their bodies. We put them alone into see-through cages, never allowing them to be part of a flock, to be able to preen their brothers and sisters, murmur to their mothers, or touch the beaks of their lovers.

Millions of birds, all precious individuals, are taken from their tropical homes every year and shipped to pet shops. The baby birds are usually snatched from their mothers (whole trees are hacked down in some forests to get to the fledgling macaws in their high nests) glue is spread on branches to trap birds, or mist nets are used to trap flocks of birds as they commute home from the fields to their nests at sunset. Many are fatally injured then and there. Others do not survive the trip to the pet store from South America or Asia.

The singer James Taylor once rescued a cockatoo named Cory from a New York health spa. Cory had annoyed his keepers and had been put into solitary confinement for five years. He had torn out all his feathers.

James Taylor placed Cory with another rescue case, a lesser sulphur-crested cockatoo named Charlie. Charlie once lived free in Australia until trappers caught him and made him into a "lure bird" by hacking off portions of his wings and staking him to the ground. Charlie's pitiful cries brought other birds to the trappers' nets. His wings were badly damaged, and he will never be able to fly properly because of his ordeal. Charlie was sold through the pet trade to an owner who quickly tired of him and let him go to a PETA sanctuary.

Francisco Serrano, when he was director of national parks in El Salvador, estimated that more than 60 percent of baby parrots and 80 percent of baby parakeets die during capture or soon after from stress, suffocation (some are shipped in hair curlers with their beaks taped shut), and rough handling.

Typical survivors end up on a perch in a pet store, wings clipped, traumatized, and bewildered, having lost all friends and family. And of course they are unable to escape. Some, like a macaw named Bucky, cannot stop themselves from screeching with fear or rage whenever they see a human being. They end up locked in dark closets or have things thrown at them and are constantly yelled at to "shut up."

Birds bred in captivity, the ones you often see in small cages in hotel lobbies or stuck on a gilt perch somewhere like a living decoration, come from bird factories. In those places, breeders warehouse hundreds or thousands of birds to produce offspring for the trade. Most of the breeding females never leave their nest boxes, never choose their own mates, and are denied lifetime bonding (in the wild, males and females share all parenting, and most widows or widowers will not take a new partner if the first dies or disappears).

Hand-raised birds, like those caught in the wild, often become neurotic, pulling out their feathers and self-mutilating. Graham Sam was such a bird. He spent ten years in a cage so small he couldn't spread his wings and had torn his own flesh bloody from stress. He, too, is one of the few lucky ones who found their way to a PETA-approved sanctuary.

CLEVER MINDS AND BIG HEARTS

Dr. Theodore Barber, author of *The Human Nature of Birds,* has studied how intelligent and innovative birds can be, even in captivity. He recounts how jays, ravens, and other birds have made useful tools by carefully selecting their materials. They have used strips of newspaper or sticks to make a rake for pulling in grain from outside a cage, placed solid objects in drinking bowls to raise the level of water in them, inserted something of the right size to plug up a hole in a leaking dish. They can crack walnuts by placing each nut carefully between two cross branches, using one foot to keep the nut steady, and lining it up so that its seam splits when a few sharp blows are delivered with the beak. In Scandinavia, crows catch fish by using the lines that fishers leave suspended through holes in the ice of frozen lakes. The bird seizes the line in his or her beak, walks off with it away from the hole, then walks on top of the line back to the hole (thus preventing it from slipping), and repeats the process carefully until the fish is brought up.

Dr. Barber tells many beautiful stories about bird behavior in his book, but I particularly remember one tale of a young injured jay who was found on the ground and brought to a wildlife clinic run by Robert Leslie, a naturalist. Leslie and his wife nursed the injured little bird and got him back on his feet again. They called him Lorenzo, and he lived freely in the household for nearly three years when he left to start a new life nearby with a mate.

Lorenzo communicated to the Leslies everything that appeared to matter to him, using special sounds and body language, which included movements of each part of his body supplemented by changing eye expressions. According to Leslie, Lorenzo impressed visitors with the intensity and exactness of his ability to communicate curiosity, enthusiasm, likes and dislikes, resentment, restless boredom, and once in a while, downright anger.

Lorenzo always kept careful track of the roughly two dozen toys he owned. He checked daily to see that each toy was where he had placed it, and if one was missing he complained immediately by wailing and pecking on Mrs. Leslie's hand until he got it back.

He understood the idea of trading and would tug at a visitor's ring or other jewelry, leave to quickly bring one of his toys to the visitor, then tug again at the object he wanted. Lorenzo was not above using sleight-of-hand to procure the bauble if a swap was not forthcoming. His technique was to distract and then swipe. In one case, he tweaked the earlobe of his victim, in another he mussed up the victim's hair, and in a third, he placed an after-dinner mint down the victim's shirt. When each person was distracted, he swooped down and yanked hard on the desired object.

Lorenzo was generous and understood sharing and helping. He was seen giving his own food to a mother squirrel with a hungry brood of young, and he once led Mr. Leslie to a baby bird who had fallen from a nest. He accomplished this by making agitated "hollering" sounds and pulling on Mr. Leslie's chest hair while skillfully leading him to the right tree. Lorenzo shared his food, his sleeping cage, and his toys for two months with this recuperating representative of a different bird species.

BIRDS OF A FEATHER

Humans did not invent love or friendship. But how quick we are to deny these bonds to animals. Avian couples—from parakeets to hornbills—caress, cuddle, kiss (often intertwining their tongues in each other's mouths), sing to each other, and carry out other loving interactions that may or may not be followed by mating. Birds who love each other murmur and talk to each other in complicated ways we cannot hope to understand and take enormous comfort in grooming one another and simply being together. They will even attempt to lift injured mates to safety if they cannot fly and will carry food in their beaks to help ailing loved ones when they are dying.

Of all the cruelties of thoughtlessness, including the loss of flight and liberty, this privation may be the most heartless.

ASK NOT WHAT YOUR ANIMAL CAN DO FOR YOU

When you start wondering, "How can I enrich my animal companion's life?" a new and healthier relationship begins: one based on respect, humility, and understanding, instead of on domination, impatience, and human convenience.

When that animal dies, you will not have to look back with regret and ask yourself, "Why was I always yelling at him?" "Why didn't I take her to the park more often?" "Shouldn't I have known not to fly her in the hold of a plane?" "Did I make her as comfortable as possible in his old age?" or "How could I have waited to take her to the vet when there was blood in his urine?" You will have diligently learned all you could about him and his nature and needs, his desires and peculiarities; you will have sacrificed some things you wanted to do, often, and truly have done your best to love him with all your heart. That love will have been returned a thousandfold.

Thomas D. Murray of Franklin, Ohio, penned a beautiful essay called "What George Taught Us" when his beloved spaniel died. He wrote,

> I'd tried to teach him with a rolled-up newspaper to stop barking and dancing through the house every time the doorbell rang or he heard a car in the driveway. I think he was trying to make me understand that a friend at the door, or even a stranger or the mailman, can be a nice little diversion on a humdrum day, and something to celebrate with a little excitement.
>
> I thought he should be more patient as we fixed his food instead of prancing around the kitchen, standing on his rear legs and then gulping down the full bowl almost before it was set in front of him on the floor. But he never stopped his kitchen parade, likely to remind me of the pure joy of wanting and waiting for something and, by always wagging his tail the entire time he

was eating, demonstrating that gratefulness is a priceless part of good manners and doesn't cost a thing.

Early on I had tried to teach him to quickly finish his business in the yard so we could come inside. In time, he taught me the joy of a much longer sunrise walk to see the new day, even in winter, and another after dinner to help put the day's work and worries in perspective.

We thought maybe a big red ribbon on his collar and some special treats might make him sense some of the season's spirit at Christmastime. But on all the days that weren't Christmas, he tried to teach us to erase the boundaries and limits we drew around the holidays by showing us they didn't start for him when the tree came into the house or the holly went up, but when the family came in on any day or night of the year. I think he was trying to show us how to simplify the spirit of Christmas and spread it out over the other 11 months, and perhaps point out that the only presents that meant much of anything to him were those waiting for him, not just on Christmas, but every morning of the year—his family, his friends, his food, his freedom, and not too many baths.

No one in our family will ever forget George. But, of all the memories, the only one I'm a little ashamed of is that right up until the end, I was still trying to teach him things.

If we open our eyes and our hearts, there are a million ways to thank the animals who, whole and complete as they are, find themselves at the mercy of our race.

What You Can Do

Companion Animals

- **Spay and Neuter.** "Neuter Is Cuter!" Spaying or neutering not only helps fight the tragic cat, dog, and rabbit overpopulation problem, it also eliminates diseases of the ovaries, uterus, and testicles and drastically reduces the risk of prostate and mammary cancers, both common in older animals. Many municipalities and humane societies have low-cost spay/neuter programs, or try calling SPAY USA at 1-800-248-SPAY. Even paying top dollar for this once-in-a-lifetime surgery beats the tragedy of bringing unwanted litters into the world.
- **Support Your Local Animal Shelter.** Never patronize pet shops and breeders—they contribute to dog and cat overpopulation. The animals at your local shelter have personality, affection, charm, and looks. You could be their lifeline.
- **Support Pet Supply Stores.** Buy leashes, toys, and other supplies for companion animals only at stores that don't sell animals.
- **Give Gifts Carefully.** Don't give anyone an animal as a gift unless you have discussed it with the person beforehand to make sure he or she is fully prepared to care for a companion animal for *life.*
- **Clean Up Your Pound.** Volunteers can transform grim, neglected pounds into nice places to visit, and comfortable places for animals. Volunteers walk and groom dogs, assist with calls, and collect blankets and newspapers.

- **Educate Others.** If you attend a fair, flea market, or other event at which animals are being given away, educate those responsible. If people are offering a litter of kittens or puppies, explain the risks of giving animals to unknown passersby: Some people sell dogs and cats to laboratories or dealers, and others abuse, neglect, or abandon them. Ask PETA for fliers on spaying and neutering and copies of the brochure "Finding the Right Home for Your Companion Animal" to share with these people.
- **Liberate Your Language!** An animal is "he" or "she"—not "it." Avoid using animal-derogatory terms such as "sly as a fox" or "He's an animal."
- **Be Considerate!** Think of your companion animal's needs for exercise, companionship, and stimulation. Don't leave him or her alone for long periods of time. Set aside some time each day for interaction with your animal companion. Provide a second companion of the same species to help alleviate loneliness and boredom.
- **Give Them a Door.** Provide a dog or cat door (into a fenced yard, of course). No one expects human beings to keep their legs crossed for eight to ten hours a day! Because cats and cars don't mix, if cats can go outside, be sure to add a 45-degree interior angle to the top of your fence.
- **Make Them Food.** Avoid off-the-shelf commercial food, which is made from chemical-laden slaughterhouse reject meat. Instead, buy a vegetarian pet food or make food for your companion animals yourself. (Even cats can have a vegetarian diet now, thanks to a supplement called Vegecat.) Write PETA for more information.
- **Bake for Your Dog or Cat.** Try these recipes:

  Vegan Dog Biscuits

  9 cups whole wheat flour
  1 cup nutritional yeast
  1 tbsp. salt
  1 tbsp. garlic powder

  Mix dry ingredients. Add approximately 3 cups water. Knead into a pliable dough. Roll out until ⅛" thick. Cut into shapes. Bake for 10–15 minutes at 350 degrees F. After turning off oven, leave biscuits in oven overnight or equivalent so they become hard and crunchy.

Garbanzo Cat Chow

⅜ cup sprouted or cooked garbanzo beans
1½ tbsp. nutritional yeast powder
1 tbsp. chopped or grated vegetables
1 tbsp. oil
½ tsp. Vegecat (see Appendix E: Recommended Products for address)
⅓ tsp. soy sauce

Mix all ingredients together. Refrigerate any unused portions.

■ **Get Information.** Learn about your friend's needs, instincts, and natural behaviors by reading up on that species. You may be surprised at the motivation behind some behaviors.

■ **Make a Bed.** Provide a foam pad to rest and sleep on. This will keep dogs and cats out of drafts and provide relief from arthritis and protection for joints, especially older ones.

■ **Buy Cruelty-Free Toys.** Buy only safe, cruelty-free toys and products for your companion animals. Don't buy rawhide, which is a slaughterhouse by-product.

■ **Create a Network.** Swap information on good and bad experiences with boarding facilities, veterinarians, groomers, "pet sitters," and even dog-door suppliers. Keep a card file for neighbors' reference.

■ **Pay Attention.** Never ignore stray animals on the street, where they can become victims of disease, starvation, cars, and the cruelty of humans—as well as being able to reproduce and add to the overpopulation problem.

■ **Help Them Get Home.** When you find lost animals, your principal aim is to reunite them with their families, without alerting unscrupulous people to their plight. Most newspapers will place a free ad if you find an animal—but make your description less than thorough; the person looking for a lost companion should be able to describe the animal *in detail*.

■ **Warn People.** Call people who place "Free to a good home" ads in newspapers, warning them that "bunchers" are known to scan such ads for animals they can sell to laboratories. Write to PETA's Literature Department to request a copy of PETA's "Guidelines for the Sale or Give-Away of Your Companion Animal" to assist you in finding a warm and loving home for your companion animals.

■ **Apply Your Business Skills.** Gwendolyn May uses proceeds from her thrift shop to pay for veterinary care and food for companion animals of needy elderly people. She also runs a twenty-four-hour advice-about-animals hotline.

■ **Be Persistent!** Call the humane society as often as needed to report cruelty and get action. (You can request anonymity.)

■ **Alert Schools.** If a school is keeping animals—either as "pets" or as teaching "tools"—protest to the teacher, the administrator, and if necessary, the school board. Ask school boards to forbid the use of animals in classrooms.

DOGS

■ **Fence Your Yard.** A kennel is not enough. If dogs must ever be left outside, they would like nothing better than to be able to explore every nook and cranny of their yard. A 6-foot privacy fence is safest—it's harder for them to escape and harder for people to hurt your pup. If a fence is out of your budget, attach a swivel hook to a running line that enables the dog to run back and forth without getting tangled. Never leave a choke collar on an unsupervised dog—dogs can strangle if the collar becomes snagged, or they can hang themselves.

■ **Use a Harness.** Swap that collar for a harness. Pressure on a dog's neck can be stressful and lead to injuries.

■ **Let Your Dog Be a Dog!** For example, don't flat out prohibit digging—give dogs their very own special places to dig. Teach them to use their "sandbox" by burying favorite toys in it.

■ **Be Gentle.** Avoid giving your dog orders except when essential for the dog's safety. Try to make suggestions and ask questions, too. Learning the meanings of words and phrases like "Cookies," "Outside?" "Water?" "All done," and "Wanna go for a walk?" can make your dog's life happier.

■ **Take a Class.** Enroll your dog in a humane training class that you attend too. If your dog is outdoors because of behavior problems, confinement and isolation only make the problems worse. Humane training teaches you to communicate with your dog, who is eager to please but isn't always clear on what you expect.

■ **Bring Your Dog Inside.** Don't kid yourself that dogs "get used to" living outside. Unless you or other dogs are out there to share it with them, the dull, unchanging scenery of the backyard quickly loses its charm. If their constant barking (really cries for attention) has finally stopped, it's not because they're content but because they've given up hope of rescue.

■ **Get Exercise.** Provide your dog with lots of exercise. Dogs crave running, sniffing, and exploring. Go for long walks daily, if possible, and use a retractable leash that allows your dog to run ahead and check out interesting fire hydrants.

■ **Look Out for "Hot Dogs."** Dogs don't perspire, so in hot weather they should never be left in a car. Even with car windows cracked, a dog can quickly suffer brain damage or death.

■ **Watch Out for Lamppost Dogs.** Jim Yeargin waits with dogs tied outside stores to apprise their guardians that the dogs could be stolen and sold to the vivisection industry. If he can't wait, he ties a tag reading, "I could have stolen this dog to sell to a laboratory," to the animals' collars.

■ **Provide Information.** Develop and distribute seasonal alerts (for example, "Remember not to leave cloth bedding in dog houses in winter—it freezes when wet" and general tips (for example, how to secure a water bucket and how to make homemade biscuits for the health-conscious dog).

■ **Be a Friend.** Offer to take "forgotten" dogs for walks, and visit them regularly. Fix a running line and/or attach a swivel (available at hardware stores). Make sure the dog can't get tangled up and that his or her water is accessible and in a container that can't be knocked over. Your kindness means the world.

■ **Offer Tips.** Whether you talk to them in person, send an anonymous letter, or contact the humane society, let owners of neglected dogs know exactly what needs to be done. Although it may seem unlikely that simply pointing out the neglect will be enough to remedy it, sometimes that's all it takes.

CATS

■ **Trim Your Cat's Claws.** Don't declaw. To prevent furniture damage, those hooks simply need to be snipped off. Have your veterinarian trim the nails or invest in a decent pair of nail clippers (available from your veterinarian and from pet supply catalogs and stores). Press the paw between your fingers and thumb to unsheathe the claws. Trim just enough to blunt claws but not enough to cut into the quick. Only do kitty's front paws. Hind paws pose no threat except during cat ninja kicking contests and will help kitty climb trees to safety if he or she accidentally slips outside. Write to PETA for more tips on furniture saving.

■ **Buy or Make a Scratching Post.** Vertical scratching posts should be sturdy and tall enough for a cat to stretch out fully (a wobbly post will frighten cats away). Posts should be covered in sisal or carpet turned inside out. Cardboard posts need to be changed when worn out or your cat will lose interest.

■ **Watch Their Diet.** Cats' special dietary needs are more critical than dogs'; for example, cats can suffer loss of eyesight and die if they are deprived of taurine, which until recently was virtually impossible to find in a non-animal form (now available as a derivative of an organic, renewable, non-animal source). While most cats appear to do well on a vegetarian diet, some have not adapted so well. Monitor your companion *closely* when you switch her or him to a non-meat diet. Harbingers of a New Age can answer any questions you might have. (See Appendix E: Recommended Products for address and phone numbers.)

■ **Give Digestible Treats.** Many adult cats have trouble digesting the milk sugar lactose. Instead, give treats like corn (maize), peas, squash, sweet potatoes, and melon.

■ **Use a Leash.** Train your cat to walk on a leash; just be sure to use an ultra-lightweight leash attached to a harness (not a collar). Start by getting your cat used to the harness and leash for short periods of time indoors; then bring along some favorite treats and pick an open area (away from trees and fences) to walk.

■ **Wear a Collar.** Use a quick-release collar with an ID tag for every cat. Even cats who never set a paw outdoors can slip out accidentally. One PETA member outfits her cats with tags that simply say, "I'm lost," with the phone number printed below.

■ **Give Cats a Room with a View.** Windows are cat "TV"—a bird feeder placed near a window beats the most gripping soap opera!

■ **Look Out for Ferals.** A colony of feral cats (domestic cats gone wild) exists (and multiplies!) in almost every community. Feeding them from time to time is helpful but not enough. These animals or their recent ancestors probably once lived in homes and are lost or were abandoned. They are subject to disease, starvation, injury, and accident; and they need help. Borrow a humane box trap from your local animal shelter, or have neighbors chip in to purchase one from a hardware store. Take the cats to the vet or the local shelter to have them examined, given the appropriate shots, and spayed or neutered—or euthanized if ill or if adoption efforts fail in your neighborhood and beyond. Preventing feral cats from continuing to reproduce is the best and kindest assistance you can give them.

What You Can Do

129

FISH

- **Keep Company.** Don't buy fish, but if you already have done so: Most fish enjoy companionship. If you have a single fish, check with friends and neighbors to find another loner whom you may be able to adopt (but don't support the fish trade by going to a dealer).
- **Clean the Fish Tank.** Clean the tank regularly, about two to three times a week. The natural waste of fish emits ammonia, which can accumulate to toxic levels. Also be sure to clean the glass well with a pad or brush so algae doesn't form.
- **Give Your Fish Plants.** Plants provide oxygen, shelter, and hiding places, and fish enjoy snacking on them as well. Provide live plants, not plastic ones.
- **Make It Fun.** Create places for your fish to hide and explore. Ceramic, natural rock, and driftwood all work well. Make sure objects are thoroughly cleaned and disinfected before putting them in the tank. Do not use metal objects, as they will rust.

BIRDS

- **Boycott Cruel Hotels.** Refuse to stay at resort hotels that keep birds caged as "decorations." Let your travel agent and the hotel managers know that you will not support this cruelty.
- **Don't Buy Birds.** Never buy or cage a bird (except for the bird's safety). Birds were born to fly and, being flock animals, live with others of their species. Wild birds make sad, lonely, and sometimes dangerous "pets." Captive-bred birds are more docile, but breeders must constantly introduce new genes from wild-caught birds, so even buying only captive-bred birds supports the wild-caught bird trade.
- **Work Your Town.** Discourage pet shops from carrying birds. Work to get your city or town to pass an ordinance banning the sale of birds.

■ **Care for a Bird by Providing:**

A private place, like a screen to go behind, in their room or flight enclosure.

"Special time" with you every day.

Baths or mistings when the birds desire them. Provide shallow containers or a birdbath with lukewarm water. Some birds like to be sprayed with water from a spray bottle. One person built a perch in her shower; the birds sit on the shower curtain rod, and when the (lukewarm) shower is turned on they can descend to the perch if they so choose.

Between eight and twelve hours of sleep a night, preferably from dusk on, in a draped flight enclosure or a covered cage.

Regular nail and beak trims to avoid difficulty in eating. If birds are allowed to chew hard toys, beak trims may not be necessary.

Bird-safe toys, including wood, on a rotating basis for chewing and playing. Make sure the wood is not poisonous. Apple tree branches are good if they haven't been sprayed. Companion animal supply companies sell suitable wooden bird toys. It may take months before interest in a toy is stimulated.

Classical music, especially Mozart, during the day.

RABBITS

■ **Hug Your Bunny.** Rabbits need lots of love and attention. Tame rabbits are social beings who are happiest living indoors with you. Isolated rabbits become bored, withdrawn, and depressed. They can make friends with other rabbits, cats, and some dogs.

■ **Groom Your Bunny.** Groom at least twice a week with a small, fine soft wire brush or soft-bristled cat brush. Grooming shows affection and lets you examine the rabbit for signs of illness.

EXOTIC ANIMALS

■ **Don't Keep Exotics as Pets.** Regardless of their size, exotic animals should never be kept in captivity. If you want to share your home with an animal companion, please visit your local shelter—millions of unwanted animals are literally dying to be someone's friend.

TRAVEL TIPS

■ **Don't Fly Your Animal.** If you must, use only a direct, non-stop flight, making sure to fly at night in summer, during the day in winter, and never during temperature extremes (animals can freeze to death, suffocate, or die of heat prostration in cargo holds—especially if there is a delay). Be sure you or someone very reliable sees the animal safely aboard, meets the arriving flight, and knows how to raise Cain if the animal doesn't arrive on time. If your companion animal is high-strung, your veterinarian may give him or her a tranquilizer. Sturdy, roomy, well-ventilated carriers and clear identification are essential (accustom the animal to the kennel at home long before the departure date). Recommended carriers must be USDA approved, and can be purchased from most airlines.

■ **Take Your Friend Onboard.** If your animal friend is small (can fit into a carry-on kennel that goes under your seat), choose an airline that allows him or her to fly in the passenger compartment with you. This is far less frightening to animals and much safer than riding in the cargo space. Avoid heavy traffic days, such as holidays and weekends. Reserve space for your companion well in advance, as airlines limit the number of other-than-human spaces per flight. Don't feed your companion animal solid food for at least six hours before flight time, but a little water and a peppy "walk" are a must before boarding.

■ **Provide Reassurance.** If you go away on vacation, remember your animal companions love you and will miss you, so greet and leave them with this foremost in your mind. Always remember to say good-bye. Use a kind, "stay," look directed into your friend's eyes and say, very reassuringly and firmly, "I'll be back." The idea that your absence will not be forever is reinforced in this simple way.

■ **Keep Them at Home.** Keep your dogs or cats safely at home, rather than boarding them out with strangers. There's a lot to be said for familiar surroundings; they are generally the safest and least stressful. Try to find a responsible (adult) friend or relative to stay at your home or to come by *at least* three times a day to keep an eye on the animals and tend to their needs (allow them to relieve themselves). Even if there are ample provisions, accidents happen and someone should make safety checks often. If you can't find someone you know and trust, explore a "pet sitting" service that has *several* verifiable and reliable references—from a humane society, veterinarians, and bona fide clients. Make sure the chosen caretaker has all the important information posted near the telephone, including emergency numbers (veterinary night service and numbers where you can be reached).

■ **Thoroughly Investigate Boarders.** If you *must* board your animal, veterinary hospitals are not recommended because animals can be exposed to illnesses and can often sense the pain of others around them. Be very careful when choosing a boarding facility—smiling people can run little shops of horrors. Humane officers have frightening stories to tell, such as animals stacked in crates during peak boarding seasons, and families returning home to find that their animal friends had "escaped." Ask friends for references, and check with your local Chamber of Commerce and Department of Consumer Affairs for possible complaints against the facility. Make sure that you inspect the *entire* premises. If you are told that this is inconvenient or that insurance regulations prevent your inspection, head out the front door, pronto.

ANIMAL THEFT

- **Use Tattoos.** Tattoo your animal companion. Use a pain-less, permanent tattoo (tags can be lost or removed, render-ing the animal conveniently anonymous). Veterinarians, shelters, pounds, and laboratories often check for tattoos, and many animals have been happily reunited with their families because they were "wearing" tattooed identifica-tion on their skin (on the inner thigh, as ears can be cut off). Organizations that can help:

  National Dog Registry (NDR). NDR has tattooed and regis-tered more than 2.4 million dogs—identified by the guardian's social security number. NDR charges a one-time fee of $35, which covers all animals in a household. NDR has agents throughout the country and claims a 97 percent recovery rate. To report a lost dog with a social security number tattoo, call 800-NDR-DOGS. (See Ap-pendix C: Recommended Groups for address.)

  Tattoo-A-Pet (TAP). TAP has approximately one million dogs registered—coded by state, agent doing the tattoo, and a number for each animal—and two thousand au-thorized facilities nationwide. Claiming a 99 percent re-covery rate, TAP has two thousand agents around the United States. The fee is $10 plus $10 for the tattoo. (See Appendix C: Recommended Groups for address.)

- **Safeguard Against Theft.** Never leave dogs unsupervised in a yard or chained or tied up alone. Cats should be al-lowed out only with you. Animals left unattended in cars are a favorite target for thieves.

- **Watch for Cars.** Write down license tags of unfamiliar vehicles in case they belong to "bunchers" who steal animals for labs.

- **Run an Ad.** Place an ad in the classified section of your newspaper that says: "PET THEFT ALERT: Don't let your companion animal end up in a research experiment. Don't leave animals alone outdoors. Check out new homes thor-oughly before you give an animal away. Call _____ (your phone number or PETA's) for more information."

■ **Read a Book.** Read *Stolen for Profit* by Judith Reitman. This book exposes a national pet-theft conspiracy.

IN CASE OF EMERGENCY

■ **Be Prepared.** Carry an animal rescue kit (nonperishable food, a cardboard cat carrier, a leash, a bandage for a muzzle, and emergency phone numbers of vets and shelters) in your car.

■ **Get Help.** In case of emergency, seek veterinary help right away. Describe symptoms or injuries clearly, and take careful note of instructions. Generally, keep the victim quiet and still; in the case of traffic accidents, move victims carefully and gently out of danger, and then follow these procedures: When waiting for a veterinarian, the general principle is to stem any bleeding (without cutting off circulation) and keep air passages clear of obstructions while disturbing the animal as little as possible. If you need to carry an injured dog, make a stretcher out of a blanket, board, coat, or sack; put it on the ground and gradually slide it under the animal. Keep the stretcher taut. Stem bleeding with a clean handkerchief, piece of sheet, or any cloth by making a pad and securing it to the wound, then elevate the injured body part.

An injured animal, however familiar, may snap or bite out of fear and pain. A bandage or belt can be used as a makeshift muzzle, looped around the snout a couple of times and then tied behind the head. Make sure the animal can breathe easily (watch out for heaving sides, a sign of breathing difficulty) and isn't vomiting, or she or he may choke. Release the muzzle as soon as you can.

Shock is a basic problem with any form of trauma; keep animals as quiet and warm as possible. If possible, put one person strictly in charge of monitoring the animal.

■ **Heads Ups!** Take the following symptoms seriously. Get help immediately!

Bleeding from any orifice: nose, mouth, ears, rectum, sex organs

Any problems with eyes: watering or half-closed, third eye-
   lid exposed
Straining to urinate or repeated trips to the litterbox
Bloating or collapse after eating, exercise, or rapid intake of
   water
Unusually lethargic or agitated behavior
Drinking lots of water
Fur standing on end
Loss of appetite
Continuous vomiting
Dragging or holding limbs
Sudden weight loss
Diarrhea
Coughing
Lumps

■ **Use Care with Antifreeze.** Be careful not to spill antifreeze,
which is highly toxic to animals, who like its sweet taste.
Better, shop for Sierra antifreeze, a nontoxic and biodegradable alternative.

What Do They Really Do to Animals in Laboratories?

Look Mommy, isn't he cute?
Can he really fly?
Of course, my dear, watch him.
How do they teach him, Mommy?
See those little wires
coming from his head.

Yes, what are they for?
Every time he makes a mistake
he gets an electric shock.
Doesn't it hurt him, then?
No, of course not. . . . Or they
wouldn't do it.

—PAUL HAGGARD

Some months after founding People for the Ethical Treatment of Animals (PETA), Alex Pacheco led the police into a laboratory called the Institute for Behavioral Research (IBR), in Silver Spring, Maryland. Once inside, police officers served their warrant, seizing seventeen small macaque monkeys, survivors from a group originally twice that size.

The monkeys were in bad shape. Many had open, festering wounds, and much of their lustrous hair was missing. Their normally bushy tails were bare because of malnutrition, and they had pulled out whole clumps of fur on their arms and legs from frustration, anger, and misery. Although once vigorous and even fierce defenders of their jungle homes, after years of confinement in feces-encrusted cages barely larger than their own bodies, they were now frail and vulnerable. They stared up anxiously at the crowds of uniformed officers and media, almost blinded by the sunlight they had not seen since being snatched, many years before, from their families in the Philippines.

As the state's veterinary witnesses would later testify in court, many of the monkeys had been operated on, their backs cut open and their nerves severed, making movement of their arms difficult or impossible.

One timid little monkey named Billy had not only lost the use of both his arms, but both were broken. He had been forced to push himself on his elbows across the cage grating and to eat his food by bending over and grasping it between his teeth, although his teeth were painfully infected.

Alex would relate how the monkeys would injure their deadened limbs, sometimes catching and then tearing off their fingers on the jagged, broken, and rusted wires that protruded from their cages. (Police documented thirty-nine of the fingers on the monkeys' hands were severely deformed or missing.) He recounted how the experimenters forced the monkeys into a dark, blood-spattered refrigerator and a jerry-rigged restraint chair, tying them down with duct tape and burning them with a cigarette lighter, squeezing their flesh, including their testicles, with surgical pliers, and administering electric shocks to them to "test" the feeling in their limbs.

Was the Silver Spring case an isolated incident?

Most people believe, or want to believe, that animals would not be used in experiments if their use weren't absolutely necessary. After all, who wants to believe we are needlessly cruel? Moreover, people hope that only a few animals, or as few as possible, are used, that all of them are destined for experiments that are potentially life-saving, and that they are treated humanely.

Nothing could be further from the truth.

Millions of animals are used in experiments every year. More often than not, they are acquired almost casually, housed abysmally, and denied anything remotely like a life. In addition to suffering through the experiments, they are under constant stress from fear, the loss of control over their lives, and the denial of all that is natural and meaningful to them, such as enjoying the company of others of their own kind and choosing.

Animals from giraffes to gerbils are used for everything from forced aggression and induced fear experiments to tests on new football helmets and septic tank cleaner. Baboons are given AIDS-infected rectal swabs, great apes are purposely driven mad to make them crush their infants' skulls in child abuse studies, and researchers are changing the genes of pigs so they can no longer walk and chickens so they can no longer fly.

Animals are burned alive in the cockpits of planes, exploded in weapons tests, and forced to inhale pollutants until they choke to death. They are starved and shot; they have hallucinogenics and electrical shocks administered to them; they are force-fed poisons and used to demonstrate already well established surgical procedures. They are commonly thought of as nothing more than disposable "test tubes with whiskers."

There are countless examples of wasteful and ludicrous experiments. This "rubbish research" comes at a time when many Americans do not have health insurance, scores of alcohol and drug treatment clinics have closed due to the loss of funds, the elderly and disabled go without new eyeglasses or dental care, and unless they can afford to buy them themselves, disabled people are left without state-of-the-art wheelchairs and home aids that would allow them to participate more fully in society.

WOULD YOU FUND THESE STUDIES?

At the University of California in Santa Barbara, experimenters sewed plastic swords to the hindquarters of male fish to see if females preferred males with or without swords (try to guess the applicability of this jewel). Elsewhere, rats were killed by being fed huge doses of Louisiana hot sauce (the human equivalent of half a cup per 10 pounds of body weight). Monkeys at the University of Texas had electrical probes inserted into their brains and were then awakened every night with loud noises to see the effect on their sex drive; rats were forced to swim to their deaths at Georgetown University to study "executive stress" (female rats stay afloat longer); more University of California studies had experimenters shoving toy snakes into monkeys' cages to see how the monkeys reacted (they were scared); and fish were given a choice between gin and vodka (whatever their preference, who cares?).

Forgetting the just plain daft experiments, there are tens of thousands of experiments that cause enormous suffering to animals every day in the name of medical research. For example,

- at Rockefeller University, experimenters have forced cats to vomit up to ninety-seven times in three and a half hours after severing the connections between the cats' brains and spinal cords;
- at the University of Iowa, pregnant rabbits have been given daily doses of cocaine, and baby rabbits were shocked in the head to study "maternal drug abuse";
- at Louisiana State University hundreds of cats were shot in the brain to show that such wounds "impair breathing";
- the U.S. Fish and Wildlife Service got into the act by spending $600,000 after the Exxon Valdez oil spill to capture birds, shoot them, outfit them with radio tracers, douse their corpses with oil, and throw them into the sea to "prove" that birds were killed by the spill;

■ University of Illinois researchers cut open cows' stomachs, inserted bags of newspapers into them, then checked the bags to see if cows can survive on a diet of 40 percent newsprint;

■ NASA has sent monkeys into space with electrical coils threaded though the backs of their eyes;

■ the tobacco industry has forced dogs and mice into smoking masks and compelled them to inhale tobacco fumes twenty-four hours a day for years;

■ half a dozen universities have kept cats awake for days at a time, forcing them to balance on narrow planks above water-filled tanks or lowering their cage temperatures to well below freezing.

As if that weren't enough, hundreds of household product and cosmetics companies and big pharmaceutical houses, many marketing the fortieth version of basically the same old antidepressant or headache remedy, still contract with laboratories that conduct the "standard four" tests. These crude tests, first hurriedly devised between 1920 and 1930, when large quantities of new pills and lotions were flooding the market, are carried out on large groups of animals every day.

Here's how unsophisticated these tests are: You take a substance—say, an acne medication or a nail polish remover—and (1) drip it into restrained rabbits' eyes; (2) thrust massive quantities of it down dogs' or monkeys' throats; (3) force rats to inhale it through a mask or by spraying it into their sealed cages, and/or (4) smear it on the raw, shaved backs of guinea pigs. Then you sit back and record the damage.

Obviously, if you force-feed a pint of drain cleaner to a monkey, the monkey's internal organs will be eaten away, along with the lining of his or her throat, and he or she will probably go into convulsions and die. His or her pain will not soothe or save the person who tries to commit suicide by swallowing drain cleaner, nor will it help in the least little bit the person who, somehow or other, inadvertently gets drain cleaner in his or her eye. We already know the likely result and the proper treatment, and these tests are not designed to determine how to treat injury.

HOW DOES IT FEEL
TO BE A GUINEA PIG?

Rabbits, guinea pigs, and other small animals suffer silently, their convulsions violently wracking their bodies without disturbing the peace of the rooms in which they "live": rooms containing row after row of plastic "shoeboxes" or stainless steel cages. The dogs will have been debarked—their vocal cords severed to cut down on the noise.

Add to all this the sort of scenes filmed secretly in 1998 inside the British headquarters of Huntingdon Life Sciences, a laboratory that tests for some of the top names in the industry worldwide. Workers were caught punching dogs in the face, screaming at the animals, and even simulating sex with each other while trying to inject a frightened beagle. In the United States, Huntingdon moved quickly in court to prevent PETA from showing exactly what its investigator had videotaped when she worked in their New Jersey facility the same year. The bubble of public assurances that animals are well cared for was in danger of being burst.

Luckily, the PETA investigator's tapes were aired on television in Cincinnati, Ohio (home of Procter & Gamble), and Norfolk, Virginia (home of PETA), before the gag order took effect. The tapes showed monkeys who were scared out of their wits being taped to an operating table. Their fear is almost palpable. The animals were supposed to be kept calm and quiet to facilitate accurate readings from an electrocardiograph, yet joking staff played loud rock music, yelled in the faces of the restrained monkeys, yee-hawed at the top of their lungs like drunken cowboys, and stuck lotion bottles into the helpless animals' mouths. Following these high jinks, workers body-slammed the primates back into their steel cages.

Should you harbor the illusion that most researchers would immediately denounce such cruelty, dream on. They will defend almost anything, as indeed the top U.S. research lobbying groups did, openly applauding Huntingdon for trying to bar PETA from allowing the public to see the photos and tapes and judge for itself. In fact, Huntingdon's injunction went so far as to specifically prohibit PETA from answering the federal government's questions about the lab or giving the tapes to members of Congress. However, Huntingdon was too late: PETA had already turned over its eight months of investigation notes, hundreds of photographs, and hours of videotapes and had filed a thirty-seven-page formal complaint with the U.S. Department of Agriculture (USDA).

Federal authorities found Huntingdon in violation of the Animal Welfare Act (AWA), the only federal law that offers any protection whatsoever to animals in laboratories.

Perhaps some researchers defend abhorrent practices because they are inured to the suffering of those around them. Perhaps, just as some people can stare at a Picasso for hours without "getting it," they can't understand for the life of them what all the fuss over animals is about. Or perhaps they see any acknowledgment that there are problems as a chink in the armor that could one day crack the whole suit.

There are certainly some truly arrogant experimenters, like Robert White, the Cincinnati man who performs horrific head transplant experiments on monkeys and watches the anguished eyes on their disembodied but live heads follow him about the room. One morning in Cincinnati, White told me it is "never acceptable" to put limits on science. Later, when he and I addressed a group of high school students, White railed to them, "Who are *you* to question a scientist?"

The Silver Spring monkeys prosecutor, Roger Galvin, learned how researchers unite to protect their own kind, like a mob defending itself against the authorities. When given every opportunity to distance themselves from the disgusting cruelty, filth, suffering, and unscientific conduct in that case, what did the research community do? Did it condemn a facility in which police found dead monkeys floating in barrels of formaldehyde, their infected limbs and rotted bandages weighed down with auto parts? Hardly. Its distinguished members flocked to the courthouse to testify *in support of* the accused, Dr. Edward Taub, a researcher many of them had never met or spoken to.

George Bernard Shaw may have hit the nail on the head when he said, "He who would not hesitate to vivisect, would not hesitate to lie about it." After each glowing endorsement, Mr. Galvin would ask the witness for the defense whether he or she had bothered to visit this laboratory. "No." "Did you ask to see the police photographs?" "No." "Did you bother to speak to the state attorney's office about the charges?" "No." The defense witnesses mocked concerns for the animals, describing the monkeys as "nothing more than defecating machines" and a cockroach infestation as an "ambient source of protein" for the primates. They described Taub as a "modern day Galileo," an apt comparison perhaps, given that, in his time, Galileo's opinions allowed experimenters, like the evil René Descartes, to nail live animals to a board, eviscerate them, and disregard their screams as nothing more important than the sound of squeaking wheels.

As with everything, there are exceptions. One is Donald Barnes. Once an experimenter for the United States Air Force, Barnes used to torture rhesus monkeys. His job was to irradiate them, then strap them to treadmills to run, vomiting, to their deaths. Over time, a light came on in his head. He realized that the experiments had yielded nothing of use and were simply a line item on the base budget that his superiors would never sacrifice.

Barnes also came to see that what he was doing was unethical. In his own words, he decided one day to "call in well," and never went back. Mr. Barnes testified for the prosecution in the Silver Spring monkeys case.

Dr. Roger Ulrich is another example. Dr. Ulrich received many professional awards and honors for his rather nasty research, using monkeys to study the relationship between pain and aggression. One day, he wrote to the American Psychological Association.

When I was asked why I conducted these experiments, I used to say it was because I wanted to help society solve its problems of mental illness, crime, retardation, drug abuse, child abuse, unemployment, marital unhappiness, alcoholism, over-smoking, over-eating . . . even war! Although, after I got into this line of work, I discovered that the results of my work did not seem to justify its continuance. I began to wonder if perhaps financial rewards, professional prestige, the opportunity to travel, etc., were the maintaining factors and if we of the scientific community, supported by our bureaucratic and legislative systems, were actually part of the whole problem.

One spring I was asked by a colleague, "Dr. Ulrich, what is the most innovative thing that you've done professionally over the past year?" I replied, "Dear Dave, I've finally stopped torturing animals."

MS. BEA AND OTHER BEINGS

When I ran the District of Columbia animal shelter, my dog, Ms. Bea, came to work with me every day. She was a mixed shepherd who looked and acted a little like the imposing grande dame in the old Marx Brothers movies.

She had several functions. At the front desk, she greeted frightened dogs being turned in. When they saw her moving toward them with self-assurance, obviously at home and happy, they stopped shaking so much and got involved in a sniff-fest with her, tails wagging.

She was also in charge of preliminary interviews for dog adoptions. Ms. Bea would turn that corner, no small dog she, and if the potential puppy adopter shrank into the corner, screaming "Does it bite?," they were in trouble.

Ms. Bea worked long hours, as we did, but she loved it. She ate what we ate—Indian take-out was her favorite—and she rode the truck into the "best" and the most troubled neighborhoods, looking out of the window at them all. We loved her very much.

She only fell down on the job once, but I couldn't blame her, because by that time she was very old, had lost her hearing, and was inclined to nap a lot. One very late winter night, some men tried to jump me as I was getting back into my van. It was only because I saw them coming, one with a tire iron in his hand, and because I used to run the heater for Ms. Bea with an extra key in the ignition that I managed to escape. Oblivious to the commotion, Ms. Bea slept through it. I never told her about the incident. It would have been a terrible blow for such a responsible girl.

Ms. Bea was seventeen years old when she died. She had lived a full life and brought much joy to the world. I think of Ms. Bea constantly. When people ask me how anyone can justify breaking into labs and "stealing" the animals, all I know is that if anyone had Ms. Bea on the operating table, I'd be through that door in a minute, lock me up if you will.

Ms. Bea is my litmus test of whether it is right to do things to animals. Ms. Bea was not a thing. She had gender, individuality, life and love and understanding inside her. No one could ever convince me that it would have been all right to burn her or sink electrodes into her head and shock her. Not to save me, my child, or my other dog, if that were the case, and I believe it is never the case. It wouldn't have been right.

They are *all* Ms. Bea, in their own way. Even the smallest of them, the ugliest or weirdest of them. I remember thinking exactly that one day when I toured the National Institutes of Health's (NIH) Poolesville Primate Laboratory.

Entering a barren room in a seemingly endless corridor of sterile, whitewashed rooms, I found a baboon. I actually *heard* him first because he was banging his head so loudly against the solid steel sides of his cage.

In this totally dull, windowless environment, he was so alive and so gaudy, almost surreal: a huge hydramus baboon, the size of a small man. He had a long dog snout that looked as if he had painted it with crazy red and pink and white and gray stripes. His long multicolored hair stood out from his body like a big colorful cloak. You could imagine him on his way to a costume party.

How must he have felt when aliens snatched him from his jungle and transported him to this cold lonely world to die in a steel cage? Most primates avoid making eye contact, yet this baboon stared straight at me. His eyes were filled not with despair, as one might expect, but with deep loathing.

I made inquiries, and my questions became embarrassing for NIH. It transpired that the baboon and several others in his "group" had been forgotten. Originally shipped to the United States from Russia, they had been used for eight years in a cancer study, but the study had been casually abandoned when the principal investigator had taken a job in another state. They would have been hosed down and fed "monkey biscuits" until the day they died. I pushed for a resolution. Eventually NIH told me it had killed them. I hoped it was true, for the baboons' sake.

THE GOLDEN RULE

If "Might does not make right," as we tell our children, then we cannot possibly justify using others *against* their own best interests *just because we aim to get something out of it*. We cannot suddenly suspend our belief in such a fundamental tenet simply because we find it inconvenient to relate to some victims.

Because might does not make right, we have condemned experimenters for having used slaves and poor Irish women to practice gynecological surgeries in the not too distant past; for giving LSD to enlisted men without their knowledge; for secretly exposing Asian women to chemical warfare agents; and for feeding retarded schoolboys cereal laced with radioactive isotopes. Because might does not make right we recoil in horror at the tuberculin experiments using human orphans, the infamous Tuskegee experiments in which black men were deliberately allowed to go untreated for syphilis, and the tests in which prisoners of war were submerged in freezing water.

If might does not make right, it can't suddenly do so when it comes to animals, any more than it can do so for retarded children or poor women.

The white rat is a case in point. Although they are mammals who feel hunger, thirst, pleasure, and pain as any other, they are laboratory favorites, in part because they are not the objects of wide public sympathy. Researchers do not use these tiny animals for scientific reasons. When it comes to feelings, a rat *is* a dog *is* a pig *is* a child, but not when it comes to physiology. Rodents are not little humans: Their blood-clotting factors and pulse rates are vastly different from ours. They manufacture their own vitamin C (we do not); their protein needs are ten times those of a human being; and, unlike us, they are nose-breathers. Researchers use them because they are cheap, readily available, easy to handle, and easy to overlook when it comes to concerns about pain, stress, or suffering.

Should rats' feelings be so easily dismissed? Not according to Dr. Neal Barnard, president of the Physicians Committee for Responsible Medicine (PCRM). The introductory course in psychology at his college used rats who were deprived of water for three days and then put in a "Skinner box" (a cage developed by B. F. Skinner that delivers a few drops of water when a bar is pressed by the thirsty animal inside). The point of the lab was to show how learning occurs. For example, if an animal is rewarded (reinforced) for an action such as pressing a bar, the animal will probably repeat the action. At the end of the course, the rats were put together in a trash can, chloroform poured over them, and the lid closed.

Students could sign up to implant electrodes into a rat's skull to show that electrical stimulation of the brain can affect behavior. During the implantation procedure, a stereotaxic device held the rat's head still, its metal bars thrust into both ear canals, breaking the eardrums. Dr. Barnard says, "My professor's response to my concern about the effects of this procedure on the rats was a joke: 'Well, I guess he won't be able to listen to his stereo in the morning.' But while I was struck by the callousness of his remark, I was sufficiently desensitized myself that I proceeded."

One day, Dr. Barnard took a rat home from the lab. "Ratsky" lived for some months in a cage in his bedroom. And, in her cage, she behaved the way he assumed rats behave. But when he started leaving the cage door open so she could walk around, he began to see things he hadn't anticipated. After several days of cautious sniffing about at the cage door, she began to investigate the world outside. As she explored the apartment, under Dr. Barnard's watchful eye, she took an interest in him and his friends.

> She gradually became more and more friendly. If I was lying on my back reading, she would come and stand on my chest. She would wait to be petted and if I didn't pay her enough attention, she would lightly nip my nose and run away. I knew that her sharp teeth could have gone right through my skin, but she was always playfully careful.
>
> I realized that rats can be as outgoing and gentle as any person. Given food, water, and warmth, most rats are friendly, fun, and meticulously clean. If not forced to live in an unclean cage, their skin has a distinct perfume-like scent. If I left a glass of ice water on the floor for her, she would painstakingly take out each ice cube and carry it inch by inch in her teeth away from the glass until all the ice had been cleaned out. One day she labored for hours to pull all my dirty clothes out of a laundry bag. Like a cat, she spent hours carefully grooming herself.

One day, Dr. Barnard noticed a lump in Ratsky's skin. With time, it grew, and it was all but impossible to find a veterinarian who would treat her, since she was not a dog, cat, or farm animal. One said Ratsky was a male and the lump was "his" scrotum. Others called it a fat pad. Finally Dr. Barnard convinced a vet who specialized in "laboratory animals," to take the lump out, whatever it was. It was a tumor.

The vet put Ratsky in a heavy cast and said the operation was successful.

Because rats are meticulous about their bodies and work tirelessly to rid themselves of any dirt, they have to be put in body casts after surgery to prevent them from removing their sutures. When Dr. Barnard cut her out of the cast, Ratsky painfully tottered a few steps, trembling. He discovered that the vet had not only removed the tumor, but had also inadvertently removed her urethra, the tube that leads to the bladder, so that urine spilled from her bladder into the abdominal cavity and was a caustic irritation under her skin.

The vet tried to correct his mistake in a second operation, but he was very uncertain whether it would succeed. While friends could understand caring for larger animals, Dr. Barnard found that few people could understand the suffering of this little mammal. "Her suffering was very apparent. At night I slept with her in the palm of my hand so I would wake up if she tried to chew out her sutures."

Before long it became clear that Ratsky's condition was worsening. The reconstructed urethra closed off, causing her great distress. Finally she was euthanized.

I carry with me the vivid image of this tiny animal tottering painfully out from her body cast, of her in the palm of my hand trying to pull out the sutures that were a constant irritation to her. In the months that followed, I began to think about all the other animals whose suffering I had taken so dispassionately, and I realized that each one was an individual who can suffer as acutely as the little rat who I had held in my hand. And that suffering was just as real whether the animal was a dog, a dolphin, a rat, or a mouse, whether the animal was "bred for the purpose" or chained up in someone's back yard.

Now, as a practicing physician, I continue to be puzzled about the resistance to compassion that I see so commonly in others and that I, too, experienced for so long. Cruelty to animals is diagnosed as a psychiatric symptom predictive of antisocial personality, yet we fail to recognize the cruelties we perpetuate so casually in our own lives.

Not too long ago, my alma mater sent me a survey asking, among other things, who had been my most effective teacher. I'm not sure they understood my reply.

It is because of prejudice alone that millions of rat bodies hit the biological waste containers annually, each one having lived a brief life as a little, once-inquisitive being like Dr. Barnard's Ratsky—each one snuffed out casually and not always quickly or cleanly.

A RAT IS NOT A LITTLE MAN

If animal experiments were as marvelous as some have claimed, we would surely have eternal life by now. After all, the unfettered use of animals has been going on, with vigor, for hundreds of years. The "war on cancer," declared with much fanfare in 1950, and then again by President Nixon twenty years later, has been deemed a qualified failure, with cancer rates remaining so high that one in every three Americans is eventually diagnosed with the disease. Small wonder when, in a study of cancer in mice and rats, 30 percent of chemicals found to cause cancer in one species were safe in the other. We have no cures for AIDS, spina bifida, diabetes (one slogan of the American Diabetes Society is "Insulin Is Not a Cure"), or virtually any serious disease you can name. Not surprisingly, everything important we have learned about diabetes has come from human studies. The link between pancreatic disease or dysfunction and diabetes was discovered in human autopsies, and it was J. B. Collip's work in test tubes that laid the groundwork for today's standard treatment. A fifteen-year study of Pima Indians revealed how we can tell who is most likely to get Type II diabetes, and autopsies on teenagers led to the discovery of viral diabetes. The most exciting work involved a ten-year study of human beings in clinical settings. In fact, although for more than a hundred years, experimenters have tried to reproduce diabetes in millions of dogs, mice, rats, and other animals, little has changed and no cure is in sight.

AN ANGRY DIABETIC

Despite a history of failures, animal experiments continue, a fact that particularly galls Mary Beth Sweetland, PETA's director of Research, Investigations & Rescue, herself a diabetic. At NIH, one vivisector has removed beagles' eyeballs to study vision problems in diabetics. The beagles don't receive painkillers after the surgery, even though veterinarians say they need them.

Mary Beth had to start taking daily doses of insulin when she turned twenty-five, in 1979. Before she realized what was wrong, her weight had fallen to just over 95 pounds, her eyesight was blurry, if she cut herself the cut didn't heal, and she was always hungry, thirsty, and very tired. But when she began injecting herself with pork and beef insulin, she quickly lost muscle mass in her thighs and stomach and her blood sugar level was a mess.

Mary Beth credits three things with changing all that and saving her life. Today she checks her glucose level five or six times a day with a monitor and takes up to four to six low doses of Humulin, a synthetic, non-animal insulin that has restored her muscle mass. She has also cut her insulin dosage from 50 units a day to only 15 a day.

Mary Beth discovered, the hard way, that the key to being a healthy diabetic is to eat a vegan diet, avoid all fat, and walk briskly or do exercises for at least thirty minutes a day.

Mary Beth says, "The best part is that I can now look my fabulous Beagle Boys (her rescued beagles) in the eye with a clear conscience."

BARKING UP THE WRONG TREE

Judging side effects in animal tests is often impossible. Even our fellow primates cannot tell us if they have a crushing headache, ringing in the ears, double vision, or nausea. More important, different species react very differently to what goes into them. Parsley is poisonous to some birds, penicillin kills guinea pigs, and chloroform is so toxic to dogs that doctors searching for anesthetics in years past avoided using it for human patients.

It is common knowledge that you can't bathe a cat in a flea shampoo meant for a dog, yet drug companies marketed DES, or diethylstilbestrol, on the strength of animal tests. Over one million women taking DES came down with uterine cancer. Intrauterine devices also passed animal tests with flying colors, as did silicone breast implants. Formaldehyde, dioxin, asbestos, and other chemicals toxic to humans were extensively tested on animals. Drugs are removed from the marketplace when the insurance claims for side effects reach a level that challenges the profitability of the company that markets them.

Perhaps even more important were the drugs we missed because animal tests did not point to them as being useful. Amazingly, even aspirin was initially rejected because it causes deformities in infant rhesus monkeys.

Now, grave new worries are coming to light. All animals harbor viruses. Experimenting on animals or animal tissues, or using animal organs in transplant experiments, carries a serious risk of disease transmission. The AIDS epidemic, for example, is believed to have been caused when a virus from a green vervet monkey jumped the "species barrier" to Africans whose immune system had already been weakened by inoculation against smallpox.

HTLV, a virus that causes leukemia, has crossed the species barrier, too, causing Marburg disease and Lassa fever. "Foamy viruses" are common in baboons, and another monkey virus, named SV40, is implicated in cases of human brain cancer after lying dormant for thirty years. It is believed to have infected people who were injected with a polio vaccine administered worldwide in the 1950s.

In 1997, scientists discovered that pig genes harbor viruses called PERV-A and PERV-B. While harmless in pigs, these viruses can be fatal in humans. In 1998, strains of avian flu crossed from chickens into children and poultry workers in

Pennsylvania and Hong Kong. The same year, Britain and Switzerland outlawed xenografts (animal-to-human transplants) calling the procedure "too risky" and, in the United States, Harvard University's Dr. Fritz Bach joined other xenotransplantation scientists in calling for a moratorium, citing the risk from the operations of unleashing a new AIDS-like epidemic.

There is something very primitive and ignorant in a blind trust in the use of animals to cure our ills. It is worth remembering that just 150 years or so ago, medical "experts" were able to persuade people to impale live snails on thorns to cure themselves of warts and to bury a live rooster to end epileptic fits. Physicians severed the left ear of cats and mixed blood from the wound into a potion to abate measles. Minced mouse was a common prescription for bladder trouble. Laypeople dutifully took this advice and footed the bill. Today, we are just as trusting for our time.

ARE THERE ALTERNATIVES?

Experimentation and even training in human and veterinary medical practice can be done without the pitter-patter of little feet. Especially in this day of technologically advanced research methods, such as *in vitro* cell culture tests in which human cells can be bombarded with diseases and show results in a matter of hours, the use of virtual organs, whole *human* DNA, and computer assaying. We have mass spectrometry, microscopy which allows us to detect minute, precancerous tumors, and detailed analysis of the human genome itself. Gone are the days when a rabbit was killed to determine whether or not a woman was pregnant.

When Dr. Nedim Buyukmihci, a veterinary ophthalmologist at the University of California at Davis, decided to change the old way of teaching veterinary students how to operate on dogs' eyes, he caused a huge stir. Traditionally, the university had purchased dogs from a breeder, deliberately damaged their eyes, and then allowed the students to practice corrective surgeries on the dogs. The dogs were then killed.

Dr. Ned believed there had to be a better way. He decided to find dogs belonging to the elderly and others with fixed incomes and have his students perform a real service, under his expert tutelage, by correcting the dogs' vision problems free of charge. These were dogs whose owners could never have afforded such operations.

The university administration went wild. When they couldn't "reason" with Dr. Buyukmihci, they suspended him from teaching and denied him tenure. Luckily for his students and the animals, Dr. Buyukmihci is a man of principle, and he fought back, suing the university.

Today, Dr. Buyukmihci is tenured and his teaching methods have replaced the old ways.

Dr. Peter Henricksen, a veterinary scientist, recounts his experience. He remembers a dog the students called Rodney, a tall, gangly shepherd mix.

Dr. Henricksen was in his third year of veterinary school when Rodney was delivered from the local dog pound. For the next quarter, four students would practice surgery techniques on him—the first of their small animal surgery training. Rodney was always happy to see them—tail thumping wildly against the walls of his small steel cage. "From the looks of him," says Dr. Henricksen, "Rodney hadn't much of a life, so a pat and a little walk around the college complex made his day."

Dr. Henricksen remembers:

The first thing we did was neuter him, a seemingly benign project except it took us an hour to complete the usual twenty-minute procedure, and an anesthetic overdose kept him out for thirty-six hours. Afterward he recovered his strength quickly and felt good.

Two weeks later we did an abdominal exploratory, opening his abdomen, checking his organ inventory, and closing him again. This was the first major surgery for any of us, and with inadequate supervision we did not close him properly. By the next morning, his incision had opened and he was sitting on his small intestine. Hastily, we sewed him up again, and he survived. But it was a week or more before he could resume the walks he had come to eagerly anticipate. He would still wag his tail when we arrived and greet us with as much enthusiasm as he could muster.

The following week, again when he was under anesthesia, we broke his leg and repaired it with a steel pin. After this Rodney seemed in almost constant pain, his temperature rose, and he didn't rebound as he had in the past. His resiliency gone, despite antibiotic treatment, he never recovered completely. He could no longer manage his walks, and our visits generated only a weak thump of his tail. The shine was gone from his brown eyes. His operated leg remained stiff and swollen.

The quarter was ending, and Rodney's days were numbered. One afternoon we put him to sleep. As the life drained from his body and his eyes lost their focus, my attitude toward animal research began to change.

In 1997, a Harvard student named Rachel Freelund helped modernize teaching methods for young doctors at that august institution. Rachel went to medical school because she wanted to study medicine and save lives. When she was accepted to Harvard, she never dreamed she would be asked to *take* a life.

Like all first-year medical students at Harvard then, Rachel was supposed to participate in the "dog lab" to witness firsthand how certain drugs affect the body. The students were to anesthetize a dog, slice open his chest, and watch the reaction of his beating heart as various drugs were injected into him.

At the end of the "exercise," the healthy dog would be killed.

Horrified, and believing there had to be a better way, Rachel went to her instructor, who told her she would not be forced to do the lab if she thought it unethical. That started Rachel thinking: If she could meet the course requirements without the lab, why couldn't all the students? "I didn't want anybody to do the dog lab," she says.

Thanks to Rachel's initiative, Harvard medical students can now choose to visit Boston hospitals to observe heart bypass surgeries on human patients instead of participating in the death of a dog. Dr. Michael D'Ambra, the cardiac anesthesiologist who directs Harvard's operating room program, says that this helps students understand the human physiology they need to know. "The *only* thing a student can do in a dog lab that we don't cover in the operating room is kill the animal," he says.

Happily, the majority of medical schools in North America have rapidly done away with live animal labs, and in England they are illegal.

OUT WITH THE OLD, IN WITH THE NEW

Before he died, Dr. Carl Sagan once lamented the use of chimpanzees in AIDS experiments. "What crime have they committed," he asked, "that they are imprisoned for life? It is time to let them out." They have not been let out, although HIV was isolated in human blood, not in that of other animals; how AIDS spreads was determined through human studies, and how the virus mutated was determined by looking at human cells.

Despite the deliberate infliction of these diseases on animals, it was *not* medical research that stamped out tuberculosis, diphtheria, pneumonia, and puerperal sepsis; the primary credit for those monumental accomplishments must go to public health, sanitation, and the general improvement in the standard of living brought about by industrialization.

Despite decades of feeding high-fat diets to every animal under the sun, it was not those studies, but the Framingham heart study, a continuing study of people who live in and around Framingham, Massachusetts, that identified the risk factors for heart disease and how to prevent it, including the fact that heart attacks virtually do not occur in people with a cholesterol level of 150 or less.

The most impressive studies of hardening of the arteries have occurred not in baboons or dogs, despite their use, but in human autopsy studies. Similarly, the connection between lung cancer and smoking was shown to be unequivocal because of human studies: Decades of research on every kind of animal under the sun rendered findings so inconclusive that they worked very much in the tobacco industry's interest.

A SLICE OF THE PIE

We should rejoice that there are alternatives to animal-based vaccines. The old ones used to be made of monkey tissue, duck embryos, and other bits and pieces that caused such allergic reactions as anaphylactic shock and death. Today's vaccines can be fashioned from human diploid cells and synthetics. Beef and pork insulin have been replaced by nonallergenic *human* insulin, or Humulin, virtually pushing them off the market by January 1998.

In 1985, the cosmetics industry insisted animal tests were indispensable. Today there are almost six hundred companies that won't touch animal tests. When the Gillette corporation made the switch, after an intensive PETA campaign that spanned ten years and included every tactic from crashing board meetings to, dressed as rabbits, climbing the flagpoles outside Gillette's corporate headquarters, one Gillette executive said, "It's so much nicer to sit down with you now instead of seeing you dangling from a rope outside our building! But we needed the push."

Yes, there is an alternative to every cruel deed. In fact, if we direct our resources and energy away from animal tests, we stand to gain tremendous benefits as human beings.

Look at the case of Baby Fae, the infant who made national news when Dr. Leonard Bailey of Loma Linda University put a baboon's heart into that child's tiny, ailing body. All the public remembers is a photograph of a baby in a crib and a doctor holding a giant phone up to her so she could hear her mother's voice. Sadly, her mother was alone, not very sophisticated, and much too trusting.

There was no happy ending for Baby Fae. She died in just three weeks, leaving in her wake freezers packed full of the bodies of more than three hundred animals who had provided the trial runs to her failed surgery. The university's news releases, the media stampede, the public appeal of a "heroic" operation to try to save a baby's life—all combined to squash the sensible questions that needed to be asked and which might have saved the baby's life.

Only when the dust cleared, the baby's body had rejected the organ, and the baby was no more, did we discover how bleak the prospect for her had been with a baboon heart. None of the animals Dr. Bailey had experimented on had lived for more than six months; there were two reparative procedures that the baby could have had instead, and which would have offered her a 45 percent chance of living (as opposed to the zero known chance of surviving a baboon heart transplant); and no effort had been made to search for a matching *human* heart. When the Animal Liberation Front broke into Dr. Bailey's Loma Linda University laboratory, they found baby baboons lying in the freezer there. Their hearts had been cut out and, as a joke, someone had pinned little homemade buttons reading, "We already gave at the office."

Money spent on animal experiments should go into far superior research methods: the new studies on cloned human skin for burn victims, instead of blowtorching pigs, for example. It should also go into prevention, which, now more than ever, is worth a pound of cure. How much better to fund dietary education programs that would spare people heart attacks, cancer, high blood pressure, and stroke instead of causing these miseries in animals.

It's not the animals who need their heads examined. Animal experimenters have spent $240 million on an artificial heart that did not buy us good health; killing three hundred baboons and cows did not save babies' lives; decades of alcohol and heroin experiments on macaques and rats have not kept people from the bottle or needle; and forcing decades of beagles to run on treadmills has not reduced air pollution. British studies also show that for every dollar spent treating heroin addiction, there is a three-dollar reduction in the amount spent fighting crime.

We could use the money from animal experiments to provide prenatal and infant care in low-income areas. As it stands, the United States spends more on animal experiments than the next top four countries combined, but has an infant mortality rate ranging between the nineteenth and twenty-second in the world. That means, in any given year, a baby born in eighteen other far poorer countries has a better chance of surviving than one born here. That is truly shameful.

Sometimes the alternative to doing something cruel and ugly to animals is not to do anything at all, as in the case of giving liquor to quail, pigs, and crayfish and recording their impairment. And someone needs to tap all the "Joe Six-Pack scientists" on the shoulder and say, "Excuse me. You haven't discovered anything from your years of animal experiments other than how to get paid. We're going to redirect your energies, retrain you, and make you into a productive citizen of society."

The only obstacle standing between the end of cruel animal experimentation and the beginning of sensible and humane health programs is that too many people still accept the unacceptable. Our job is to expose the myths and demand a change. In the next section, you will see how many ways there are to do just that.

What You Can Do

Help Get Animals Out of Laboratories

CHANGE YOUR LIFE

- **Clean House.** Rid your household of animal-tested and animal-ingredient products. Almost six hundred companies now test their products in sophisticated ways without the use of animals. Get a free list of which companies do test and which ones don't test on animals from PETA. You can also request PETA's "Cruelty-Free Shopping Guide." This wallet-sized reference guide is easy to carry with you when shopping. When friends visit, make sure you prominently display the products in your bathroom or on your kitchen counter, and offer them samples and literature.
- **Join a Society.** Join an animal rights professional society if you are a veterinarian, physician, scientist, or psychologist. (See Appendix C: Recommended Groups.)
- **Take Care of Yourself.** Reduce your risk of disease by becoming a vegan. Don't let vivisectors use you as an excuse for torturing animals in needless experiments.
- **Use Cruelty-Free and Natural Cleaners.** They don't pollute rivers or poison the Earth. They are available in health food stores and from the PETA "Catalog for Cruelty-Free Living."
- **Write to Companies.** Ask them to use a "Not tested on animals" logo. Ask local store managers to stock products with the logo.

- **Save Receipts.** Save your receipts from purchases of cruelty-free cosmetics and hair care products, then send them to Procter & Gamble, one of the few companies still testing on animals, with a note saying, "See what you're missing!" or "If you'd stop testing on animals, my business could be yours." (See Appendix F: People to Contact for address.)

- **Be a Donor.** If you are at least eighteen years old, obtain and fill out a human research donor card from PETA and the United Network for Organ Sharing (1-800-243-6667) to keep with your driver's license or ID card.

- **Boycott Procter & Gamble.** Ask your office's orders manager to talk to suppliers about replacing Procter & Gamble products at work. P&G products include Tide, Crest, Bounty, Comet, Ivory, and Charmin. Check your office kitchen too: P&G makes Folgers, Sunny Delight, Pringles, Jif, and Crisco. Call PETA for a P&G action pack, which includes a full listing of P&G products, poster, stickers, leaflets, and other information to share.

- **Use 1-800 and 1-888 Numbers.** 800 numbers are your chance to express your feelings about animal tests free of charge! When you have politely griped and discussed alternatives with the usually uninformed-on-the-issue operator, ask to be transferred to another or to a supervisor. To learn a company's toll-free number, call 1-800-555-1212.

- **Organize.** Mobilize your community to encourage a company to go cruelty-free. Circulate a petition among your friends, family, neighbors, and school. Collect products manufactured by the company and send them in, asking for a refund.

- **Know Your Neighbors.** If you have a corporate bad guy in your town (like John Pepper, CEO of Procter & Gamble), organize a house call. Everyone should know who lives in their neighborhood, so perform a public service and let residents know to keep their animals safe inside!

- **Don't Cooperate with Cruelty.** Chris Aldous, a mature student, returned his Bachelor of Education degree from Lancaster University in protest of animal experiments in the university's psychology department. His action received widespread media coverage. Aldous said, "Things aren't going to change overnight, but hopefully my protest will be added to those of many others protesting in equally valid ways."

■ **Don't Deliver.** Joel Carr runs J. R. Crickets restaurant in Decatur, Georgia. When he learned of experiments conducted at nearby Yerkes Regional Primate Research Center, he and restaurant employees refused to deliver carry-out food to the institution.

■ **Quit Your Job.** Susan Buettner and Regina Palmer quit their jobs because they were disgusted to learn that the companies they worked for and believed in still used animals instead of modern testing techniques.

■ **Don't Sell Out.** Radley Hirsch, owner of San Francisco Audio, refused to sell loudspeakers to the University of California San Francisco (UCSF) to blast squirrel monkeys with high-frequency-range sounds (louder than jet engines) to study the hearing loss suffered by people attending rock concerts. Radley contacted PETA, who then brought the matter to the attention of Paul McCartney and The Pretenders' Chrissie Hynde, who joined the protest.

■ **Form a Team.** Join PETA's National Action phone tree and team up with others.

■ **Fill Out Cards.** Pick up consumer request cards at your supermarket or drugstore and have friends join you in requesting brand-name, cruelty-free products. If possible, speak to the store manager.

■ **Paint a Bus.** That's what one British group did and visited forty towns with anti-vivisection materials. Thousands of people visited the vehicle, signed ballot papers, and gave an overwhelming thumbs-down to cosmetics tests on animals.

■ **Perform.** Use street performance art to enlighten people. Dressing up as vivisectionists and animals is bound to get people's attention. Make sure there is a bucket available for donations and fliers that explain what is wrong and what can be done.

DEMONSTRATE YOUR FEELINGS

■ **Scale a Crane.** Activists from In Defense of Animals scaled a crane at the building site of a new laboratory at the University of California in Berkeley. From the crane top they hung a banner reading, "No Toxic Animal Lab." Their action delayed construction for a week and generated articles in newspapers across the country.

■ **Block a Bus.** Trish Tereskowicz persuaded two friends to join her in blocking three busloads of physicians en route to Georgetown University to observe endoscopies on live dogs. (An endoscopy involves directing a tube down the patient's throat and into the stomach.) The protesters, standing in front of the buses with signs, delayed the doctors for more than an hour and monopolized discussions for a week.

■ **Haunt a House.** When Dr. John Draize, inventor of the hideous Draize "rabbit-blinding test," retired to "get on with (his) gardening," never having expressed any regret at the suffering this test has caused animals since its introduction in 1994, activists, dressed as the spirits of animals killed in product tests, "haunted" his Maryland home. Draize failed ever to even advocate anesthesia for the rabbits' eyes used to test bleach and drain cleaners. It is little known that Draize also invented a test in which harsh chemicals were repeatedly applied to the penises of live animals.

BLOW THE WHISTLE

■ **Investigate.** On a field trip to Aurora University in Illinois, a gifted 15-year-old student from Downers Grove, Illinois, found herself in a room "filled with animals." The hosting adults at first evaded the student's questions, but finally admitted that the animals were used in experiments. She wrote to PETA for help, and we discovered that Aurora University *was not registered* with the U.S. Dept. of Agriculture (USDA) as required by law!

■ **Get a Job.** Take a job in your local lab or, if you're already inside, blow the whistle. Whistle-blower cards are available from PETA. One lab employee had this to say about his experience, "I work in the lab. Every few months I take home another Norwegian rat or a rabbit. But my presence here and people knowing how I feel stops any spontaneous sadistic things that can happen. Before I came, there were many weekends when these animals didn't even have water."

■ **Join a Campaign.** Acting on whistle-blower tips, PETA discovered that Palmer College of Chiropractic in Iowa had surgically implanted stainless steel rods into the spines of rabbits who were then kept that way for up to one year, and that the National College of Chiropractic (NCC) in Lombard, Illinois, surgically exposed beagles' spines and glued their vertebrae together. More than four hundred chiropractors joined the campaign and protests were held. Palmer College contacted PETA to say that the "research has been discontinued and our animal facility is not currently operational."

■ **Get in Touch.** In another case, a call from a member of a film crew making a training film at Washington's Children's Hospital saved the life of a dog now called Guinness. For demonstration purposes, Guinness, originally from a pound in Virginia, had a tube inserted into his chest. After the film, he was to be killed. PETA contacted the hospital staff who agreed to save him. Guinness now lives in a loving home.

■ **Make a Call.** A call from nurses at the Huntington Research Institute in Pasadena, California, helped PETA stop experiments in which cats were being drowned, then given heart attacks and resuscitated. Four cats had already died within eighty-four hours of having their lungs flooded with water. PETA pressured the hospital to suspend the experiments pending protocol review by our experts. Experts on drowning, including Dr. Henry Heimlich, whose Heimlich maneuver is used to expel water from the lungs of drowning victims, showed that the experiments would yield nothing applicable to human drowning victims and that they were extremely painful for the cats. The experiments were stopped.

■ **Use Your Voice.** Rick Smith, a law student at a private university in Ada, Ohio, walked in on a "Drug Awareness Demonstration" conducted by the school's pharmacology department. He was too late to keep one rat from being injected with alcohol and another with phenobarbital, but, as the third animal was prepared to receive an injection of a controlled dangerous substance, Rick said, "I won't allow you to do that," and put a protective hand over the cage opening. Rick, who placed his law school career on the line and opened himself up to peer criticism, received much support from people who admire his courage—one of them being his law professor.

■ **Brighten Their Day.** Cheryl Mcauliffe collected donations of toys and treats from area pet stores to give on Valentine's Day to animals imprisoned in Emory University laboratories. When she and DeKalb Coalition activists, along with TV film crews, arrived at the university to deliver their gifts, the experimenters refused to accept them. That evening the networks broadcast the experimenters' denial, displaying their cruelty to the public.

■ **Educate Yourself.** See our Appendix A: Recommended Reading for books that reveal the staggering range of experiments on animals and why vivisection is scientific fraud.

■ **Educate Others.** Borrow or buy one or more of PETA's startling casework videotapes on animal experimentation, and show them to friends, at demos—wherever you can. This footage of actual experiments and/or labs, shot from inside by PETA undercover investigators, whistle-blowers, or the vivisectors themselves, is the most persuasive evidence of cruelty we know. Call or write PETA for a video brochure.

■ **Give a Talk.** Schedule yourself to give a ten-minute talk (with handouts) at civic association meetings, to church groups, classes, or humane societies. Set up a display in a library, school, or community center.

■ **Use Message! Checks.** Most people write about three hundred checks a year, and each check is seen by merchants, clerks, tellers, and others. Every time you order a supply of checks from Message! Products (1-800-243-2565), your chosen charity makes about a dollar. Among organizations offering Message! checks are the Humane Society of Utah, In Defense of Animals, the Michigan Anti-Cruelty Society, the Michigan Humane Society, PETA, and the Vegetarian Resource Group. (See Appendix E: Recommended Products for more information.)

■ **Make a Display.** Display literature and posters at your local veterinarian's office, humane society, health food store, dry cleaner, and at any other place that is sympathetic. Brenda Crawford puts out animal rights books, magazines, and literature at her beauty salon for customers to read. She also uses and promotes cruelty-free John Paul Mitchell products.

■ **Hang a Poster.** Use PETA's posters on your lunchroom and office bulletin boards and in grocery and other store windows with permission.

■ **Display Stickers.** Use PETA's "Liberate Laboratory Animals" bumper stickers, put PETA's "Stop Animal Tests" stickers on all your mail, and include a PETA animal experimentation brochure with your next batch of bill payments.

■ **Send a Message.** Record an animal rights message on your answering machine; for example: "Three animals die every second in U.S. labs—for more information, call 757-622-PETA." Update the facts on your message every two weeks.

■ **Plant a Tree.** Organize a tree-planting ceremony in your area to commemorate the animals killed by Procter & Gamble.

■ **Boycott Beef and Pork Futures.** If you are a broker or investment banker, follow the lead of vegetarian commodities broker Susan Sjo, who refuses to trade beef and pork futures and tells her clients why.

■ **Invest Responsibly.** If you own stock in companies that test on animals, either cash it in, or use it as leverage to change corporate practices. Join PETA's Corporate Responsibility Project, or draft your own resolution. For example, lend your name to an animal protection shareholder proposal: If you have owned $1,000 worth of stock in a company for one year or longer, you are eligible to sign on to existing shareholder proposals. Typical proposals ask companies to disclose detailed and closely guarded information to shareholders regarding their use of animals. Other proposals ask for an outright ban on animal tests.

■ **Support Ethical Companies.** Buy and give stock that supports ethical practices, choosing companies such as the Body Shop, John Paul Mitchell Systems, and Aveda.

SAVE THE PREMARIN HORSES AND FOALS

■ **Make a Switch.** Switch from Premarin or Prempak-C to synthetic and plant-based estrogen drugs to manage menopause symptoms naturally. After Doris Thompson learned that mares are confined for their urine and their foals even slaughtered, she stopped taking Premarin and alerted the local newspaper. It ran a full-page story, and both Doris and the newspaper were flooded with calls from interested women.

■ **Make a Call.** Call Wyeth-Ayerst, maker of Premarin, toll-free at 1-800-999-9384. Let the company know what you think of its treatment of horses and foals.

■ **Take a Picture.** Have your photo taken and send it in to PETA's giant album filled with hundreds of pictures of women who have stopped taking Premarin or never will take it. The album represents millions in lost sales to Wyeth-Ayerst from compassionate women.

■ **Write a Letter.** Write to PETA for a free Premarin pack, which includes information on effective, non-animal hormone-replacement therapies, to distribute to friends, newspapers, doctors' offices, and horse clubs.

- **Dress Down.** Volunteer to dress as Lady Godiva in a demonstration to spread the message that Premarin is cruel to mares and foals. Call PETA.
- **Make a Display.** Set up a Premarin exhibit, booth, or table at area horse shows and competitions.
- **Make a Delivery.** Dressed in a Santa Claus suit, deliver a sackful of coal or yams (a natural alternative to Premarin is made from wild Mexican yams) to Wyeth-Ayerst at Christmas.

STOP VIVISECTION IN SCHOOLS

- **Educate Students.** Schedule a cruelty-free makeover demonstration during a personal hygiene class. Encourage junior and senior high school students to set up information tables outside the school cafeteria. For example, Brandeis Students for the Ethical Treatment of Animals educated hundreds of their fellow students about product testing with a "Dorm Inform Campaign." Going door-to-door in all campus dorms, SETA handed out PETA's wallet-sized "Cruelty-Free Shopping Guide," explained the many non-animal alternatives, and collected products tested on animals for a campus display. (After the fair, all the cruel products were sent back to the companies.)
- **Lobby Administrators.** Urge school principals to replace animal programs with ones that use plants instead. (4-H has programs on soil and plant science, weather, trees, and a bicycle program that includes a bike rodeo.) Make the same request of your school district and state board of education.
- **Report Violations.** Contact PETA if you know of any experiments in your area schools.

MISCELLANEOUS

- **Report Reactions.** Have you or anyone you know ever had an adverse or injurious reaction to a household or cosmetics product? If so, call or write PETA today.

7

Fur, Feathers, Baubles, Bits, and Bones . . .

W hen you think of fur, you think of wildlife, but the stories of two dogs, Aurora and Cindy, paint the picture just as well.

Aurora was a stray dog who, one winter, stumbled into a steel-jaw leghold trap set for a coyote. In a haze of pain, she limped along, taking one slow agonizing step after step, the trap clamped like a vice to her swollen leg. After three long weeks, the infection in her leg was making her woozy. She had lost a lot of weight because she had been unable to find enough food to sustain herself.

Exhausted and worn out, Aurora saw an unused camper shell in someone's backyard and crawled under it to lie down to die, still dragging the deadly trap with her.

Then, miraculously, along came a local dog named Ranger, who discovered Aurora's hiding place and set out to rescue her. Ranger was very bright, and he figured out how to bring Aurora mouthfuls of snow for water. He also snuggled up to her, covering her body with his own to keep her warm as the fever swept through her. Sensing the urgency of Aurora's condition, Ranger stood beside the camper and howled incessantly, refusing to budge when called.

Not sure what to do, a woman in the neighborhood put a plastic cup filled with food next to Ranger. While she stood and watched, Ranger carefully picked up the cup and carried it under the camper shell to his friend. Although reluctant, Ranger let Aurora be carried out and taken to the veterinarian. Her mangled leg was amputated, but Aurora pulled through.

Beautiful Aurora—a priceless treasure whose photographs show her jumping with joy in the snow with her new family—is what fur trappers call a "trash animal." Trash animals by the thousands are crippled or killed "by mistake" in traps set for other animals like foxes. Aurora was lucky. She escaped with her life. Another "trash catch," Cindy, did not fare as well.

Cindy, a hound with floppy ears and a long, sweet face, had been let out to play in the woods and had not come home. Although the family searched the area and called her name, it was days before her cries were finally heard and Cindy was found. The poor dog had leghold traps clamped on both back paws and one on her front leg.

Animal control officer Joy Bannister said of Cindy, "When I came up to her it was clear that she had been trying to chew off her own paw to break free and was crying in pain."

Cindy was taken out of the traps, but it was too late. Her injuries were so severe the veterinarian had to euthanize her. I wish I could show you the last picture ever taken of her, looking so brave, her little white hound face gazing hopefully up at the photographer, three bloody stumps of sinews and bone where her feet should have been.

"Target" animals—foxes, lynxes, minks, raccoons, and coyotes among them—die badly in the traps or when, like Cindy, they try to chew their own paws off to escape. Some are driven to such desperate measures because they know they must return to their young in the den who depend on them for food. If a foot or paw comes off, gangrene and infection sets in, and that, or the loss of blood from the wound, is usually enough to kill them.

If they stay in the trap, after a day or two, perhaps longer, the trapper will arrive, causing their hearts to pound in their chests like steel drums. The trapper will beat them to death with a club or baseball bat, shoot them in the head (although shooting is not favored because it can damage the value of the pelt), or stand on their chests and jump up and down to squash their ribs and puncture their hearts.

It is a bloody business, and the amount of blood shed is far from minor—not counting the "trash catch," it can take more than forty raccoons or one hundred squirrels to make a coat.

In 1998, the European Community voted to ban the importation into Europe of any fur from countries still using this barbaric device. Then, at the eleventh hour, in an unforgivable move, President Clinton used his influence to persuade the Europeans to exclude the United States from the ban. PETA has since made sure that Germans, Italians, the Swiss, and others who buy furs on the international market fully realize that North American furs include an unseen toll of family dogs and cats, songbirds, and even a few bald eagles.

Not that U.S. fur farms are necessarily any more humane than trapping. The animals in them are not coddled, and they do not die in their sleep on fluffy pillows. PETA investigators who went to a chinchilla "ranch" in Michigan to learn first-hand how the animals were killed found it was by genital electrocution. The animals were given an electrically induced heart attack while fully conscious.

The electrocution was carried out cheaply, a metal "alligator clip" attached to the chinchilla's ear, another to her labia, then into the socket on the wall goes the lead end, a switch is flipped, and a jolt of electricity passes through the animal's skin and down the length of her body.

According to biologist and wildlife specialist Leslie Gerstenfeld-Press, the current causes unbearable muscle pain, and death can come slowly, yet the chinchilla is paralyzed, unable to scream or run away.

"Nope, still beating," one fur rancher told PETA's investigator, feeling for the heart, then shocked the chinchilla again. Another rancher admitted that he had come back into the room after electrocuting a chinchilla, only to find the animal had revived and had to be electrocuted again.

Before the First World War, it was considered impossible to farm chinchillas. No one could get these little animals, who live in altitudes of 11,000 feet or more above sea level, to survive a move to lower ground. Then, sadly, an American trapper embarked on a six-year project to slowly move the animals "down mountain," resting for a full year every few thousand feet, then taking them by sea to Los Angeles. Chinchilla ranches boomed.

Fur farmers, like experimenters, do not like anyone to see what goes on inside their operations. But they have not always succeeded in keeping animal-friendly people out. As a result, farmers have been caught using anal electrocution; leaving animals out in open pens in blizzard conditions (in nature, the animals would burrow or dig into the ground or keep moving to stay warm); throwing live chickens, feet first, into a grinder to create ground meat for the caged fur-bearers; and killing animals by injecting weed killer into their chests.

On one fur ranch in Illinois, where anal electrocution was carried out in full view of other foxes who were next in line, a PETA investigator made a deeply disturbing video showing raccoons and foxes whirling like dervishes in their filthy, tiny cages and tearing at the mesh until their feet were bloody. Sir Paul and Lady Linda McCartney's daughter, the designer Stella McCartney, said she felt sick when she watched it and was determined to help. She went into the studio, stuck a pair of headphones on and narrated the video, then popped it in the mail to every design house. "Please stop using fur," she wrote.

There are millions of reasons not to wear fur garments, counting the millions of beautiful ocelots, beavers, nutria, and other wonderful beings who get their necks broken and worse to make them. When people didn't care, the late Fund for Animals founder, Cleveland Amory, asked them to consider that wearing a fur coat makes a person look "fat and uninformed." Environmentalists remind dishonest furriers who tout fur as "a natural" that it can only be "natural" while it is on its original owner's back. Treat the coat with mortants (a horrid but descriptive word) and other cancer-causing chemicals, as is always done, and it will break down about as fast as a soda can, that is, perhaps never. It also smells when it gets wet.

As for the energy conscious, it may matter to know that it takes 7,845,000 more BTUs (British Thermal Units of energy) to make a ranched fur than to produce a "fashionable fake." Brigitte Bardot points out, "Fur is very old-fashioned. We wore it when we didn't know any better. Now, who wants to appear like a cavewoman?" Not the 94 percent of readers who responded to a 1998 *Cosmo* poll, saying animals should not be killed for their pelts.

WOMEN (AND OTHER HUMAN BEINGS) IN SHEEP'S AND SNAKE'S CLOTHING

Twiggy, fabulous and famous in the 1960s as the world's first "skinny minny" model, has also written to all the top couturiers in the world. She wants them to stop using exotic animal skins, like alligator, boa, Siberian Steppe pony, and crocodile. Twiggy's kindness contrasts sharply with U.S. *Vogue*'s icemaiden editor, Anna Wintour, who advocates wearing anything that moves and even sings the praises of French fries cooked in pony lard, although it is hard to see how eating them would give anyone that "model look."

Some skins even come from supposedly protected species. In the nineties, the U.S. Fish and Wildlife Service fined Chanel, Saks Fifth Avenue, Gucci, and Fendi for illegal use of endangered species for shoes, handbags, and watch straps.

An estimated 25–30 percent of imported crocodile shoe leather and other wildlife items are made from poached animals.

According to Beauty Without Cruelty (BWC), which keeps track of the trade in exotic skins from India, the most common way snakes are skinned is simply to nail them, alive, to a tree and run a knife down their bellies, then strip the skin away and toss the writhing body aside.

Alligators and crocodiles are hard to kill, so their deaths are agonizingly slow. A PETA investigator who visited the back rooms of a Florida "alligator farm" that runs a gift shop jam-packed with alligator purses, belts, and knickknacks found the 'gators kept in half-sunken tin-sided tubs in the dark. The room reeked of rancid meat, alligator waste, and stagnant water.

He videotaped teenage employees wading into the water, armed with metal baseball bats. The kids smashed the young animals repeatedly in the head. Wounded alligators tried to escape and had to be chased down and struck again.

The investigator wrote, "The animals continued to move and writhe minutes after they had been struck. The workers then took out switchblade knives and slit the base of the alligators' necks. Still some of the alligators moved. One had enough strength left in him to slowly edge himself over the door sill and onto the ground below."

British herpetologist Clifford Warwick studied slaughter methods used at another alligator farm that were even worse, although they are described as "humane" by industry standards. This scenario involved three workers: One stood on the alligator's mouth, another on her tail, and another attempted to slice through her spinal cord with a steel chisel and hammer. Warwick says it took five to eight blows for the chisel to break through the vertebra, and even then, the spinal cord was not always completely severed. Of course, severing the spinal cord doesn't kill. It paralyzes. Some alligators remained conscious for two hours.

Nearly all crocodile skin comes from animals taken from the wild. Crocodile hunters typically catch these massive animals with huge hooks and wires, reeling them in when they become weak from blood loss or drown. One eyewitness account describes how men with hammers and picks smash with all their might at a group of cornered crocs.

Like alligators, these animals are thought of as ugly and frightening, although they are excellent and skilled mothers and have actually enjoyed the company of people when raised with them from hatchlings. The Pedersons of Illinois lived for forty-two years with a six-footer named Alice. They called her "an ideal companion" who had a personality of her own, who sat and smiled beside them while they watched television, and who was particularly fond of bubble baths. Who isn't?

HANNAH SURVIVES

If there is no justification for picking on fierce animals with thick skin, how can there be any for hurting a gentle sheep? I remember Patty Mark, an Australian campaigner and sheep rescuer, telling me, without thinking how odd it sounded, about a sheep "sitting ever so politely" on the seat of her car as she drove about town. I could easily imagine it, having myself ridden in my car with a very polite goat (who stuck her head out of the window as dogs do and sat on her haunches when we came to a stop sign, as if it was the most natural thing in the world).

Wool producers love to mock pro-sheep people for "objecting to the sheep getting nicked during shearing," as if that is the problem. The truth is, millions of sheep used in the wool trade suffer cruelties that would make any decent person pale.

No matter where you buy it, most wool comes from Australia. There, about 148 million sheep are kept in flocks of many thousands each, making individual attention to a sick animal a silly proposition. A mind-boggling eight million mature sheep there die every year from untreated illnesses, heat exhaustion (most are imported European Merinos with very thick wool, and so they have a hard time coping with summer temperatures), lack of shelter in winter and shade from the blistering sun, and other forms of plain out-and-out negligence.

Up to 40 percent of lambs born each year die at birth or before they reach the ripe old age of eight weeks. If they do live, the lambs have their tails and the *skin* (not the wool, the flesh) cut off the backs of their rumps to keep flies from laying eggs in the folds of their wool. The wounds are stanched with tar, and the pain is so great that the little lambs, when they can rise to their feet, walk sideways like crabs for days.

The next assault occurs when the lambs are sheared. This happens before they would naturally shed their winter coats and results in about one million deaths a year from exposure. Shearing is not a gentle art when there are so many sheep to deal with. It is quick and dirty and the electric machines sometimes slice off a nipple or a tumor.

The older sheep are sold and shipped to the Middle East for slaughter. To get there, they must travel huge distances overland to the coast and be herded aboard enormous fourteen-tier-high ships. The journey takes about three weeks, the whole time spent standing in their own waste. It would be a terrifying ordeal even for a healthy sheep, and few are that robust after the life experiences they've already endured. The sick and newborns are left among the living or weeded out and thrown overboard. When the ship docks, the rest of the sheep are prodded down the ramp and sold at market. They have their throats slit while fully conscious.

Hannah is a sheep who didn't make it as far as Tehran. She collapsed in the field where she was born and where she gave birth.

A member of Animal Liberation in Australia spotted her lying about twenty feet from the fence, clearly visible from the road. She stopped the car, crawled through the fence, walked over, and knelt down beside her. The sheep was not even aware of the woman's presence.

The ewe had given birth to twin lambs. One was lying behind her, still covered with afterbirth, dead. The other was cuddled up to her flank, also dead. The woman lifted the sheep's head gently. Both of her eyes were sealed with thick crusts of pus. One ear was full of maggots, as was one of her hind legs. The woman had seen this before, too many times. This poor animal needed help. Immediately. Her life was hanging by a thread.

There was a house close by. The resident rented the house from the farmer who owned the sheep. The farmer lived some distance away, and the resident said it was pointless calling him as he would not come out for "just one sheep." She had told him three days before that a sheep was down. He had done nothing.

Thankfully, there was a gate nearby. The woman who had stopped for the sheep lifted the animal into the back of her car. She was light as a feather, nothing but skin and bones. The woman picked up the two dead baby lambs and placed them on the seat beside her. They would be buried on her plantation, along with many others, and would have a tree planted for them.

Before driving away, the woman looked back over the paddock. It was dotted with the remains of more than a dozen dead ewes and lambs. She wondered what kind of monster would allow this to happen. She wondered why the law didn't protect sheep from such appalling neglect.

After driving a few kilometers, she turned off onto a side road. She managed to clean out most of the maggots in the ewe's ear and scrape those from her leg. She lifted the sheep's head and poured a trickle of water into her mouth. The sheep swallowed and tried to raise her head but was too weak. The ligaments along her neck were so taut that, when the woman removed her hand, the sheep's head was jerked to one side or the other.

The plantation was a good hour's drive away. "Please, hold on. We will help you, sweetheart. No one will hurt you anymore. Please don't give up." The woman spoke these words out loud, over and over, all the way home, giving way to tears, as she had done so many times before.

When she arrived home, she placed the ewe on some old blankets on the lounge room floor and gave her some electrolyte solution. It was a start. She cleaned out her ear with fly repellent and warm paraffin oil, and bathed the sheep's eyes with boric acid and warm water. It was impossible to find sufficient muscle mass for an intramuscular injection of penicillin, so the woman injected it under her skin.

When the sheep became more comfortable, the family went on a "medicine hunt" around the grounds, returning with a bucketful of grasses and weeds. It must have seemed like a smorgasbord to her, for suddenly she showed life. At that moment, the family realized the ewe—they decided to call her Hannah—had a chance, but there was still a long way to go.

Over the following weeks, her caretakers gradually increased Hannah's food intake and introduced her to such goodies as apples, fresh lucerne from the garden, willow leaves, whole oats, grass, and the occasional biscuit. She began to improve and was soon able to hold her head up. A mattress was placed on the floor, and her rescuer slept alongside her every night, changing her position every few hours and replacing wet towels (because Hannah was too weak to get up to urinate).

After fourteen days, Hannah could be held up and helped with her feeble attempts to walk. It was almost three weeks before she could stand, supporting her own weight for a couple of minutes before collapsing into the waiting arms.

When Hannah was able to rise unassisted, she was moved into the laundry room and the door was left open. Hannah came and went as she pleased. She wore a coat to protect her bare skin from the sun. Her wool had fallen away in tufts, a result of extreme stress.

There was also an orphaned lamb called Babby on the farm. Babby had lost her mum. Hannah had lost her babies. They adopted each other and grazed together by the house. Whenever Babby came to the laundry for a bottle, Hannah would come, too, for an apple or a biscuit.

Eventually, Babby was weaned and Hannah's instinct to join the flock returned. They would wait at the gate each morning to be let out with the other rescued sheep, always returning in the evening for their treats and settling down by the house for the night.

The picture of Hannah lying totally helpless and slowly dying remains vivid in her rescuer's mind.

SISTERS UNDER THE SKIN

The thought of wearing bits of Hannah or any other animal brings back to me the song from Dr. Doolittle that goes,

> When you dress in suede or leather
> Or some fancy fur or feather
> Do you stop and wonder whether,
> Are you wearing someone's brother,
> Perhaps it's someone's mother.

With suede and leather, should you see a sale of cheap goods, couches perhaps or jackets, you may be looking at rain forest leather. This is the hide of cows grazed in South and Central America to make cheap burgers for the international meat market. To create grazing land, the forests must come down, and when the multinational corporations bring in their bulldozers to fell the trees, along with them go the homes of countless birds, insects, mammals, and reptiles.

Vegetarians are sometimes asked, "What about your shoes?" Well, we may not eat our shoes, but there is no denying that leather supports the meat industry, and skin accounts for a whopping 50 percent of the by-product value of cattle. To stop supporting the cruelties of factory farming and the slaughterhouse, one must stop subsidizing their existence through leather purchases.

If you have ever priced a "fancy" pair of leather boots and calculated how many pairs it would take to rebuild a cow, you know how much money that leather "side business" puts in a farmer's pocket. Even the veal calf can be squeezed for a few extra dollars. His skin is made into high-priced calfskin gloves, wallets, and car seat linings.

Tanneries use a variety of substances to treat the hide, including anti-decomposition chemicals, mineral salts (aluminum, iron, chromium, and zirconium), formaldehyde, coal-tar derivatives (phenol, cresol, and naphthalene), and various oils and dyes, some of them cyanide-based. The incidence of leukemia among residents near one Kentucky tannery has been found to be five times the U.S. average, and one study found that more than half of all testicular cancer victims work in tanneries.

Other animals made into clothing and accessories include lizards, ostriches (whose beautiful eyelashes are—believe it or not—made into false ones), and, in Australia, approximately five million kangaroos every year. The kangaroos are run down by hunters in jeeps, killed when poison is purposely put in their water supply, or impaled on sticks embedded in the ground. Their leather is made into everything from dog collars to sneakers.

FOES TO FINE FEATHERED FRIENDS

Our trappings spare no animals, from those who swim to those who fly. Just over one hundred years ago, a spot check of the hats worn in New York by women out for a stroll showed that 542 out of 700 of them were decorated with the mounted heads of birds! Kathryn Lasky wrote a book about this phenomenon, called *She's Wearing a Dead Bird on Her Head!*, pointing out that whatever tiny shreds of power women had at that time in politics or the community were easily swept away by their ludicrous get-up. Says Lasky, "Who is going to listen to a woman with a dead bird on her head?"

In 1998, the British designer Alexander McQueen sent his models down the runway in Paris wearing whole bird bodies on their shoulders and hats. Perhaps this is a sign of progress at least as far as hats go, for feathered headdresses have left the street and only appear onstage in fashion's latest shock theater.

As for the use of feathers for other purposes, the news for birds is still bleak. In 1992 North Korea's president, Kim Il

Sung, celebrated his eightieth birthday, and the occasion caused a panic in the land as his hangers-on tried to pick the perfect presents for a man who already had everything. The *Wall Street Journal* reported that the North Korean government sent citizens into the countryside to collect ginseng root, live frogs and ducks, as well as snapping turtles, whose blood is thought to be an aphrodisiac. The *pièce de résistance*, however, was a quilt. Seven hundred thousand tiny sparrows were killed for the feathers that filled it.

Today, larger birds bear the brunt of our desire for old-fashioned stuffing material for comforters, jackets, and pillows. The softest and warmest down is supposed to be that of the Eider duck, who uses her breast feathers to line her nest and cover her eggs. Other down and feathers may come from birds killed for meat, as with feather dusters and boas made from chicken feathers, but the greatest horror of the down industry is in the way in which feathers are plucked from live geese and ducks.

Most down comes from Hungary and other East European countries where birds are force-fed for foie gras production. These geese and ducks suffer live plucking as a second major insult, and their lives, albeit short, are extraordinarily miserable. Feathers are ripped from the birds' bodies, then allowed to grow back four or five times before they are slaughtered. After being restrained (their legs are "hog-tied" and they are strung upside down) and having their feathers pulled out of their flesh by hand, the birds make a pathetic sight. They huddle together or scrunch up against a fence or stall, seeking isolation in their pain, their bodies shaking uncontrollably from shock. They are so physically distressed that it takes days for them to recover.

Down is for the birds. Or it should be. For spoiled human beings living in this century, alternatives are easy to find—just as they are for silk, which is acquired by immersing silkworms in scalding water, steaming them, electrocuting them, or drying them in a hot oven or by microwaving the cocoons (the threads of about nine hundred of which go into one shirt).

THE FINISHING TOUCH

One also has to watch out for fashion accessories. Some bracelets and earrings are made from the "old man of the sea," the turtle. How many shoppers realize that the traditional method of separating turtles from their shells was to suspend the turtles, alive, over a furnace until the heat peeled the plates off their bodies? There is no card at the jewelry counter that advises you that, even today, no anesthetic or courtesy blow is delivered to turtles before their shells are cut away from their flesh, the oil squeezed from them for ointments and creams, and their bodies macheted into steaks. One has to wonder if helping mother turtles find a safe place to hatch their eggs is really a service, given that a fair number of the hatchlings will be killed in vile ways *if* they reach adulthood. In fact, they will more than likely end up in parts; a foot clunking around in the bottom of a soup tureen, or a bangle worn to the disco.

All this gives extra meaning to the phrase "Buyer beware!"

What You Can Do

Make Your Closet Cruelty-Free

....

- **Speak Up.** When you see cruelly produced clothing and accessories in stores, please let the clerks and managers know you object to the sale of animal parts.
- **Write Letters.** When businesses advertise fur, exotic leathers, and other animal-derived fabrics in your local papers, write letters to the editor explaining how the products are obtained and urging readers not to buy them.
- **Buy Non-leather Products.** Purchase only non-leather shoes, clothing, and accessories (including watchbands, soccer balls, upholstery, belts). Today there are many comfortable, well-made, and fashionable non-leather alternatives, such as satin dress shoes, synthetic running shoes, and canvas recreation shoes. (Get a current list of companies that make non-leather clothing and accessories from PETA.)
- **Choose Non-animal Fabrics.** Avoid eelskin, ivory, pearls, feathers, angora, and felt, which is usually made from animal hair. Choose instead canvas, ramie, cotton, vinyl, nylon, linen, rayon, straw (hats and bags), faux pearls, plastic, rubber, or even hemp.
- **Avoid Down.** Choose cotton, cotton corduroy, natural fibers, satin evening coats, parkas, and quilts stuffed with cruelty-free synthetics, like Fiberfill II, Polarguard, and Thinsulate.
- **Don't Buy Silk.** Silk is used in cloth (including taffeta), silk-screening, and as a coloring agent in some face powders,

soaps, and other cosmetics. It can cause severe allergic skin reactions, as well as systemic reactions if inhaled or ingested. Alternatives include rayon, milkweed seed-pod fibers, kapok (silky fibers from the seeds of some tropical trees), and synthetic silks.

- **Never Buy Ivory.** Ivory comes from elephants and from marine mammals such as whales, walruses, and narwhals. It is often carved into figurines, curios, or jewelry.
- **Avoid Tortoiseshell Products.** Don't buy tortoiseshell jewelry or combs; leather, eggs, or food products from turtles; or creams or cosmetics made with turtle flesh extract. Twenty thousand endangered sea turtles are slaughtered every year in Mexico, many as they are crawling back to sea, exhausted, after laying their eggs.
- **Boycott Furs from Endangered Animals.** Reject rugs, pelts, hunting trophies, and articles such as handbags, compacts, coats, wallets, and key cases made from skins or furs of jaguars, leopards, snow leopards, tigers, ocelots, margays, and small tiger cats. Earth Island Institute reports that more than 90 percent of Nepal's fur shop coats are made from protected species. Approximately four rare snow leopards are killed to make coats that sell for $3,200 apiece; and it takes at least thirty "common" leopard cats to make one full-length coat.
- **Protect Birds.** Don't wear feathers or buy mounted birds. Up to 70 percent of "exotic" birds imported into the United States die during capture, transit, and the required thirty-day quarantine.
- **Speak Up!** Tell merchants, catalog companies, vendors, and hotels why they should never order such goods again.
- **Walk On By.** Leave lovely shells and coral behind. Fish and crabs use empty shells as homes.
- **Buy a Souvenir.** Don't bring home living "souvenirs"— hermit crabs belong in the ocean, not in a tank. Steer clear of once-living "trinkets" too, like starfish and seahorses.
- **Protest.** Always write and call in protest when you see an ad for fur in a newspaper or magazine or hear one on the radio.

- **Write or Call.** Write and call the producers of television shows, especially soap operas, and tell them that, if a character must wear fur, it should be an obvious fake fur and be announced in the credits.
- **Complain.** Complain if mall managers include fur in fashion shows.
- **Stay Current.** Keep your eyes open for sweepstakes and beauty pageants that still offer fur prizes, and charities that feature fur in fund-raising. Write and call the promoters of such events and ask them to join the twentieth century.
- **Talk Loud.** Strike up a conversation within hearing distance of a fur-wearer about the gruesome facts of fur.
- **Give Out Cards.** Hand out fur cards (available from the Humane Society of the United States and PETA) to fur-wearers. Slip anti-fur cards into fur coat pockets at department stores.
- **Wear a Button.** Make an anti-fur button a permanent part of your winter wardrobe.
- **Give to Charity.** Convince others to donate their furs to charity. If one of your relatives still has a fur stashed in the back of her closet, use your powers of persuasion to convince her to get rid of it with a tax deductible contribution of it to PETA, or give it to a wildlife rehabilitator to use as a cuddly "surrogate mother" for orphaned wild babies to snuggle up to.
- **Make a Donation.** Donate to a local campaign action group or national organization to help fund anti-fur billboards and ads.
- **Talk to People.** Approach people who are wearing fur and politely tell them how animals suffer.
- **Demonstrate.** Contact your local animal rights organization or PETA for fur demonstrations near you, or organize your own.
- **Be an Activist.** Write to PETA for an anti-fur activist pack.
- **Use Your Plates.** Turn every rush hour and trip to the store into an educational opportunity by sporting a "NO FURS" or "BAN FUR" car license plate.

■ **Build a Cow.** Build a life-sized cow out of cast-off leather goods and display it in a library, school, art gallery, town square, or even in your front yard.

■ **Dress Up.** Jeanie Brown got the last laugh when she won a Halloween "Elvira Look-Alike" contest in which the prize was a fur coat. Brown and other activists were disgusted when the prize was announced, particularly given Cassandra "Elvira" Peterson's support of animal rights. (Cassandra's personalized license plate reads, "BAN FUR.") Brown donated the coat to PETA for use in educational presentations and demonstrations.

■ **Dress Down.** Outside the Seattle Fur Exchange, baseball manager Tony La Russa led activists in a "fur funeral." Dressed in black and bearing a fur-laden coffin, they captured media attention while, inside, the pelts of hundreds of thousands of animals went on sale. Sales of furs slumped, however, due to "cruelty consciousness" worldwide.

■ **Bare It All.** Activists all over the world have "gone naked" to protest fur. From Paris to Tokyo, Italy to the United States, animal rights activists have grabbed international headlines, telling the world loud and clear they'd rather go naked than wear fur!

CHAPTER

8

Dissection Busters

ALL CUT UP ABOUT ANIMALS

The excerpts you are about to read come from a report made by a PETA investigator who worked incognito at a leading dissection supply house, a place where all sorts of animals were prepared for shipment to schools throughout North and South America.

> The cats were roughly shunted from their transport cages into one large cage for gassing by being jabbed with a hooked metal bar. The cats are so tightly packed that their fur is pushed through the openings in the wire. They are put into a small carbon monoxide chamber and gassed for less than five minutes. This brief time is not always sufficient to kill them.
>
> The rabbits were thrown into a wheelbarrow and covered with water. One rabbit was trying to get away. The man put the rabbit underneath the other rabbits. Soon he started to laugh, "Look, he's trying to crawl out from underneath." He grabbed the rabbit, repeatedly picking him up and dunking him back into the water, holding him under for a few seconds before pulling him out for a few seconds.

The rats are strapped by rubber bands to small boards for processing. This morning, one of the rats was moving and trying to get loose. One of the men pulled the band out of the rat's mouth and laughed. "This one's still alive." He pulled her off the board as she struggled with the band around her belly. Everyone was laughing. They began to toss the live rat around. Someone said, "That thing's gonna bite somebody." Another man threw the rat into a bucket of water that contained dead rats. The rat was scrambling to get out of the bucket. A worker held her under until she stopped moving.

A live frog was hopping around the floor by the gas chamber. One of the men laughed and said, "Hell, let's just stick a needle in it."

The animals described in the investigator's notebook all lost their lives just so a child somewhere could say, "Yuck!" Of course, the students and their teachers never realize how the animals' deaths take place. All they see is a creepy-looking body in a plastic bag.

Adam Pitre, an eighth-grade student in Ontario, didn't need to witness such scenes to know there is something wrong with dissection. When he was told to slice up frogs, worms, rats, and fish in his biology class, Adam refused. His teacher told him he would have to drop out, but Adam chose to go to the school board instead. Not only did the board permit him to use other learning methods, but it decided to adopt a policy that requires teachers to inform students of their right to seek alternatives.

Animal experimenters fight vigorously against replacing dissection with more sophisticated teaching methods because they see it as a slippery slope. No doubt they think that if little Jimmy and Sally can be made to overcome their healthy aversion to cutting into animals while they are young, they may be less likely to object to experimentation later.

Luckily, many students are sharp enough to want to use one of the hundreds of teaching methods that are more interesting, more relevant, more technical, and more humane than slicing into a formaldehyde-filled cat corpse or bull's eye.

Proof of student interest in alternatives to dissection, even in the face of resistance, comes in the form of students like Oregonian Julie Grizzel-Meyers, who sued her school when her science teacher told her to pick up her scalpel, "or else"; Erin Sharp, a straight-A student in Flower Mound, Texas, whose honors biology course required dissection until Erin convinced her school to switch its requirements; and Ryan Ugstad, Ceilidh Yurenka, and Ian Hatton, three New Hampshire youngsters who got 73 percent of students to sign a petition that resulted in replacing dissection school-wide.

The young movie star Alicia Silverstone has volunteered her time to promote modern alternatives to dissection and believes in the project with all her heart. She has recorded a television public-service spot in which she asks that frogs be respected, not dissected. She worries where the cats come from (PETA's investigator found collars and tags on some cats at the supply house) and wonders what the demand for frogs for "classroom cut-ups" is doing to the wild populations so important to our ecosystem.

NATURE'S BOUNTY ON THE SLAB

There is far more spirit and respect in this poem by an anonymous French Canadian poet than in any dissection lesson:

> What a wonderful bird the frog are!
> When he walk, he fly almost;
> When he sing, he cry almost.
> He ain't got no tail hardly, either.
> He sit on what he ain't got almost.

When you think about it, it makes no sense that so many frogs are destroyed simply so that someone can observe where these little animals' hearts lie in their bodies. Looking at a diagram, a three-dimensional model, or a computer software program would serve the purpose just as well—although what the purpose is, I'm not sure. After all, no student is going to grow up to be a frog doctor. Is there more need to study a frog's skeletal structure than that of a wombat? It's all so arbitrary and archaic. For the most part, the frogs are used simply as "generic animals," to demonstrate where the various organs are.

Cats, rats, sharks, squid, rabbits, starfish, and a host of other animals come ready-to-buy and ship through the mail in sealed packs, but frogs are still the top-selling favorite. They are small, easy to catch and kill, and cheap, but the study of biology should not be based on those factors at all. More properly, it should be the respectful study of life rather than the debasement of it. How precious to teach students to watch animals in their natural world, from a distance, without interference, and to be in awe of their ways: to see how carefully and cleverly they fashion a home without power tools, feed themselves without going to a supermarket, and raise their children, without books or classrooms.

HARDENING YOUNG HEARTS

Does dissection in schools tend to desensitize young minds? To take an extreme case, Jeffrey Dahmer, the serial killer, told television reporters that he had enjoyed dissection and that it was through dissection that he had first experienced the "thrill" of taking life. Obviously, not everyone who dissects is going to go on to lobotomize and cannibalize human beings, but there is certainly enough violence in the world without encouraging students to contribute to it at all.

George Angell, founder of the Massachusetts Society for the Prevention of Cruelty to Animals, realized that back in 1884. When he was asked why he was so concerned about preventing cruelty to animals, Mr. Angell replied, "I am working at the roots. Nearly all the criminals of the future, the thieves, burglars, incendiaries, and murderers, are now in our public schools and we are educating them. We can mold them now if we will. We may teach a child to shoot a little songbird in springtime, with its nest full of young, or we may teach him to feed the bird and spare its nest. We may go into the schools now and make neglected boys merciful, or we may let them drift, until, as men, they become lawless and cruel."

Luckily, resources abound, and a new world of learning that does not involve bloodshed or gore is available to any teacher or child who wants access to it.

"The things that are on the market now are just phenomenal," raved one Massachusetts science teacher. "There's so much to chose from, it is mind-boggling."

The future belongs to the young, and, happily, there are great young pioneers out there, actively changing the world into a kinder place for all forms of life.

What You Can Do

Stop Dissection in Your School

··

- **Don't Dissect.** If you are a student, refuse to dissect. Put your feelings in writing to your teacher and principal, and try to involve your parents if you can. Parents, support your child's right to nonviolent education. The Dissection Hotline, 1-800-922-FROG (3764), exists *specifically* to help you protest animal dissection in the classroom; the Animal Legal Defense Fund (ALDF), 415-459-0885, sponsors the hotline and provides legal support for students who object to dissection. Don't be afraid to ask for help. (See Appendix C: Recommended Groups for ALDF's address.)
- **Participate in National "Cut Out Dissection" Month.** Green ribbons, symbolizing the millions of frogs who have been dissected, go up in high schools around the country throughout October. "Dissection busters" wear green armbands and put up "Cut Out Dissection" locker posters, banners, stickers, and cafeteria cards; petition and leaflet their classmates; ask their principals and school boards to institute alternatives; and ask their PTAs to pass resolutions banning dissection. Students also clean up local ponds to make them habitable for frogs.
- **Assert Your Rights.** Stand up for your right to a violence-free education. Contact PETA for a "Cut Out Dissection" pack and to borrow or buy "Classroom Cut-Ups," a video about dissection.

■ **Ask Questions.** The next time you receive a call or letter requesting a donation to your alma mater, ask if the school funds animal experiments. Do not contribute until you have a guarantee in writing that animals are not being used.

■ **Find Out.** If you live near a medical or veterinary school, find out whether or not animals are used in classroom training. If they are, approach the administration and faculty about modernizing their curriculum to exclude animal labs. Educate students about the alternatives to using animals in their training. Contact PETA for a list of alternatives. (For additional help, see the organizations listed in Appendix C: Recommended Groups.)

■ **Persuade Local Universities.** If your local universities use animals to teach physiology, ask if they will work with you to switch to a non-animal teaching technique. Nassau Community College (NCC) routinely abused turtles in the school's "turtle heart lab." In the experiments, turtles' brains are pithed, their shells are cut, and their hearts are exposed and subjected to varying intensities of electrical stimuli, even though these experiments and the results were documented long ago. With the help of Legal Action for Animals and the New York Turtle and Tortoise Society, PETA determined that New York State public health laws require experimental facilities to prove that their experiments benefit human or animal health before they can be approved. NCC did not have the required certification to experiment on any animals. The New York Department of Health (DOH) moved quickly to prohibit all animal experiments at NCC, and the turtle heart lab was stopped. DOH is considering legal action to prohibit any experiment involving animals when a non-animal method is available.

■ **Organize Meetings.** Use your state's "open meetings" law to open up animal care and use committee meetings at your local state-funded universities. These meetings are required by the federal Animal Welfare Act and are supposed to provide a forum for discussing research protocols. Groups in Washington, Florida, and Vermont have already opened up meetings in their states. For further information, have your attorney contact ALDF. Contact the Progressive Animal Welfare Society (PAWS) for information on how they opened up meetings at the University of Washington. At the University of Florida (UF), where the battle over animal rights has been particularly controversial, activists began using the state's liberal Sunshine Law in their fight. That law requires that all public records and meetings be open for scrutiny by the media and the public. By gaining publicity at meetings on the use of animals, activists have been able to influence the outcome of various research proposals. (See Appendix C: Recommended Groups for PAWS's address.)

■ **Pass Laws.** Pass laws that outlaw the harmful use of animals at science fairs and in classrooms in your community. Find out what's happening in your own community, then speak out and educate others.

■ **Inform Medical Students.** Make sure your local medical students know their rights to refuse. PETA and ALDF will help any student who objects to animal labs. Show them the video *Dog Lab,* and send $2 to PETA for the booklet "Alternatives to the Use of Animals in Medical Education."

■ **Be an Ethical Medical Student.** Refuse to use animals. The American Medical Student Association will back you up. Many medical schools in the United States have now decided that animal laboratories are ineffectual and misleading and have eliminated them.

■ **Go on TV.** Ask your local television stations to let you tape a free-speech message concerning a student's right to refuse to dissect animals.

Dealing with Animal "Pests"

I n 1910, a crowd gathered at an intersection in Boulder, Colorado. They had spotted a dog running about with white froth coming from his mouth.

"He's mad," someone yelled out, and the police were called.

The dog stood with wide-open eyes, either too mad or too frightened to move. The crowd called for the police officer to shoot. Then a tall woman pushed through and went to pick up the dog. A dozen men yelled at her to stand back and two or three grabbed her. The police officer was firm.

"Madam," he said, "the dog is mad. He must be shot. Look at the foam coming out of his mouth."

"Foam?" the woman said contemptuously. "That's not foam. That's the cream puff he's just been eating!"

That story, from *The First Pet History of the World,* illustrates nicely how people can overreact to animals. "Pest control" companies like nothing more than a rabies scare that they can use to drum up business. The embarrassing old stereotype of the woman screaming and jumping on a table to avoid a two-ounce mouse in her kitchen did not disappear with women's liberation. It has been joined by general hysteria over the minor inconveniences that are caused by wildlife. It is hard to miss stories of such "problems" as those of "animal messes" from goose droppings on golf courses (wouldn't *you* stop migrating and decide to raise your family at the sixteenth-hole pond if people were always shooting at you when you tried to go back north?) to the guano delivered by crows, grackles, and starlings doing nothing more threatening than resting in the corporate fruit and nut orchards planted on their plowed-over ancestral homes.

A "live and let live" ethic might require an occasional broom or scrub brush or the bother of sealing up entrance holes into buildings. But too many people choose the Wyatt Earp approach: "exterminators," sticky glue traps, bait boxes, poisons, and anticoagulants (causing the animals to bleed to death) such as zinc phosphide, aluminum phosphide, and gut-wrenching red squill.

Flying from one coast to the other, it is impossible not to be stunned at how little forest and woodland remains. In fact, in the Pacific Northwest, 1,200 acres of ancient forest, critical to owls, eagles, and as many as forty species of animals who share just one tree, are felled every week for timber. Starlings, foxes, tree frogs, squirrels, and raccoons don't need much: a little nourishing food, some clean water, shelter from the elements, and air to breathe. Humans, on the other hand, are quite needy. We want everything, from highways and office blocks to pop-top bottles, plastic trash bags, snack foods, air conditioning, lounge chairs, and beauty salons. And so it is that the construction of our malls, housing developments, golf courses, and other "necessities" has become the single greatest threat facing wildlife.

In Chevy Chase, Maryland, a pregnant raccoon was trying hard to find just the right spot to make a nest for her babies. She was about to deliver, but the tree in which she had been raised had been felled, together with all the others in that patch of woods. In their place, there were now big houses. She was very tired when she spotted the opening under the eaves of a corner house one night, and she crawled inside and found a huge wooden cavern—she thought it was heaven. Everything would be all right, she could give birth here.

Her two babies were beautiful when they were born, and mother was proud. The den she had found was perfect for them to learn to run and play in, and high enough up and sheltered so well that they were safe from dogs, storms, and, of course, people.

The people below heard the tiny raccoon feet scampering about in the attic and took out the Yellow Pages. A "pest control" man arrived with a box trap and assured the couple he would release any "coons" he caught into the woods. They trusted him because he had a state license and a nicely painted truck that said, "Your wildlife problems solved."

The next morning when the mother raccoon came back from foraging, her babies were gone. Wild-eyed with worry, she ran through the attic, making her click call to them, but there was nothing. Nothing except a metal box that smelled of fish. She entered cautiously and her second nightmare began. Almost as soon as the cage door slammed behind her, she heard heavy steps, then a piece of wood in the den floor swung back and a man with a flashlight appeared just feet away from her. Still frantic about her babies, and now in fear for her own life, the mother raccoon thrashed at her cage, tearing her paws on the wire as she tried to dig out of the metal box.

There is no happy ending for the mother raccoon and her babies. No matter what they tell people, for the truth would lose them a lot of business, wildlife trappers commonly bludgeon and drown animals or turn the animals over to be killed by animal control agencies. It is a rare "nuisance trapper" who has built a relationship with a wildlife rehabilitator. In many states, a fear of rabies has led to extreme laws that prevent certain species from being released back into the community.

Kevin Happell will never forget seeing a Critter Control employee beat baby raccoons to death in his apartment building. The man used a metal rod and "visibly broke multiple bones in their bodies. . . . The raccoons, being babies, offered no resistance whatsoever. . . ."

As we force the animals into ever-decreasing spaces and plant ornamental shrubs where their sheltering and berry trees once were, what can they do? Smelling food in our vegetable gardens or even our trash cans, and seeing holes in our attics and gables in which to shelter their young, who can blame these displaced families for trying to reclaim a little of the land, trees, and food sources stolen from them? They have no options.

THE TINIEST OF MAMMALS

Rats get bad press, and they really don't deserve it. They are still associated with the plague and biting babies in cribs, although the plague was caused by rats simply *spreading* filth created by a slightly larger animal, *homo sapiens*. In New York City alone, in any given year, rats bite only a tiny fraction of people compared to the number bitten by other human beings.

D. O'Hara recalls looking out of her window on a scorching hot day. She had put water out for a stray cat, but as she watched, she saw a mother rat lay her head on the cool rim of the water bowl and fall fast asleep. O'Hara says the rat had such a look of peace on her little face, she seemed to say, "I've found Heaven."

The mother rat had had her babies in a nest of eucalyptus leaves near the O'Haras' porch, and Ms. O'Hara could watch from her window as the mother groomed them and taught them to shell the unsalted peanuts Ms. O'Hara left out for them. The mother rat took impressive care of her brood: dipping their little paws in the cool water and smoothing the fur around their ears and faces. Each baby put his or her arms around the mother's neck and paid attention while being bathed. The mother also taught them to dart and run if danger approached.

Everyone told Ms. O'Hara the rats would become a problem, so she swept out the nest, only to see the mother rat work tirelessly to build another and gather more food to store for them.

Although simple and effective solutions to rodent invasions abound, other common "solutions" are grotesquely cruel. Typical back- and neck-snapping traps do not cause instant death. Death comes from slow suffocation, internal bleeding, or eventual starvation and dehydration. Another wretched death is caused by the sticky glue trap in which the animal's tiny face and limbs get stuck. Animals struggling in these traps pull out their hair and bite off their toes in desperation trying to escape. The traps can be left unattended for days, so that the exhausted, panicked mouse or other small creature dies of dehydration, or the whole trap, mouse and all, may be tossed into the garbage where, again, the animal dies slowly and miserably.

At PETA, wildlife experts send out information on such humane devices as "beaver bafflers" (wire mesh tunnels that allow beavers to remain in their family lodge without flooding houses built on low-lying land) and tips on how easy it is to rodent-proof a home. They hear from landowners who want to get rid of prairie dogs without calling in the pest control companies who vacuum the dogs out of their holes and gas them or sell them to pet shops, and they hear from gardeners who have found nests of snakes or wasps.

Simple, effective, and humane solutions exist for almost any "nuisance" problem. Author Gregg Levoy was raised in a household "equipped with pest spray or rolled-up magazines for every genus and species," where his father would "sometimes crouch in an upstairs window, Luger in hand, and try to pick off tomcats." In *A Better Mousetrap*, Levoy wrote that, after experiencing pain firsthand, he decided to live his life without administering it.

> I don't strip the leaves off twigs anymore as I walk along the sidewalk, and I work around the ant colony when I'm clearing the back yard. Sometimes I feel so isolated from the proverbial web of things, living in the city, that a part of me is even glad to have something resembling an ecosystem about. The spider webs in the window do wondrous things with the light that slips in at sunset.

Also, I cannot shake the feeling that somewhere there is a tally being kept of these things—my cruelties, my compassions—and that it will make a difference somewhere down the line when I go to cash in my chips. Besides, there is a slight question, in my mind, of relativity. Who is the pest here, me or the mouse?

As I stand in the checkout line at the hardware store, an elderly man taps me on the shoulder. "Good for you," he says, surveying my $17.50 "Have A Heart" boxtrap. "You'll probably come back as a mouse."

What You Can Do

Wildlife

··

When trees are cut down and fields stripped of natural vegetation, squirrels, skunks, raccoons, and opossums who would
never have ventured beyond the edge of the forest are suddenly homeless and hungry. Here is what to do if you must
keep them out of your home:

- **Provide Wildlife Sanctuary.** Leave a good part of your yard
  natural, with bushes and ground cover. The more diverse
  your bushes, seeds, and berries, the greater variety of birds
  and small mammals you will attract and nurture. Cherish
  rare, huge, great-granddaddy den trees as well as brushy
  hedgerows—which are vital as homes for wildlife along the
  edges of woodlands and mowed areas. Two books that can
  help you attract and nurture wildlife are *Attracting Backyard
  Wildlife: A Guide for Nature Lovers,* by Bill Merilees, and *Land-
  scaping for Wildlife,* by Carrol L. Henderson.
- **Keep Dead Wood.** Dead wood is ecological gold and crucial to kicking our pesticide habit. More than 150 species of
  birds and animals live in dead trees and/or feed on the insects there. Top off, rather than chop down, dead trees
  twelve inches or more in diameter. Fat dead logs, woody
  debris, and underbrush are also precious to wildlife. Before
  cutting any wood, check for nests and dens.
- **Provide Birdbaths.** Keep water in a birdbath and in a
  ground pan all year long. Use heating elements to keep

them unfrozen in cold weather. Be sure neither is too close to a bush or other cover where a cat might hide.

■ **Install a Martin House.** Mosquitoes will disappear from your woodsy yard as elegant swifts, swallows, and purple martins sweep through the air.

■ **Make a Ramp.** Lean planks or branches in uncovered window wells so creatures who may fall into them can climb out.

■ **Leave Them Alone.** If an animal has a nest of young in an unused part of your house and is doing no significant harm, leave the family alone for a few weeks until the youngsters are grown. They will probably then move out on their own. Squeals above your fireplace usually mean baby raccoons in your chimney. DON'T light a fire! They will move out in a few weeks. If you can't wait, put a radio tuned to loud talk or rock music in the fireplace and hang a mechanic's trouble light down the chimney. (Animals like their homes dark and quiet.) Leave these in place a few days, to give Mom time to find a new home and move her children. You might also hang a thick, knotted rope down the chimney, secured at the top, in case your tenant is not a raccoon and can't climb out unaided.

■ **Seal Up Your House.** Seal all entry places and cap your chimney (or a relative's)—*after* making sure no animals are inside. A mother animal will (justifiably) tear your roof apart if you seal her young inside.

■ **Avoid "Pest Control" Companies.** Don't capture and kill or relocate an animal by calling in "pest control agents" whose promises of humane destruction or relocation can be a fraud. You may be separating them from loved ones and food and water sources.

■ **Build a Bat House.** A bat consumes three thousand or more mosquitoes and other insects nightly. Bats won't get in your hair and the chances of them being rabid are minuscule—less than that of your dog. Bats are responsible for up to 95 percent of the seed dispersal essential to the regeneration of tropical rain forests. For more information about bats, write Bat Conservation International. (See Appendix C: Recommended Groups for address.)

- **Turn Off the Lights.** If bats should enter your home, turn off all lights and open the doors and windows. If they still don't leave, they can be caught in a large jar or net and released outside. Wear thick gloves, since a frightened bat may bite. Then seal the point of entry, which may be as narrow as three-eighths of an inch.
- **Get Certified.** Find out what you need to do to certify your yard in the National Wildlife Federation (NWF) Backyard Wildlife Habitat Program. (See Appendix E: Recommended Groups for address.)
- **Buy Metal.** Use metal garbage cans with tightly fitting lids, and latch dumpsters.
- **Feed Pets Inside.** Never leave dog and cat food outside.
- **Be Smart.** If you must set a mousetrap, use the plastic "Smart Mousetrap," available from PETA (1-800-483-4366). When using these, be sure to check them every few hours, as frightened rodents, with their high rate of metabolism, quickly become stressed, thirsty, and hungry.
- **Complain.** Complain to stores that sell glue traps, explaining how inhumane the traps are. Recommend that they sell humane box traps instead.
- **Set Them Free.** If you encounter an animal stuck to a glue trap, pour a small amount of any kind of cooking or baby oil onto the stuck areas and gently work them free.
- **Don't Feed Them!** Don't feed geese (or other wildlife), as tempting and kind as it seems. Feeding wildlife weakens their natural (and necessary!) fear of humans and can cause them to become "pests."
- **Help Out Birds.** Place hawk silhouettes, wind chimes, or streamers in the window, and close drapes or blinds whenever possible to prevent birds from flying into windows (they can suffer concussions or mandible or eye damage). Birds see their own reflections and mistake them for "intruders," are attracted to something inside, or see the sky reflected in the window.

- **Open a Window.** If a bird enters your house, wait until dark, then open a window and put a light outside it. Turn out all house lights, and the bird should fly out to the light.
- **Throw Bird Seed.** At weddings, throw bird seed instead of rice (which can swell in birds' stomachs, proving fatal to them).
- **Cut Down on Plastic.** Avoid buying unnecessary plastic products. Buy juice in cardboard cartons, use wax paper instead of plastic wrap, and so on. (Your garbage can be a trap—a potentially lethal picnic for animals in your neighborhood.)
- **Provide an Escape.** Put a vertical branch in every dumpster so animals can escape.
- **Recycle.** Recycle paper, aluminum, plastic, and glass. Call the Environmental Defense Fund hotline, 1-800-CALL-EDF, for the recycling center nearest you.
- **Dispose of Jars.** Rinse out jars and other containers in which animals' heads can get caught. Screw lids back onto empty jars before disposing of them, and put sharp tops and tabs inside empty tin cans so they cannot slice tongues and throats. Crush the open end of cans as flat as possible.
- **Tear Up Containers.** Tear open one side of tough plastic and cardboard containers so that squirrels and other small animals cannot get caught in them. Many have died, unable to back out of inverted-pyramid yogurt cups.
- **Cut Rings Apart.** Snip apart plastic six-pack rings, including the inner diamond. The rings are commonly found around the necks of wildlife ranging from turtles to waterfowl. In a celebrated case in Maryland, Mary Beth Sweetland rescued a duck who, for months, had been ensnared in a plastic six-pack holder and was wasting away. Winning the duck's confidence took time. Mary Beth eventually lured him out of the water with cracked corn, and, with a garden stake she had hidden up her sleeve, gently speared the plastic rings to the ground, and cut them off.
- **Patrol Beaches and Parks.** Join, create, or consider yourself the sole member of a beach brigade or park patrol. Pick up

string, fishing line, and all plastic litter (bags, bottles, six-pack rings, lids, and disposable diapers) near streams and woods. Birds, turtles, dolphins, and even whales and otters can get tangled in or swallow such trash, and the result is injury and, often, death. Beach clean-ups are usually held in the fall. For information on where and when one may be held near you, write Coastal States Organization or the Center for Environmental Education (See Appendix C: Recommended Groups for addresses.)

■ **Be Careful!** Never dispose of razors and other dangerous items by dropping them in loose with your other garbage. One activist places used razor blades inside empty, rinsed-out, *sealed* cartons.

■ **Clean Up Antifreeze.** Take care to clean up antifreeze spills carefully (and rinse out the rags you use to do so!); it is toxic, and animals are attracted to its sweet taste. Do not wash antifreeze down storm water grates. For more information about disposing of hazardous chemicals, call the Environmental Protection Agency (EPA) hotline: 1-800-424-9346 or 202-382-3000.

■ **Use Your Own Bags.** Carry your own string or canvas bags to the grocery store (cotton string bags are available from Seventh Generation) or, at least, choose paper bags over plastic. In the kitchen, use only biodegradable or photodegradable food storage bags, such as those available from Earth Card Paper Company and Co-op America. (See Appendix E: Recommended Products for addresses.)

■ **Make a Directory.** Keep names and telephone numbers of wildlife rehabilitators handy (they are available from your local humane society or park authority) in case of emergency.

■ **Be Aware.** If you find a young animal who appears orphaned, wait quietly at a distance for a while to be certain the parents are nowhere nearby. If they are not, take the little one to a professional wildlife rehabilitation center for care and eventual release into a protected wild area.

■ **Volunteer.** Volunteer to help local wildlife rehabilitators nurse injured wildlife back to good health and prepare them for release. Wildlife rehabilitation operations, like shelters, need soft bedding materials, newspapers, and other supplies.

■ **Don't Use Poisons.** Never use poison or sticky repellent caulk to control pigeons, starlings, or other birds. A stretched-out Slinky, nailed to a board and placed on a window ledge or roof, will keep birds from roosting. If your city or town poisons birds, urge them to substitute humane forms of control (write to PETA or the Humane Society of the United States for a fact sheet).

■ **Talk to Children.** Always politely explain to children whom you see chasing pigeons or seagulls that this frightens them. Most understand when told. Approach their parents, if necessary.

DETER INSECT INVASIONS HUMANELY

■ **Use Spices.** Ants in your pants—or your kitchen, bathroom, or basement? Pour a line of cream of tartar, red chili powder, paprika, or dried peppermint at the place where ants enter the house—they won't cross it. You can also try washing countertops, cabinets, and floors with equal parts vinegar and water or a citrus-based cleaner.

■ **Try Bay Leaves.** If cockroaches have moved in, never fear—simply place whole bay leaves in several locations around the infested rooms, including inside kitchen cabinets. Bay leaves smell like dirty socks to cockroaches!

■ **Get Gentrol.** PETA pick: Gentrol, an insect-growth regulator, eliminates the reproductive potential of a cockroach population without killing them. (See the listing for Professional Pest Management in Appendix E: Recommended Products for information on purchasing Gentrol.)

■ **Keep Clothes Fresh.** A humane and great-smelling alternative to mothballs: Place cedar chips around clothes or store sachets made out of dried lavender or equal parts dried rosemary and mint in drawers and closets.

■ **Use a Jar.** Are there spiders sharing your home? If you must move them on, carefully trap them in an inverted jar and release them outside.

■ **Fly Away!** Hang clusters of cloves in a room, or leave an orange skin out. Both smells repel flies.

■ **Plant Chives.** Avid gardeners are all too familiar with aphids, those little insects who like roses as much as we do. Planting chives near your rose bushes will help keep them from the area.

■ **Keep Them.** If you find predators such as ladybugs, snakes, and praying mantises in your yard or garden, the best policy is to let them stay.

■ **Close Holes.** Prevent insects from entering your home in the first place by filling holes and cracks in walls with white glue (it's less toxic than caulk).

■ **Keep Clean.** Don't give insects a food supply; keep living areas clean. Be careful to sweep up crumbs, wash dishes immediately, store food in tightly sealed containers, and empty garbage frequently. Often this will be enough to make bugs move on in search of more fertile ground.

■ **Use Citronella.** Deter flying insects gently with citronella candles or other incense. Forget bug zappers. They kill insects who are essential for pollination of night-flowering plants and for people's aesthetic senses—fireflies and moths are priceless flying jewels.

10

Choosing a Health Charity

I n 1997, a group of physicians discovered that the March of
Dimes had given donation money to experimenters to sew
newborn kittens' eyes shut, wait a year to see how depriv-
ing cats of normal vision alters brain development, and then
kill them. The doctors felt the experiment was not only cruel,
but a waste of time and money. They decided to take a closer
look at the March of Dimes research. What they found was
that the charity was also funneling donors' contributions into
experiments in which cocaine, nicotine, and alcohol were
given to animals, although it is already known that these substances are harmful to developing babies and can cause learning defects and other disabilities.

The Physicians Committee for Responsible Medicine
(PCRM) went directly to the March of Dimes with their concerns, pointing out that the charity ought to be using its research funds to track down the causes of birth defects in
human populations rather than spending money on rat and
mouse tests. But executives there brushed them aside and de-
fended the charity's policies. The March of Dimes went so far

as to refuse to allow donors who disapprove of animal experiments to earmark their donations for non-animal research.

The doctors grew angry and decided to duke it out with the charity, insisting on an end to cruel tests of dubious value at a time when birth defects are rising. They issued public statements calling on the March of Dimes to reform its practices and commissioned a poll that found that more than half of all Americans prefer to support health charities that avoid funding animal tests. They also pointed out that a similar children's health charity was getting the job done: Easter Seals opposes animal tests and uses its funds on clinical and other studies that have direct bearing on child health and on diverse services.

NOT SO CHARITABLE ACTS

What PCRM had uncovered was the tip of an ugly iceberg. Many charities perform animal experiments without their donors' knowledge. A person approached at an intersection by high school students soliciting for the American Heart Association (AHA) probably has no idea that AHA has severed the nerves in dogs' hearts, cut holes in the throats of newborn lambs and obstructed their breathing, and forced chickens to breathe concentrated cigarette smoke—even though scientists have known for years that smoking causes cancer and heart disease.

Even the Red Cross, publicly associated with disaster relief, runs its own animal laboratory in Rockville, Maryland— not that you'll find any mention of it in Red Cross public service announcements or news.

It is not only animal-friendly donors who become upset when they realize what horrors they may be funding when they write a check to a health charity; people who have the very diseases and ailments that these charities profess to be trying to cure are upset, too.

Kit Paraventi has had diabetes for more than twenty years. She has experienced debilitating complications, including two years of blindness, dialysis, and a kidney transplant, and she is outspoken in her rejection of animal tests. She regularly writes to the American Diabetes Foundation to ask that it adopt a "No animal tests" policy and feels that, as pressure mounts, the charity will be compelled to switch.

Larry Carter has cerebral palsy and was once a poster child for the campaign to find a cure. He is incensed that animals suffer in his name. "Nobody knows pain and suffering better than those of us who have endured it ourselves," he says, "and we owe it to ourselves and the animals to see that they do not suffer in our supposed behalf. If we are willing to kill innocent animals in our quest to be healthy, then what we lose in the bargain—our sense of compassion and empathy—is much, much greater."

Mr. Carter also wants people to know that the only important breakthroughs in cerebral palsy research have come from human studies, including the finding that pregnant women who receive magnesium supplements have a dramatically reduced risk of having a baby born with mental retardation or cerebral palsy.

Women with breast cancer or whose mothers had breast cancer are uniting to fight charities' animal experiments. Groups of people living with AIDS and families of Alzheimer's disease patients want to stress that animal "models" of human disease only hinder, confuse, and mislead. They want charities to modernize and they are putting their money where their mouths are, giving only to charities like the Elton John AIDS Foundation, Cancer Care, and others on PETA's list of charities that do not test on animals.

Helping hasten that day are youngsters like Harry Grimm, a nine-year-old who refused to collect donations for the American Heart Association through a school program and sent the money he collected to a cruelty-free health charity instead.

What You Can Do

Health Charities

....

- **Ask Questions.** Question health charities carefully. When you get a fund-raising appeal or are approached for a donation from a foundation, ask whether your donation would be used to fund animal experiments. (For example, the March of Dimes funds animal experiments, while Easter Seals does not.)
- **Get a List.** You can get a free list of charities that do and that don't fund animal tests from PETA. Don't give any money, and tell the charity why you won't, if they fund or conduct animal research. Send copies of any responses to PETA and to the Physicians Committee for Responsible Medicine (PCRM). (See Appendix C: Recommended Groups for addresses.)

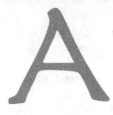

APPENDIX

A

Recommended Reading

VEGANISM

150 Vegan Favorites by Jay Solomon. Fresh, easy, and incredibly delicious recipes you can enjoy every day.

The Compassionate Cook by Ingrid Newkirk. Favorite recipes from PETA staff and members. Available from PETA.

Cooking with PETA. In addition to more than two hundred recipes, this book includes helpful information on how and why to become vegetarian. Available from PETA.

Diet for a New America by John Robbins. Exposes the cruelty, wastefulness, and ecological impact of mechanized meat production. Available from PETA.

Eat More, Weigh Less: Dr. Dean Ornish's Life Choice Program for Losing Weight Safely by Dr. Dean Ornish. Available from PETA.

Eat Right, Live Longer: Using the Natural Power of Foods to Age-Proof Your Body by Neal Barnard, M.D. Available from PCRM and PETA.

Enemies: A Love Story by I. B. Singer. This farcical comedy is also a subtle exploration of the parallels between Holocaust refugees and nonhuman victims of persecution.

Instead of Chicken, Instead of Turkey by Karen Davis. Features vegan alternatives to poultry and eggs. Available from PETA and United Poultry Concerns.

The Jungle by Upton Sinclair. The classic novel that exposed corrupt conditions in the Chicago meat-packing industry.

The McDougall Plan for Super Health by John McDougall, M.D., and Many McDougall. An easy-to-understand explanation of how to "look better, feel better, and stay better."

Slaughterhouse by Gail Eisnitz. The shocking story of greed, neglect, and inhumane treatment inside the U.S. meat industry.

Vegan: The New Ethics of Eating by Eric Marcus. A thorough and engaging overview of the health, ecological, and ethical issues surrounding the human diet.

The Vegan Gourmet by Susann Geiskopf-Hadler and Mindy Toomay. Full flavor and variety with over 100 delicious recipes.

Vegan Nutrition Pure and Simple by Michael Klaper. Clarifies the consequences of eating animal products and expounds the benefits of a vegan diet.

Vegetarian Times (periodical), 4 High Ridge Road, Stamford, CT 06905; 1-800-829-3340.

ANIMALS IN ENTERTAINMENT

Beyond the Bars: The Zoo Dilemma by Virginia McKenna, Will Travers, and Jonathan Wray.

The Rose-Tinted Menagerie by William Johnson.

HUNTING AND FISHING

The American Hunting Myth by Ron Baker. Hard facts about the state and federal agencies that perpetuate the "sport" of hunting.

What's Wrong with Hunting compiled by the Fund for Animals. This book takes an entertaining and educational look at the practice of sport hunting in America; includes accounts from sport and Hollywood celebrities. Available from the Fund for Animals.

COMPANION ANIMALS

250 Things You Can Do to Make Your Cat Adore You by Ingrid Newkirk.

The Compassion of Animals by Kristin von Kreisler. True stories of animal courage and kindness.

Dr. Pitcairn's Complete Guide to Natural Health for Dogs and Cats by Richard Pitcairn, D.V.M.

The Dog Who Loved Too Much: Tales, Treatments, and the Psychology of Dogs by Nicholas Dodman.

Mother Knows Best: The Natural Way to Train Your Dog by Carol Lea
   Benjamin.
Preparing for the Loss of Your Pet by Myrna Milani, D.V.M. Saying
   good-bye with love, dignity, and peace of mind.
Stolen for Profit by Judith Reitman. Exposes the pet theft trade.
Understanding Your Dog by Michael Fox, D.V.M.
Vacationing with Your Pet by Eileen Barish.

VIVISECTION

Monkey Business by Kathy Snow Guillermo. This inspiring true story
   of Alex Pacheco and Ingrid Newkirk describes how they met,
   founded PETA, and took on the case that put animal rights in
   the spotlight: the Silver Spring monkeys. Available from PETA.
Free the Animals! by Ingrid Newkirk. This is a riveting account of
   daring animal rescues from laboratories, fur farms, and food
   factories. Behind-the-scenes looks at real-life rescues reveal the
   true nature of animal liberators. Available from PETA.
Animal Liberation by Peter Singer. Includes in-depth examinations of
   animal experimentation, vegetarianism, and animal rights phi-
   losophy. Available from PETA.
*Future Medical Research Without the Use of Animals: Facing the Chal-
   lenge* edited by Nina Natelson and Murry Cohen, M.D. Available from Concern for Helping Animals in Israel, P.O. Box 3341,
   Alexandria, VA; 703-658-9650.
The Human Cost of Animal Experiments by Dr. Robert Sharpe. Awareness Publishing Ltd., P.O. Box 553, Sheffield S11 9YU, England.
Lethal Laws: Animal Testing, Human Health and Environmental Policy
   by Alix Fano. This book offers an analysis of the scientific problems that have plagued animal tests for decades. St. Martins
   Press, Inc., 175 Fifth Avenue, New York, NY 10010; 1-800-446-
   8923. Also available from PCRM.
Slaughter of the Innocent by Hans Ruesch. Debunks the claims advanced by the vivisectionist establishment and its allies. Available from The Nature of Wellness (818-790-6384).
Naked Empress by Hans Ruesch. This book exposes the corruption of
   the chemical and pharmaceutical industries. It further exposes
   vivisection as a racket that has become an endless source of
   profits and new diseases. Available from The Nature of Wellness
   (818-790-6384)
Secret Suffering: Inside a British Laboratory by Sarah Kite.

The Plague Dogs by Richard Adams. Two dogs escape from a laboratory where they have been horribly tortured. Fiction.

Doctor Rat by William Kotzwinkle. A witty but gruesome tale of animals in one laboratory. Fiction.

Caught in the Act: The Feldberg Investigation by MacDonald. Evidence collected in a cruelty investigation that nullifies any pro-vivisection arguments.

Animal Experimentation: A Harvest of Shame by Moneim Fadali, M.D. Examines the ethical and practical difficulties involved with animal experimentation.

Natural Progesterone: The Multiple Roles of a Remarkable Hormone by Lee. A technical guide to the uses of plant-derived, natural progesterone, which is more effective and safer than estrogen-replacement therapy. Available from PCRM.

Health with Humanity by Steve McIvor. Available from the British Union for the Abolition of Vivisection (BUAV), 16A Crane Grove, London N7 8LB, England.

CLOTHING

Trapping Animals for Fur by Tyler and Jordan. Available from Care for the Wild International, 1 Ashfolds Horsham Road, Rusper, West Sussex RH12 4QX, England; tel.: 44-1293-871-596; fax: 44-1293-871-022.

Pulling the Wool by Christine Townend.

DISSECTION

Vivisection and Dissection in the Classroom: A Guide to Conscientious Objection by Gary L. Francione and Anna E. Charlton. Available from the American Anti-Vivisection Society.

Animals in Education: The Facts, Issues and Implications by Lisa Ann Hepner.

WILDLIFE

Wild Neighbors: The Humane Approach to Living with Wildlife by Hodge, Grandy, Hadidian, and Hadidian. For people who want solutions to human–animal conflicts without causing harm.

Living with Wildlife: How to Enjoy, Cope With, and Protect North America's Wild Creatures Around Your Home and Theirs by Landau, Stump. Resolves—in the most humane ways possible—

common conflicts that arise from human–wildlife contact (such as with deer, baby birds, and bear).

The Human Nature of Birds: A Scientific Discovery with Startling Implications by Theodore Barber. A provocative new study of birds, humans, and the deepest prejudices of Western science—developed from six years of independent research by a behavioral scientist.

Common Sense Pest Control by Olkowski, Daar, Olkowski. Covers nontoxic pest management.

RELIGION

Animals and Their Moral Standing by Stephen R. L. Clark. The major writings of Stephen R. L. Clark, an international authority on animal rights, that trace the development of the animal rights movement.

Animal Theology by Andrew Linzey. Based on a series of lectures given to the theology faculty at Oxford University; argues that contemporary agribusiness is theologically indefensible.

Animals on the Agenda: Questions About Animals for Theology and Ethics by Yamamoto and Andrew Linzey.

Diet for Transcendence: Vegetarianism and the World Religions by Rosen, Cerquetti, and Greene. Explores historical and scriptural evidence of vegetarianism in many different religions.

Food for the Gods: Vegetarianism and the World's Religions by Berry. A thorough look at a variety of faiths with essays and interviews; vegetarian recipes from each tradition.

Nonviolence to Animals, Earth and Self in Asian Traditions by Chapple. Traces the vision of ahimsa in Jainism, Hinduism, and Buddhism and explores its connections to contemporary concerns for animal rights, vegetarianism, and environmentalism.

Animal Sacrifices: Religious Perspectives on the Use of Animals in Science by Thomas Regan.

Judaism and Animal Rights: Classical and Contemporary Responses by Roberta Kalechofsky.

The Slaughter of Terrified Beasts by Hyland. Documents scriptural support of the humane treatment of animals. Available from PETA.

The Souls of Animals by Gary Kowalski. Written by a Unitarian Universalist minister, it explores the world of animal consciousness and spirituality. Available from PETA.

GENERAL

Generation React by Danny Seo. A guide for young people interested in changing the world. Available from PETA.

When Elephants Weep: The Emotional Lives of Animals by Masson and McCarthy. Thoroughly and effectively explores the full range of emotions that exist throughout the animal kingdom.

CHILDREN'S BOOKS

Animal Place: Where Magical Things Happen by Kim Sturla. Two children learn how to care for animals at the Animal Place Refuge.

The Gnats of Knotty Pine by Bill Peet. The gnats of Knotty Pine Forest avert the horrors of the hunting season.

Kids Can Save the Animals! 101 Easy Things to Do by Ingrid Newkirk. Available from PETA.

The Lady and the Spider by Faith McNulty. A story about respect for even the smallest of creatures.

So You Love the Animals by Zoe Weil. Hundreds of games and activities to help young people become involved in protecting animals.

Victor the Vegetarian by Vignola. Victor saves two lambs.

Victor's Picnic by Vignola. An easy lesson in vegan nutrition for young readers.

William's Story by Deborah Duel. After the girl who befriended him moves away, a stray cat goes on the prowl.

Recommended Videos
and Audiotapes

VEGANISM

Live Longer, Live Better. Audiotape by Neal Barnard, M.D., author of the top-selling book *Foods That Fight Pain*. This powerful yet simple approach to trimming your waistline, lowering your cholesterol, and controlling your blood pressure includes interviews with Dean Ornish, M.D., on reversing heart disease; Dennis Burkitt, M.D., the medical pioneer who made fiber a household word; and other leading experts. 90 minutes. $9.95. Available from PCRM 1-800-695-2241 or PETA.

Dairy Farm Investigation. 1996. This footage documents what life is like for cows on a typical dairy farm: Cows with huge, swollen udders are chained in a filthy barn, forced to stand and lie in their own excrement; dead calves are abandoned in their stalls; and a downed cow meets a horrible end, eyes wide with fear, as she is dragged onto a truck. 7 minutes. Available on loan from PETA.

Diet for a New America. This powerful video is the perfect vehicle to introduce people to the effects of the meat-based diet. It is a PBS documentary that offers an impressive range of knowledgeable, authoritative experts who disclose the environmental, health, and animal welfare issues that confront people today. 60- and 30-minute versions are available for $19.95 from EarthSave

International. Also available for purchase or loan from PETA. (See Appendix C: Recommended Groups for addresses.)

The Diner. Responsible for getting many people to "go vegetarian" on the spot. A brief but frightening look at what happens to animals in the meat industry. 11 minutes. Available on loan from PETA.

Raw Footage, Raw Pain. Secret footage obtained at a Colorado poultry factory farm shows why no one should buy eggs. Birds live and die in filthy spaces the size of half a sheet of typing paper. 12 minutes. Available on loan from PETA.

Truth or Dairy? 1994. This British youth-oriented video shows all the foods and clothing available to vegans and the health benefits of going vegan. 23 minutes. Available from The Vegan Society. (See Appendix C for address.)

Victims of Indulgence. PETA's undercover investigation of a foie gras manufacturer led to the first-ever raid on a U.S. factory farm. Sir John Gielgud narrates this look at the force-feeding of geese and ducks for foie gras. 10 minutes. Available for purchase or on loan from PETA.

A Diet for All Reasons. The foods we eat can either support our health or contribute to disease. This nutritional overview will forever change the way you think about diet. 60 minutes. $21.95. Available from PCRM, 1-800-695-2241.

The Down Side of Livestock Marketing. 1991. This video shows the commonplace abuse and negligence that downed animals endure at stockyards and auctions. It contains graphic scenes of mistreatment and animals in horrible conditions. 18 minutes. Available from Farm Sanctuary. (See Appendix C for address.)

Hens Might Fly. 1992. This video condemns the battery cage system by demonstrating how it deprives the animals of their natural interests and instincts. 8.5 minutes. Available from Compassion in World Farming. (See Appendix C for address.)

Hidden Suffering. 1992. This film shows the inhumane conditions that domestic fowl endure as a result of modern intensive farming practices. 27 minutes. Available from Farm Animal Welfare Network. (See Appendix C for address.)

Humane Slaughter? This video graphically depicts the slaughter of chickens and turkeys. It concludes with a plea to the viewer to demand that poultry be included in the Humane Slaughter Act and to become a vegetarian. Available from The Farm Sanctuary. (See Appendix C for address.)

The Pig Picture. 1995. This documentary focuses on the life of a factory-farmed pig. It also gives us a bird's-eye view of how pigs live in the wild in contrast to how the pig's life has been altered to fit human desires. 17 minutes. Available from The Humane Farming Association. (See Appendix C for address.)

Vegetarian Cooking for the Athlete. This half-hour cooking show hosted by Peter Burwash is easy to follow and beautifully done. It can be purchased separately for $19.95, or as a one-hour tape with *Healthy, Wealthy, and Wise* for $24.50. Available from Focus on Animals. (See Appendix C for address.)

ANIMALS IN ENTERTAINMENT

Cheap Tricks. Narrated by actor Alec Baldwin, this videotape provides a glimpse of how grim life is for animals in traveling animals acts. 12 minutes. $15.00. Available from PETA.

Elephants. This piece shows horrifying examples of the psychological and physiological illnesses that confinement can produce in elephants. 5 minutes. Available on loan from PETA.

Circus Life. Behind-the-scenes footage shows animal trainers beating elephants, and scars and open wounds attest to the misery of captive life. 5 minutes. Available on loan from PETA.

Zoochotic Report: A ZooCheck Investigation. This is an investigative video on mentally damaged animals in captivity. It focuses on the repetitive movements common to captive animals as a sign of madness and boredom. Available from The Born Free Foundation. (See Appendix C for address.)

The Ugliest Show on Earth. An undercover investigation of British circuses. 26 minutes. Available from Animal Defenders. (See Appendix C for address.)

Dying to Please. This video focuses on "swim with dolphins" programs and on the larger issue of the appropriate use of marine mammals in captivity. Narrated by Michael Landon. Available from Focus on Animals. (See Appendix C for address.)

When the Circus Came to Town . . . The world-famous non-animal Cirque du Soleil holds workshops for street kids in Montreal and Rio de Janeiro, teaching circus skills, culminating a performance. Suitable for grade 7 through adult. 51 minutes. Available from Bullfrog Films, Inc. (See Appendix E for address.)

The Other Barred. How do the animals feel? This sensitive documentary raises questions by showing the animals in their cages, without dialogue or commentary. 10 minutes. Suitable for all ages. Available from Bullfrog Films, Inc. (See Appendix E for address.)

A Day at the Dog Races. This documentary explores the greyhound racing business in the United States. 21 minutes. Suitable for ages 13 and up. $49.95. Available from Bullfrog Films, Inc. (See Appendix E for address.)

HUNTING AND FISHING

Stripmining the Seas. This powerful documentary, made by Earthtrust, shows dramatic footage of the destruction caused by undersea driftnets laid out over vast areas of the Pacific—30,000 to 40,000 miles in high season—in largely unregulated international waters. Suitable for all ages, mid-elementary school and up. 20 minutes. $40.00. Available from Focus on Animals. (See Appendix C for address.)

Whales and the Threat of Nets. How do great whales feed? What is so bad about modern fishing nets? Why do nets threaten whales' lives? Can entangled whales be rescued? How can you help save whales? An instructive interview showing home video footage of a rescue of a giant humpback whale caught in a fishing net. Suitable for all audiences, junior high school and up. 30 minutes. $35.00. Available from Focus on Animals. (See Appendix C for address.)

Angling: The Neglected Bloodsport. Dispels the myth that fish don't feel pain; shows the detrimental effects of angling on other wildlife. Available from Campaign for the Abolition of Angling. (See Appendix C for address.)

What's Wrong with Hunting. Questions posed in a schoolroom environment are answered by biologists and doctors; explains why pro-hunting arguments are faulty. $15. Available from the Fund for Animals. (See Appendix C for address.)

Money and Myths. Illustrates how state wildlife departments promote killing wildlife. Available from The Humane Society of the United States. (See Appendix C for address.)

COMPANION ANIMALS

Friends for Life. This video teaches young children the importance of responsible pet care. 15 minutes. $175. Available from Pyramid Film & Video. (See Appendix E for address.)

Kiss the Animals Goodbye. This documentary shows what happens inside a large animal shelter. It reveals the alarming problem of pet overpopulation. 20 minutes. $50. Available from Focus on Animals. (See Appendix C for address.)

VIVISECTION

Beyond Animal Experiments by Neal Barnard, M.D. New scientific methods are making animal experimentation obsolete. The president of the Physicians Committee for Responsible Medicine takes an in-depth look at the issue from its philosophical roots to state-of-the-art methods that are replacing animals in modern research. 90 minutes. $9.95. Available from PCRM (1-800-695-2241) or PETA.

Breaking Barriers. Dr. Jane Goodall called her visit to the SEMA laboratory in Rockville, Maryland—where this videotape was filmed—"the worst experience of my life." The conditions shown on this tape launched the international "Save the Chimps" Campaign. 16 minutes. Available for purchase or on loan from PETA.

Britches. This is an uplifting story of an infant primate rescued from a university animal laboratory and delivered into the arms of a caring adoptive mother primate. 13 minutes. Available for purchase or on loan from PETA.

Don't Kill the Animals. Singers Lene Lovich and Nina Hagen "liberate" animals from a research laboratory in this video. 7 minutes. Available for purchase or on loan from PETA.

No Gravy for the Cat. This exposé of one experimenter's ride on the federal grant gravy train tells the remarkable story of how five slated for death in a Texas Tech animal laboratory escaped on the underground railroad. 12 minutes. Available for purchase or on loan from PETA.

Inside Biosearch. A whistle-blower and an undercover investigator spent months documenting violations at a product testing laboratory. 14 minutes. Available for purchase or on loan from PETA.

Unnecessary Fuss. The abuse documented on this videotape led former Department of Health and Human Services Secretary Margaret Heckler to terminate the federally funded brain-damage experiments on primates at the University of Pennsylvania. 26 minutes. Available for purchase or on loan from PETA.

Silver Spring Monkeys. PETA cofounder Alex Pacheco documented
animal abuse during a four-month undercover investigation at
the Institute for Behavioral Research in Silver Spring, Maryland.
PETA's investigation led to the first-ever criminal conviction of
a U.S. experimenter on animal cruelty charges. 17 minutes.
Available for purchase or on loan from PETA.

Boys Town Kittens. A look at Boys Town's "deafness" experiments,
in which kittens were denied painkillers after major surgery.
3 minutes. Available on loan from PETA.

Premarin. Mary Tyler Moore narrates as we enter a barn where
pregnant mares are forced to stand on concrete for months with
bags strapped to their groins to collect their estrogen-rich urine.
2 minutes. Available on loan from PETA.

Advances in Medical Education. Narrated by world-renowned medical
innovator Henry Heimlich, M.D., this video shows Harvard
Medical School's alternative to the traditional "dog lab" method
of teaching cardiac medicine. 18 minutes. Available on loan
from PETA or PCRM.

In Defense of Animals: A Portrait of Peter Singer. This award-winning
video summarizes the ethical and practical arguments behind
the animal rights movement. 28 minutes. Cost for institutional
use and public performance is $250 to purchase and $30 to rent.
Available from Bullfrog Films, Inc. (See Appendix E for address.)

Paradise Lost. This documentary about the international primate
trade tracks monkeys as they are taken from their natural
homes and used for laboratory experiments. 19 minutes. Available from BUAV, 16A Crane Grove, Islington, London N7 8LB,
England.

Lethal Medicine. This video focuses on the misleading and false results obtained through animal research that is cruel to animals
and can be lethal to humans. 57 minutes. $25.00 plus $2.24 shipping and handling. Available from The Nature of Wellness. (See
Appendix C for address.)

Among the Wild Chimpanzees. This beautiful National Geographic
documentary chronicles the first twenty years of the pioneering
research of Jane Goodall. At the age of twenty-six, she went to
Tanzania to begin a lifetime study that spanned three generations of chimpanzees. This film record of the chimps' daily
life—and the skilled and sensitive way in which Jane Goodall
relates to them—brings us a new understanding of our nearest

relatives in the animal kingdom. 59 minutes. $40.00. Available from Focus on Animals. (See Appendix C for address.)

Henry: One Man's Way. 1997. This video tells the story of activist Henry Spira. It was written and produced by Peter Singer. 53 minutes. . $250 to purchase, and $30 to rent. Available from Bullfrog Films, Inc. (See Appendix E for address.)

Tools for Research. This award-winning film addresses the unsound reasoning behind animal research. 37 minutes. Available from Bullfrog Films, Inc. (See Appendix E for address.)

CLOTHING

Stella McCartney's Fur Farming Exposé. Shot inside an Illinois fur farm in 1997. $18.00. Available from PETA.

Skins. This classic film about the fur industry juxtaposes animals struggling in their traps and a fur fashion show. $35.00. Available from Focus on Animals.

DISSECTION

Classroom Cut-Ups. Actor Sara Gilbert narrates this comprehensive look at classroom dissection and its alternatives. 15 minutes. Available for purchase or on loan from PETA.

Dog Lab. This footage of dog surgery training class, filmed by instructors at East Carolina University, documents abuses that led to the closing of the basic science "dog lab" at that university. 16 minutes. Available for purchase or on loan from PETA.

RELIGION

We Are All Noah. Dedicated to the religious community, the film asks that we widen our circle of compassion. $50.00 Available from Focus on Animals. (See Appendix C for address.)

VIDEOS FOR CHILDREN

101 Dalmatians
Babe
Bambi
Black Beauty
Charlotte's Web

E.T.
Free Willy (I and II)
The Little Mermaid
The Secret of NIMH
Shiloh

Recommended Groups

Abolition of Angling
44-171-278-3068
B. M. Fish
London WCIN 3XX
England

Action for Animals
510-652-5603
P.O. Box 20184
Oakland, CA 94620

Alley Animals
P.O. Box 27487
Towson, MD 21285

American Anti-Vivisection Society (AAVS)
1-800-729-2287
801 Old York Road, Suite 204
Jenkintown, PA 19046

American Fund for Alternatives to Animal Research (AFAAR)
212-989-8073
175 West 12th Street, Suite 16G
New York, NY 10011-8275
Bestows grants to develop non-animal tests; publishes findings of research.

American Vegan Society
609-694-2887
P.O. Box H
Malaga, NJ 08328
Has an extensive list of available vegetarian books and sponsors annual conferences; oldest American vegetarian organization.

American Veterinary Medical Association (AVMA)
1931 North Meacham Road, Suite 100
Schaumburg, IL 60173

Animal Aid
44-1732-364546
Fax: 44-1732-366533
The Old Chapel
Bradford Street
Tonbridge
Kent TN9 1AW
England

Animal Defenders
44-181-846-9777
261 Goldhawk Road
London W129PE
England

Animal Legal Defense Fund
707-769-7771
Fax: 707-769-0785
127 4th Street
Petaluma, CA 94952
Web site: www.aldf.org
E-mail: info@aldf.org
Provides information to people in need of legal assistance in cases involving companion animals.

Animal Rights Foundation of Florida (ARFF)
954-917-ARFF (2733)
P.O. Box 841154
Pembroke Pines, FL 33084

Animal Rights Hawaii
808-941-9476
P.O. Box 10845
Honolulu, HI 96816-0845

Animal Welfare Institute
202-337-2332
Fax: 202-338-9978
P.O. Box 3650 or P.O. Box 3719
Georgetown Station
Washington, DC 20007
Web site:
    www.animalwelfare.com
E-mail: awi@animalwelfare.com
Works to ban steel-jaw traps and for the humane treatment of animals in laboratories, the use of non-animal testing methods, and farm industry reforms.

Animals Agenda
410-675-4560
P.O. Box 25881
Baltimore, MD 21224

The Ark Trust, Inc.
818-501-2275
Fax: 818-501-2226
5551 Balboa Blvd.
Encino, CA 91316
Web site:
    www.arktrust.org/genesis
E-mail: genesis@arktrust.org
Holds an annual Genesis Awards gala in Hollywood to laud the powerful voices of the media that have been used to promote an understanding of animal issues.

Association of Vegetarian Dietitians & Nutrition Educators
Tel./Fax: 607-546-4091
3835 Route 414
Burdett, NY 14818
Offers a home-study course on vegetarian and vegan diets.

Association of Veterinarians for Animal Rights (AVAR)
530-759-8106
P.O. Box 208
Davis, CA 95617-0208

Bat Conservation International
P.O. Box 162603
Austin, TX 78716

Beauty Without Cruelty
212-989-8073
175 West 12th Street, 16G
New York, NY 10011
An international organization promoting alternatives to all animal use.

The Black Vegetarian Society
770-621-5056
P.O. Box 14803
Atlanta, GA 30324-1803
National headquarters of The Black Vegetarian Society chapters.

Born Free Foundation
44-1403-240170
Fax: 44-1403-327838
3 Grove House
Foundry Lane
Horsham
West Sussex RH13 5PL
England

British Union for the Abolition of Vivisection
44-171-700-4888
Fax: 44-171-700-0252
16A Crane Grove
London N7 8NN
England

Calgary Animal Rights Coalition
403-262-3458
41 6A Street NE
Calgary, Alberta T2E 4A2
Canada

Center for Environmental Education
1725 DeSales Street NW
Washington, DC 20036

Coastal State Organization
c/o Margie Fleming
444 North Capitol Street NW, Suite 322
Washington, DC 20001

Compassion in World Farming (CIWF)
44-1730-264208
Fax: 44-1730-260791
Charles House
5A Charles St.
Petersfield
Hampshire GU32 3EH
England

Dissection Hotline
1-800-922-FROG (3764)

Doris Day Animal League
202-546-1761
227 Massachusetts Avenue NE,
   Suite 100
Washington, DC 20002
E-mail: ddal@aol.com
Provides information on federal legislation pertaining to animals.

Earth Island Institute
415-788-3666
Fax: 415-788-7324
300 Broadway, Suite 28
San Francisco, CA 94133
E-mail:
   earthisland@earthisland.org
Supports projects for the preservation/restoration of the global environment

EarthSave
502-589-7676
600 Distillery Commons,
   Suite 200
Louisville, KY 40206
Web site: www.earthsave.org
E-mail: earthsave@aol.com
An organization committed to environmental and health education; provides materials and support for people who are becoming vegetarian.

Elephant Alliance
619-454-4959
6265 Cardeno Drive
La Jolla, CA 92037

European Coalition to End Animal Experiments
44-171-700-4888
Fax: 44-171-700-0252
16A Crane Grove
London N7 8NN
E-mail: sariv@compuserve.com

Farm Sanctuary
530-865-4617
Fax: 530-865-4622
3100 Aikens Road
Watkins Glen, NY 14891
Works to prevent the abuses in animal farming through legislation, investigative campaigns, education, and direct rescue programs. Operates shelters for rescued farm animals.

Focus on Animals
540-665-2827
534 Red Bud Road
Winchester, VA 22603

Friends of Animals
203-656-1522
777 Post Road, Suite 205
Darien, CT 06820

The Fund for Animals
301-585-2591
8121 Georgia Avenue, Suite 301
Silver Spring, MD 20910
E-mail: fund4animals@fund.org

Greyhound Pets of America
1-800-366-1472
5 Carleton Avenue
Randolph, MA 02368

The Greyhound Project
617-333-6655
261 Robin Street
Milton, MA 02186

Greyhound Voice
2 Lincoln Street
P.O. Box 8981
Essex, VT 05451

Hinduism Today
107 Kaholalele Road
Kapaa, HI 96746-9304
Web site: www.hindu.org/ht

Humane Farming Association
415-771-2253
1550 California Street, Suite 6
San Francisco, CA 94109
Leads a national campaign to stop factory farms from misusing chemicals, abusing farm animals, and misleading the public.

Humane Society of the United States (HSUS)
202-452-1100
2100 L Street NW
Washington, DC 20037
Web site: www.hsus.org
Programs focus on humane education, wildlife protection, farm animals, companion animals, and animal research issues.

In Defense of Animals
415-388-9641
Fax: 415-388-0388
131 Camino Alto, Suite E
Mill Valley, CA 94941
E-mail: ida@idausa.org
Works through protest, education, and legal action to advocate lifestyles and technologies that do not exploit animals.

Interfaith Council for the Protection of Animals and Nature
2841 Colony Road
Ann Arbor, MI 48104

International Wildlife Rehabilitation Council
4437 Central Place, Suite B4
Suisun, CA 94585
Offers information and programs involving the rehabilitation of animals.

Jain Meditation International Center
212-362-6483
Box 244
Ansonia Station
New York, NY 10023-0244
Web site:
www.jainmeditation.org

Jewish Vegetarians of North America
410-754-5550
6938 Reliance Road
Federalsburg, MD 21632
E-mail:
imossman@skipjack.bluecrab.org

Jews for Animal Rights
255 Humphrey Street
Marblehead, MA 01945
Web site:
host.envirolink.ofg/jar/jews_ar

The Johns Hopkins Center for Alternatives to Animal Testing
111 Market Place, Suite 840
Baltimore, MD 21202-6709
Encourages research that will provide knowledge leading to *in vitro* or other non-animal test procedures.

Last Chance for Animals (LCA)
310-271-6096 or
888-88-ANIMAL
Fax: 310-271-1890
8033 Sunset Boulevard, Suite 35
Los Angeles, CA 90046
E-mail: info@lcanimal.org
Anti-vivisection, direct action animal rights organization that maintains an information hotline regarding demonstrations and fund-raisers.

League Against Cruel Sports
44-171-403-6155
Fax: 44-171-403-4532
Sparling House
83-87 Union St.
London SE1 1SG
England

Medical Research Modernization Committee
216-283-6702
20145 Van Aken Blvd., #24
Shaker Heights, OH 44122
Web site: www.mrmcmed.org
E-mail: mrmcmed@aol.com

Muslim Vegan/Vegetarian Society
59 Brey Towers
136 Adelaide Road
London NW3 3JU
England

National Anti-Vivisection Society (NAVS)
1-800-888-6287
53 West Jackson Blvd.,
Suite 1552
Chicago, IL 60604-3795

**National Coalition of
 Greyhound Advocates**
978-369-3574
51 Staffordshire Lane
Concord, MA 01742

National Dog Registry (NDR)
914-679-BELL
Box 116
Woodstock, NY 12498-0116

**National Greyhound Adoption
 Network**
1-800-446-8637
P.O. Box 620863
Woodside, CA 94062
Web site: www.greyhounds.org

National Wildlife Federation
1400 16th Street NW, Ste. 501
Washington, DC 20036-2266

The Nature of Wellness
818-790-6384
Fax: 818-790-9660
P.O. Box 10400
Glendale, CA 91209-3400
Web site:
 www.animalresearch.org
Offers educational resources
concerning the use of animals in
research, the problems involved,
and the alternatives.

**North American Vegetarian
 Society**
518-568-7970
P.O. Box 72
Dolgeville, NY 13329
Web site:
 www.cyberveg.org/navs
E-mail: navs@telenet.net
Dedicated to the promotion of
vegetarianism through educa-
tion, publications, and annual
conferences.

**People for the Ethical
 Treatment of Animals
 (PETA)**
757-622-PETA (7382)
Fax: 757-622-0457
501 Front Street
Norfolk, VA 23510
Web site: www.peta-online.org
E-mail: peta@norfolk.infi.net
Exposes animal abuse and pro-
motes respect for animals. Its
credo is "Animals are not ours
to eat, wear, experiment on, or
use for entertainment."

**Performing Animal Welfare
 Society (PAWS)**
209-745-2606
P.O. Box 849
Galt, CA 95632

239

Physicians Committee for Responsible Medicine (PCRM)
202-686-2210
Fax: 202-686-2216
P.O. Box 6322
Washington, DC 20015
Web site: www.pcrm.org
E-mail: pcrm@pcrm.org
Comprised of physicians and lay members; promotes nutrition, preventive medicine, and ethical research practices; publishers of *Good Medicine* magazine.

PLAN (Legislation)
717-233-5770
P.O. Box 12085
Harrisburg, PA 17108-2085

Plenty International
P.O. Box 394
Summertown, TN 38483
Web site: www.plenty.org
E-mail: plenty1@usit.net
Has worked with villages around the world since 1979 to enhance nutrition and local food self-sufficiency through vegetarianism.

Progressive Animal Welfare Society (PAWS)
425-787-2500
206-787-2500
Fax: 425-742-5711
15305 44th Avenue W
P.O. Box 1037
Lynnwood, WA 98046
Web site: www.paws.org
An all-animal protection organization that enhances public awareness of animal abuse and exploitation using intervention and legal action.

Psychologists for the Ethical Treatment of Animals (PsyETA)
301-963-4751
P.O. Box 1297
Washington Grove, MD 20800-1297

Royal Society for the Protection of Animals (RSPCA)
44-1403-264181
Fax: 44-1403-241042
The Manor House
The Causeway
Horsham
West Sussex RH12 1HG
England

Rutgers Animal Rights Law Center
15 Washington Street
Newark, NJ 07102
Web site: www.animal-law.org
E-mail: director@animal-law.org

Sea Shepherd Society
310-301-SEAL (7325)
Fax: 310-574-3161
P.O. Box 628
Venice, CA 90294
Web site: www.seashepherd.org

Society for Animal Protective
Legislation
202-337-2334
P.O. Box 3719
Georgetown Station
Washington, DC 20007
A resource organization that
tracks developments in anti-fur
legislation and factory farming.

SPAY USA
1-800-248-SPAY (7729)
Helps people find low-cost veterinarians in their local area.

Tattoo-A-Pet
1-800-828-8667
6571 SW 20th Court
Fort Lauderdale, FL 33317

United Animal Nations
916-429-2457
Fax: 916-429-2456
5892 South Land Park Drive
P.O. Box 188890
Sacramento, CA 95818
Web site: www.uan.org
E-mail: info@uan.org
Rescues animals from disasters
in the United States.

United Poultry Concerns (UPC)
757-678-7875
12325 Seaside Rd.
Machipongo, VA 23405

Vegan Action
510-548-7377
P.O. Box 4353
Berkeley, CA 94704-0353
Web site: www.vegan.org
Distributes information on
vegan diets and lifestyles and
campaigns for the increased
availability of vegan foods.

Vegan Outreach
211 Indian Dr.
Pittsburgh, PA 15238
Web site:
    www.veganoutreach.org
Distributes the informative
booklet, *Why Vegan?*

Vegan Society
44-1424-427393
Fax: 44-1424-717064
Donald Watson House
7 Battle Road
St. Leonards-on-Sea
East Sussex TN37 7AA
England

Vegetarian Resource Group
410-366-8343
Fax: 410-366-8804
P.O. Box 1463
Baltimore, MD 21203
Web site: www.vrg.org
Dedicated to health, ecology, ethics, and world hunger education; produces and sells books and pamphlets.

World Society for the Protection of Animals
617-522-7000
P.O. Box 190
Boston, MA 02130
Helps animals victimized by war and natural disasters worldwide and captive animals abroad.

ZooCheck Canada
416-285-1744
3266 Yonge Street, Suite 1729
Toronto, Ontario M4N 3P6
Canada

APPENDIX

Recommended Web Sites

Animal Aid Online
www.animalaid.org.uk
Frequently updated web site for the UK's Animal Aid.

The Animals Rights Resource Site
arrs.envirolink.org
One of the largest clearinghouses for animal rights information online.

Coalition to Abolish the Fur Trade
www.banfur.com

Compassion Over Killing
www.cok-online.org
Has links to web sites focusing on campaigns against Macy's and
Neiman Marcus fur sales. A good example of a local activist group
with a focused online presence.

The Essene Cooperative's Homepage
www.inetex.com/joanne/

FactoryFarming.com: The Truth Hurts
www.factoryfarming.com

Farm Sanctuary
www.farmsanctuary.org

The Fund for Animals
www.fund.org

HandiLinks to Vegetarian Organizations
www.ahandyguide.com/cat1/v/v26
A large site that can be difficult to navigate. If you reach a general page, just search for "vegetarian."

In Defense of Animals
www.idausa.org

Jesus Was a Vegetarian
www.jesus-online.com

Last Chance for Animals
www.lcanimal.org
Does lots of web activism and has four secondary sites.

The Mining Co. Guide to Animal Rights
animalrights.miningco.com
Has links to the latest alerts from animal rights organizations from across the country.

PETA
www.peta-online.org

Veg Source Interactive
www.vegsource.org
Lots of links on the scientific basis of vegetarianism and tons of discussion boards.

Veg Web
www.vegweb.com
Hundreds of recipes for the new vegetarian.

The Veggies Animal Contact Directory
www.interalpha.net/customer/ecoslobs/veggies/home

E

Recommended Products

VIDEOS

Bullfrog Films, Inc.
900-543-FROG
P.O. Box 149
Oley, PA 19547
Web site: www.bullfrogfilms.com

Pyramid Film & Video
310-828-7577
2801 Colorado Avenue
Santa Monica, CA 90404

MESSAGE! CHECKS

The following organizations offer Message! checks:
The Humane Society of Utah
In Defense of Animals
The Michigan Anti-Cruelty Society
People for the Ethical Treatment of Animals
The Vegetarian Resource Group
    To order checks, contact

Message! Products
1-800-243-2565
Fax: 1-800-790-6684
P.O. Box 64800
St. Paul, MN 55164-0800
Two hundred checks cost $9.95.

DISTRIBUTORS OF VEGETARIAN COMPANION ANIMAL FOOD

Harbingers of a New Age
Support: 406-295-4944
Orders: 1-800-884-6262
Fax: 406-295-7603
717 East Missoula Avenue
Troy, MT 59935-9609
Provides products and information about vegetarian cat and dog food.

Natural Life Pet Products
1-800-367-2391
Fax: 316-231-0071
1601 West McKay
Frontenac, KS 66763
Canned and kibble dog food.

Nature's Recipe
1-800-843-4008
Fax: 909-278-9727
341 Bonnie Circle
Corona, CA 91720
Canned and kibble dog food—call for closest distributor.

Pet Guard
1-800-874-3221
Fax: 904-264-0802
P.O. Box 728
Orange Park, FL 32067-0728
Canned dog food and biscuits, digestive enzymes.

Wow-Bow Distributors
516-254-6064
Fax: 516-254-6036
13-B Lucon Drive
Deer Park, NY 11729
Canned and kibble dog food and biscuits, nutritional supplements.

PRODUCTS TO PROTECT WILDLIFE

Co-op America
2100 M Street NW, Suite 310
Washington, DC 20063
Source for biodegradable or photodegradable food storage bags.

Earth Card Paper Company
100 South Baldwin Street, Department 4
Madison, WI 53703
 Source for biodegradable or photodegradable food storage bags.

Professional Pest Management
1-800-527-0512
Zoecon Corporation
12200 Denton Drive
Dallas, TX 75234
Call for location of nearest Gentrol distributor.

Seventh Generation
1-800-456-1177
Colchester, VT 05446-1672
Source for cotton string shopping bags.

CRUELTY-FREE PRODUCTS YOU CAN MAKE AT HOME

Dozens of safe and effective home recipes can be concocted from substances as inexpensive as baking soda and vinegar. Here are some suggestions:

CLEANSERS
Cooking utensils: Let pots and pans soak in baking soda solution before washing.
Copper cleaner: Use a paste of lemon juice, salt, and flour; or rub vinegar and salt into the copper.
Furniture polish: Mix three parts olive oil and one part vinegar, or one part lemon juice and two parts vegetable oil. Use a soft cloth.
General cleaner: Mix baking soda with a small amount of water.
Glass cleaner: White vinegar or rubbing alcohol and water.
Household cleaner: Three tablespoons of baking soda mixed into one quart of warm water.
Linoleum floor cleaner: One cup of white vinegar mixed with two gallons of water to wash, club soda to polish.

Mildew remover: Lemon juice or white vinegar and salt.
Stain remover, toilet bowl cleaner: Vinegar.
Wine or coffee stains: Blot the fresh spill with a cloth soaked with club soda.

INSECT REPELLENTS
Ant control: Pour a line of cream of tartar at the place where ants enter the house—they will not cross it.
Ant repellent: Wash countertops, cabinets, and floors with equal parts vinegar and water.
Cockroach repellent: Place whole bay leaves in several locations around the kitchen.
Flea and tick repellent: Feed flaxseed oil and chopped garlic or garlic tablets to companion animals. Place herbs such as fennel, rue, pennyroyal, and rosemary and/or eucalyptus seeds and leaves where the animal sleeps to repel fleas.
Mosquito repellent: Take 100 milligrams of vitamin B-complex daily during the summer months.
Mothballs: Place cedar chips around clothes; dried lavender can be made into sachets and placed in drawers and closets.

MISCELLANEOUS
Air freshener: Leave an opened box of baking soda in the room, or add cloves and cinnamon to boiling water and simmer. Scent the house with fresh flowers or herbs; or open windows (in the winter, for about fifteen minutes every morning).
Drain opener: Prevent clogging by using a drain strainer or by flushing the drain weekly with about a gallon of boiling water. If clogged, pour one-half cup baking soda, then one-half cup vinegar down the drain and cover it tightly for about a minute.
Odor remover (spills and accidents): On carpet or furniture, blot the fresh stain with a cloth soaked with cider vinegar.
Water softener: One-quarter cup vinegar in the final rinse.

For a more extensive list, write to PETA for a free pamphlet titled "Homemade Household Recipes."

People to Contact

American Cancer Society
1599 Clifton Road, NE
Atlanta, GA 30329

American Home Products
President
973-660-5000
Fax: 973-660-7026
5 Giralda Farms
Madison, NJ 07940-0874

American Red Cross
202-737-8300
430 17th Street, NW
Washington, DC 20006

Boston Chicken, Inc.
14103 Denver West Parkway
P.O. Box 4086
Golden, CO 80401-4086

Burger King Corporation
1-800-937-1800
P.O. Box 520783, General Mail Facility
Miami, FL 33152-0783
Request that Burger King offer the vegan burgers it sells in all its stores in Europe.

March of Dimes Birth Defects Foundation
914-997-4504
1275 Mamaroneck Avenue
White Plains, NY 10605

McDonald's Corporation
Jack Greenberg, CEO
1 McDonald's Place
Oak Brook, IL 60521

Muscular Dystrophy Association
800-572-1717
3300 E. Sunrise Drive
Tucson, AZ 85718-3208

Procter & Gamble
John Pepper, CEO
513-983-4602
1 Procter & Gamble Plaza
Cincinnati, OH 45202

Shriners
Louis Brantley, CEO
813-281-0300
Fax: 813-281-8174
2900 Rock Point Drive
Tampa, FL 33607

Vogue
212-880-8800
Fax: 212-880-8169
350 Madison Avenue
New York, NY 10017-3704

Wendy's International, Inc.
P.O. Box 256
4288 West Dublin Granville Road
Dublin, OH 43017

Wyeth-Ayerst Laboratories
President
800-666-7248
P.O. Box 8299
Philadelphia, PA 19101

ABC
212-456-7777
770 W. 66th Street
New York, NY 10023-6201

CBS
212-975-3247
524 W. 57th Street
New York, NY 10019-2902

CNN
P.O. Box 105366
Atlanta, GA 30348

Fox
310-277-2211
10201 W. Pico Blvd.
Los Angeles, CA 90035

NBC
212-664-4444
30 Rockefeller Plaza
New York, NY 10112-0002

PBS
703-739-5000
1320 Braddock Plaza
Alexandria, VA 22314-1649

Canadian Ministry of Agriculture
Minister of Agriculture
House of Commons
Ottawa, Ontario K1A OA6
Canada

Environmental Protection Agency
Commissioner
202-260-2090
401 M Street, SW
Washington, DC 20460

Food and Drug Administration
Commissioner
301-827-2410
Parklawn Building
5600 Fishers Lane
Rockville, MD 20857

National Park Service
Director
1849 C Street, NW
Washington, DC 20240

U.S. Department of Agriculture
Secretary of Agriculture
1400 Independence Avenue, SW
Washington, DC 20250

U.S. Department of Fish and Wildlife
202-208-4131
1849 C Street NW
Washington, DC 20240

The Honorable (representative's name)
U.S. House of Representatives
Washington, DC 20515

The Honorable (senator's name)
U.S. Senate
Washington, DC 20510
To find the name of your U.S. Senators or Representative, call the Congressional switchboard at 202-224-3121, your local library, or your local League of Woman Voters.

Samples

ZOOCHECK CHART

ACTION OBSERVED	SPECIES	DURATION
Biting bars of the cage		
Repeated licking of bars or walls		
Continuous pacing back and forth or from side to side		
Unnatural twisting and rolling of the neck		
Vomiting and eating vomit		
Walking around and around placing footsteps in same position		
Playing with and eating excrement		
Head bobbing up and down, again and again		
Rolling or swaying from side to side		
Grooming to excess, including hair-plucking; animal may have bald patches		
Repeated tail-biting, leg-chewing, head-bashing		

LETTER TO THE EDITOR

Letters to the Editor
Newspaper
Address
City, State Zip

To the Editor:

Well, it looks like the circus is in town, and, while some children might dream of running away to join one, it is likely that most performing animals dream of running away *from* them.

Behind the glamour and pageantry, the lives of animals in circuses are paradoxically dull and dreary. They spend most of their lives in cages and chains. Lions and tigers live and travel in cages only 4 feet × 5 feet × 6 feet—barely enough room to turn around in, while elephants are chained virtually around the clock. Such unrelieved confinement is understandably frustrating for animals who would, in nature, roam great distances with their families.

The tricks animals are forced to perform—balancing on balls, leaping through flaming hoops, and standing on their heads—are hardly natural. Look closely—the whips, muzzles, electric prods, and other "tools" used in circus acts—are chilling reminders that the animals are captives who are *forced* to perform. Elephants, because their tremendous size makes them potentially dangerous, are regularly beaten with bullhooks, whips, and even sledge hammers, to remind them "who's the boss." And the big cats, according to Henry Ringling North in his book, *The Circus Kings*, are "chained to their pedestals, and ropes are put around their necks to choke them down. . . . They work from fear."

Unfortunately, much of the cruelty is absolutely legal. The helpless animals have little recourse. We as consumers must put our collective foot down and refuse to patronize the institutions that imprison animals. Just as we are outraged by poachers in Africa, we must stand up and protest the abuse and murder of animals in the name of "entertainment." We can help them by choosing amusements over *abuse*ments and going to see innovative, exciting, and—best of all—totally human-powered circuses like the Cirque du Soleil.

Sincerely,

Your name
(Phone number)

Index

About the Author

photo: Motoya Nakamura

Ingrid Newkirk is co-founder and president of People for the Ethical Treatment of Animals (PETA), the largest animal rights organization in the world. Her campaigns to save animals have made the front pages of *The Washington Post* and other national newspapers. She has appeared on *The Today Show, Oprah, Nightline,* and *20/20,* among others.

Newkirk has spoken internationally on animal protection issues, from the steps of the Canadian Parliament to the streets of New Delhi, India, where she spent her childhood. She is the author of *Kids Can Save the Animals!, The Compassionate Cook,* and *250 Ways to Make Your Cat Adore You,* as well as numerous articles on the social implications of our treatment of animals in our homes, in slaughter-houses, circuses, and laboratories.

She has served as a deputy sheriff; a Maryland state law enforcement officer for 25 years with the highest success rate in convicting animal abusers; director of cruelty investigations for the second-oldest humane society in the U.S.; and chief of animal disease control for the Commission on Public Health in the District of Columbia.

Ms. Newkirk loves fur on its original owners only and shares her office with four delightful cats who were rescued from abusive homes and who take an active interest in her work.